# ONE YEAR OF

# Healthy, Hearty & Simple

# ONE-DISH MEALS

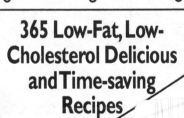

**365 Low-Fat, Low-Cholesterol Delicious and Time-saving Recipes**

am Spaude & Jan Owan-

One Year of Healthy, Hearty and Simple One-Dish Meals. © 1993 by Pam Spaude

**Library of Congress Cataloging-in-Publication Data**

Spaude, Pam.
　One year of healthy, hearty & simple one-dish meals: 365 low-fat, low-cholesterol, delicious, and timesaving recipes / Pam Spaude and Jan Owan-McMenamin.
　p. cm.
　Includes index
ISBN 1-56561-019-9 ; $12.95
　1. Low-fat diet. 2. Low-cholesterol diet. 3. Casserole cookery. 4. Diabetes—Diet therapy—Recipes. I. Owan-McMenamin, Jan. II. Title
RM237.7.S63 1993
641.5'638—dc20　　　　　93-16903
CIP

Edited by: Patricia Richter
Cover Design: Terry Dugan Design
Text Design: Liana Raudys
Art/Production Manager: Claire Lewis
Printed in the United States of America

Published by:
CHRONIMED Publishing, Inc.
P.O. Box 47945
Minneapolis, MN 55447-9727

# TABLE OF CONTENTS

**Introduction**     v

**Salads**     3

**Soups**     37

**Sandwiches**     49

**Pasta and Rice**     65

**Vegetables and Legumes**     89

**Beef and Veal**     115

**Seafood and Fish**     155

**Lamb**     249

**Pork and Ham**     263

**Poultry**     283

# INTRODUCTION TO ONE YEAR OF HEALTHY, HEARTY, AND SIMPLE ONE-DISH MEALS

This book was designed to help you cook simple healthful meals that taste good, are nutritious, and are quick and easy to prepare.

Today it seems we are all more aware of the relationship between health and diet, so we look for ways to cook meals that are low in cholesterol, fat and sodium. This book is filled with recipes to help you cook healthy.

Our collection provides a main dish meal for every day of the year, and to complete the menu nutritionally, we have suggested some side dishes that complement the entrée.

Each of our recipes includes the nutritional analysis and exchange information that lets you see for yourself exactly which components are part of the main dish. You can add your own choices to our main dishes, or add nothing, remembering that one meal does not necessarily have to satisfy your entire day's worth of nutritional components, or exchanges. Our exchanges were computed based on the guidelines from the American Diabetes Association.

We hope you'll like this collection. We're sure you'll find most meals quick and easy to prepare. So, happy, healthy eating to you for the next year and for many years to come!

*Pam Spaude*
*Jan Owan-McMenamin*

# Substitutions:

- ⅛ tsp. garlic powder for 1 clove garlic (Note: If you especially like garlic, use bottled garlic, already chopped, such as Polaner)
- margarine for butter
- Miracle Whip® salad dressing for mayonnaise

### Measures:

- dash or pinch = less than 1/8 tsp.
- 1 cup uncooked rice = 3 to 4 cups cooked

### Abbreviations:

- tsp. = teaspoon
- Tbsp. = tablespoon
- pkg. = package

### Miscellaneous Notes:

Use whole-wheat breads and pasta, and whole grain rice whenever possible for improved nutrition in your meals.

# Definitions:

**baste** to moisten food while it is cooking

**blanch** to scald briefly in hot water

**blend** to mix smoothly and inseparably together (only if specified in the recipe does it mean using an electric blender)

**confectioner's sugar** powdered sugar

**cream** to mix or beat into a creamy, smooth consistency

**diced** cut into small cubes

**dry mustard** powdered form of the spice

**garnish** to add something to a food dish that provides color and/or decoration or distinctive flavor

**julienne cut** cut into thin strips

**marinate** to soak meat in a seasoned liquid before cooking

**minced** cut or chopped into very fine pieces

**parboil** to boil partially, not to doneness

**pasta** a food paste, dried into different shapes such as spaghetti, macaroni, noodles, etc.

**prepared mustard** the paste form of this spice; usually used as a sandwich condiment

**puree** to make into a mushy, almost soupy consistency

**salad dressing** can be synonymous with a Miracle Whip® type product, as opposed to mayonnaise, which is not advertised as "salad dressing"

**sauté** to fry lightly with a little oil, usually just to beginning of tenderness, not crispiness

**score** to make shallow cuts, usually crisscrossed

**shortening** a solidified fat such as Crisco®

**simmer** to cook at or just below the boiling point

**whisk** to whip or beat with a hand utensil

Salads

1 7½ oz. can water-packed tuna
1 16 oz. can garbanzo beans, drained
⅔ cup chopped celery
⅔ cup chopped onion
⅔ cup chopped green pepper
¼ cup chopped red pepper
1 cup chopped carrots
1 large tomato, chopped
1 tsp. minced garlic
1 tsp. dried parsley flakes, crushed
⅔ cup low-cal Italian dressing
5 cups shredded lettuce
1 cup sliced mushrooms

Combine all ingredients in a large bowl and toss lightly until mixed well.

## Per serving
*202 calories*
*10 mg cholesterol*
*504 mg sodium*
*0.15 gm saturated fat*
*1.2 gm fat*

## Exchanges per serving
*1 bread*
*1 meat*
*1 vegetable*

**On the side** Honeydew melon cut into slices or served in a cup as melon balls adds a refreshing taste and completes this meal nutritionally.

## 2  Bean, Rice and Green Pea Salad

1¾ cup cooked long-grain rice
1 10 oz. package frozen peas, thawed
1¾ cups freshly cooked or drained, canned
    black beans
1½ Tbsp. vegetable oil
⅓ cup chopped pimentos
1 tsp. Dijon-style mustard
1½ Tbsp. ketchup
¼ cup red wine vinegar
⅛ tsp. pepper
6 lettuce leaves

Place rice, peas and black beans in a mixing bowl. In a blender, combine the remaining ingredients, except the lettuce, and blend. Toss with the rice, peas and beans. Chill covered for 2 hours. Serve on lettuce leaves.

### Per serving
*204 calories*
*0 mg cholesterol*
*241 mg sodium*
*0.5 gm saturated fat*
*3.5 gm fat*

### Exchanges per serving
*2 bread*
*1 vegetable*

**On the side** Serve with fresh pears and a glass of low-fat milk and you have a nutritionally complete meal.

## 3    Bean Sprout Fruit Salad

2½ cups fresh bean sprouts
¼ cup sliced water chestnuts
½ cup sliced seedless grapes
1 diced medium peach
⅓ cup diced green pepper
½ cup cooked rice
⅓ cup plain low-fat yogurt
1 tsp. curry powder
1 tsp. soy sauce

Combine bean sprouts, chestnuts, grapes, peach, green pepper and rice.

In a small bowl, mix yogurt, curry powder, and soy sauce. Pour dressing over salad. Toss and serve.

**Per serving**
*75 calories*
*0.5 mg cholesterol*
*597 mg sodium*
*0.75 gm saturated fat*
*0.5 gm fat*

**Exchanges per serving**
*1 fruit*
*½ vegetable*

**On the side** A fresh peach per person compliments this salad and adds only 40 calories and one fruit exchange. One slice of bread or a small roll and a cup of milk make this a complete meal.

# 4   Broccoli and Cauliflower Salad *Serves 4*

2 cups broccoli florets, steamed
2 cups cauliflower, steamed
4 Tbsp. unsalted sunflower seeds
½ cup raisins
2 Tbsp. light mayonnaise
6 Tbsp. plain low-fat yogurt
1 Tbsp. honey
2 Tbsp. lemon juice
½ tsp. minced garlic

In a salad bowl, combine broccoli, cauliflower, sunflower seeds and raisins.

In a small bowl, mix mayonnaise, yogurt, honey, lemon juice and garlic. Blend well. Pour over broccoli-cauliflower mixture. Toss and chill.

**Per serving**
*193 calories*
*3 mg cholesterol*
*51 mg sodium*
*1.1 gm saturated fat*
*6 gm fat*

**Exchanges per serving**
*1 fat*
*1 fruit*
*2 vegetable*

**On the side** An 8-ounce glass of milk or 1 slice of bread make this meal nutritionally complete.

⅓ cup vegetable oil

2 Tbsp. lemon juice

2 Tbsp. lime juice

1 Tbsp. minced garlic

⅛ tsp. pepper

1 6⅛ oz. can tuna in spring water

1 bunch broccoli, cut into florets

8 oz. fresh spinach, cut

1 small head red leaf lettuce, torn into bite-
   size pieces

1½ cups tomato, cut into chunks

¼ cup alfalfa sprouts

⅓ cup freshly grated Parmesan cheese

1 Tbsp. bacon bits

In large bowl, whisk oil, lemon and lime juices, garlic and pepper. Add remaining ingredients and toss to coat.

**Per serving**
*370 calories*
*42 mg cholesterol*
*227 mg sodium*
*6.0 gm saturated fat*
*18.0 gm fat*

**Exchanges per serving**
*2 fat*
*3 meat*
*2 vegetable*

**On the side** Serve with a slice bread or a small roll and a piece of fresh fruit to balance the meal nutritionally.

# 6   Cabbage and Carrot Salad

*Serves 6*

Dressing:
1 cup skim milk
2 Tbsp. cornstarch
½ tsp. mustard
2 Tbsp. vinegar
⅛ tsp. salt

Salad:
2 cups shredded cabbage
1 cup shredded carrots
¼ cup finely chopped fresh parsley
¼ cup chopped onion
1 tsp. lemon juice
1 Tbsp. finely cut chives

Mix all dressing ingredients in a small bowl. Blend well and set aside.

In a bowl, combine cabbage, carrots, parsley and onions; mix. Pour lemon juice over mixture. Add dressing to taste; toss.

**Per serving**
*29 calories*
*0.9 mg cholesterol*
*85 mg sodium*
*0 gm saturated fat*
*0 gm fat*

**Exchanges per serving**
*1 vegetable*

**On the side** Serve with fresh pears, a slice of bread and 8 oz. milk to complete the meal.

# 7   Carrot and Raisin Salad

*Serves 4*

4 cups grated carrots

1⅓ cup canned crushed pineapple (unsweetened juice)

½ cup raisins

2 tsp. lemon juice

⅔ cup low-fat plain yogurt

3 Tbsp. light mayonnaise

2 Tbsp. shredded coconut

2 tsp. sugar

In a bowl, combine carrots, pineapple, raisins and lemon juice; toss. In a small bowl, combine remaining ingredients; use a hand mixer to beat until blended well. Pour over carrot mixture and toss until salad is well coated. Chill for 1 hour.

**Per serving**
*191 calories*
*3 mg cholesterol*
*89 mg sodium*
*1.4 gm saturated fat*
*3.3 gm fat*

**Exchanges per serving**
*1 fat*
*1 fruit*
*½ skim milk*
*1 vegetable*

**On the side** Serve with low-fat plain yogurt and the meal is nutritionally complete.

⅔ cup light mayonnaise

¼ cup mustard

2 Tbsp. vinegar

½ tsp. garlic powder

¼ tsp. ground red pepper

¼ cup diced onion

4 cups cooked cavatelli pasta

1 cup diced celery

1 cup chopped green pepper

1 cup chopped red pepper

In a large bowl, combine mayonnaise, mustard, vinegar and spices. Add remaining ingredients; toss well. Cover and chill.

**Per serving**
*134 calories*
*1.6 mg cholesterol*
*120 mg sodium*
*0.65 gm saturated fat*
*2 gm fat*

**Exchanges per serving**
*1 bread*
*1 fat*

**On the side** Serve with your choice of vegetable salad, a fruit, and a cup of skim milk to complete the meal.

# 9    Chicken Apple Salad

*Serves 4*

2 cups boneless, skinned, cooked chicken breasts, diced
20 small red seedless grapes, cut into halves
2 apple, diced
⅔ cup diced celery
⅔ cup diced onion
3 Tbsp. light mayonnaise
2 tsp. vinegar
4 tsp. lemon juice
⅛ tsp. black pepper

In a mixing bowl, combine all ingredients and toss well. Refrigerate until thoroughly chilled, then serve.

**Per serving**
*255 calories*
*87 mg cholesterol*
*103 mg sodium*
*2.6 gm saturated fat*
*21.5 gm fat*

**Exchanges per serving**
*½ fat*
*1 fruit*
*2 meat*

**On the side** A cold vegetable, such as asparagus spears vinaigrette, a small dinner roll, or a small tossed salad will complete this meal.

1¾ cup chopped cooked chicken
2 Tbsp. chopped pecans
⅓ cup diced celery
3 Tbsp. grated carrots
½ cup plain low-fat yogurt
½ tsp. chopped dillweed
⅛ tsp. salt
⅛ tsp. pepper
4 lettuce leaves

Combine chicken, pecans, celery and carrots. Toss with yogurt, dillweed, salt and pepper. Serve on lettuce leaves.

**Per serving**
*344 calories*
*179 mg cholesterol*
*271 mg sodium*
*4.5 gm saturated fat*
*14 gm fat*

**Exchanges per serving**
*1 fat*
*3 meat*
*½ milk*
*1 vegetable*

**On the side** Serve with a fresh peach per person, a slice of bread, or a small roll for a complete meal.

Dressing

1 cup nonfat plain yogurt
½ cup raspberries*
1 Tbsp. raspberry or red wine vinegar
1 tsp. sugar

Blend all dressing ingredients in blender until smooth, about 15 seconds.

Salad

4 cups bite-sized pieces of mixed salad greens
2 cups cut-up, cooked chicken
1 cup raspberries*
⅓ cup thinly sliced celery
¼ cup toasted sliced almonds

Toss salad greens, chicken, raspberries, and celery. Sprinkle with almonds. Serve with raspberry dressing on the side.

* *You can use fresh or loosely packed, frozen raspberries.*

**Per serving**
*250 calories*
*60 mg cholesterol*
*130 mg sodium*
*2.4 gm saturated fat*
*11 gm fat*

**Exchanges per serving**
*½ fat*
*1 fruit*
*2 meat*

**On the Side** Add a small muffin, some carrot sticks, and a glass of low-fat milk to complete your meal.

2 cups tomatoes, cubed

1½ cup chopped carrots

⅔ cup chopped celery

2 cups chopped green pepper

2 cups cooked chickpeas

1 Tbsp. vegetable oil

4 Tbsp. lime juice

1 tsp. Dijon-style mustard

1½ tsp. mint flakes or leaves

½ tsp. honey

1 tsp. vinegar

⅛ tsp. black pepper

4 lettuce leaves

In a large mixing bowl, combine tomatoes, carrots, celery, green pepper and chickpeas. In a small bowl, combine oil, lime juice, mustard, mint flakes, honey, vinegar and black pepper; mix and blend well. Pour over chickpeas and vegetables; toss. Cover and chill 1 hour. Serve on lettuce leaves.

**Per serving**
*201 calories*
*0 mg cholesterol*
*219 mg sodium*
*1.3 gm saturated fat*
*3.5 gm fat*

**Exchanges per serving**
*2 bread*
*1 vegetable*

**On the side** Serve with fresh cantaloupe and a glass of milk for a nutritionally complete meal.

¾ cup canned pineapple, no sugar added
1 Tbsp. apple cider vinegar
1 Tbsp. light soy sauce
1 Tbsp. Dijon-style mustard
2 tsp. vegetable oil
⅛ tsp. ground ginger
1 cup boneless, skinned, cooked chicken breast, cut into thin strips
2 cups shredded lettuce
⅓ cup diced green onions
1 Tbsp. finely chopped red pepper
¼ cup water chestnuts, sliced
½ tsp. sesame seed

In a glass bowl, combine juice from pineapple, vinegar, soy sauce, mustard, oil and ginger. Add chicken and toss to coat. Cover and refrigerate 1 hour. In another bowl, combine lettuce and green onions, pineapple, red pepper and water chestnuts; mix and toss. Add chicken mixture to lettuce mixture; toss. Sprinkle with sesame seeds.

**Per serving**
*304 calories*
*85 mg cholesterol*
*589 mg sodium*
*2.15 gm saturated fat*
*11.98 gm fat*

**Exchanges per serving**
*1 fat*
*1 fruit*
*2½ meat*

**On the side** Serve with a slice of your favorite bread and a glass of milk for a nutritionally complete meal.

8 oz. dry vermicelli

1 tsp. minced garlic

¼ cup vegetable oil

½ cup lemon juice

1 Tbsp. soy sauce

2 small cucumbers, sliced

2 cups shredded cabbage

2 potatoes, boiled, peeled and cubed

⅛ tsp. pepper

Cook vermicelli according to directions on package; drain and rinse with cold water. In a bowl, mix garlic, oil, lemon juice and soy sauce. Add vermicelli, cucumber, cabbage and potatoes; mix well. Season with pepper.

**Per serving**
*311 calories*
*0 mg cholesterol*
*143.6 mg sodium*
*1.16 gm saturated fat*
*10.3 gm fat*

**Exchanges per serving**
*2 bread*
*2 fat*
*1 vegetable*

**On the side**   Serve with a glass of milk and a piece of your favorite fruit.

3 cups shredded cabbage
1 orange, peeled and sectioned, cut in half
1 tangerine, peeled and sectioned, cut in half
½ cup seedless red grapes, halved
½ cup seedless green grapes, halved
¼ cup sliced celery
1 apple, cored and chopped
1 8 oz. carton low-fat orange yogurt
⅛ tsp. nutmeg
⅓ cup sunflower seeds

In a large salad bowl, combine cabbage, orange pieces, tangerine pieces, red grapes, green grapes, celery, and apple. Combine yogurt and nutmeg. Pour yogurt mixture over cabbage and fruit; toss. Sprinkle with sunflower seeds. Chill.

**Per serving**
*88 calories*
*0 mg cholesterol*
*10.8 mg sodium*
*0.3 gm saturated fat*
*2.9 gm fat*

**Exchanges per serving**
1 fruit
½ skim milk

**On the side** Serve with your favorite bread or rolls.

1¾ cup cooked long-grain rice

2½ cups freshly cooked green beans, cut in 2-inch
  lengths

1¾ cup 96% fat-free ham, diced

½ cup chili sauce

¼ cup red wine vinegar

⅛ tsp. pepper

¼ cup rice bran

6 lettuce leaves

In a mixing bowl, combine rice, green beans and
ham. In a blender, combine chili sauce, vinegar and
pepper; blend. Toss dressing with rice, green beans
and ham. Chill for 2 hours, covered. Add rice bran
and toss just before serving. Serve on lettuce leaves.

**Per serving**
*230 calories*
*25.3 mg cholesterol*
*971 mg sodium*
*1.03 gm saturated fat*
*5.1 gm fat*

**Exchanges per serving**
*1 bread*
*2 meat*
*1 vegetable*

**On the side** Serve with fresh fruit.

# 17 Lentil Turkey Salad

¾ cup lentils, rinsed
1½ cups cooked turkey, cubed
⅛ cup sliced black olives
⅓ cup green peppers, chopped
⅓ cup chopped red peppers
½ cup sliced onions
1½ tsp. curry powder
1 tsp. vegetable oil
1½ Tbsp. light mayonnaise
2 Tbsp. plain low-fat yogurt

Place lentils in a saucepan and cover with water. Cook lentils on low heat for 20-25 minutes. Drain and rinse with cold water. In a bowl, mix lentils with remaining ingredients. Toss and chill.

**Per serving**
*240 calories*
*31 mg cholesterol*
*73 mg sodium*
*0.92 gm saturated fat*
*4.2 gm fat*

**Exchanges per serving**
*½ bread*
*1 fat*
*2 meat*

**On the side** Serve with plain low-fat yogurt, 1 cup per person, fresh vegetables, or a fresh fruit of your choice.

2 cups cooked elbow macaroni
1 cup diced celery
1 cup diced carrots
⅓ cup diced green pepper
¼ cup diced green onions
½ cup peas
1 Tbsp. Dijon-style mustard
½ cup light mayonnaise

Combine macaroni, celery, carrots, green pepper, onions and peas in a bowl; toss. Mix mustard and mayonnaise; pour over macaroni salad and toss.

**Per serving**
*188 calories*
*2 mg cholesterol*
*135 mg sodium*
*1 gm saturated fat*
*5 gm fat*

**Exchanges per serving**
*1 bread*
*1 fat*
*1 vegetable*

**On the side** Serve with cantaloupe, ⅛ melon or 1 cup per person, and a glass of milk for a nutritionally complete meal.

1½ cups small shell macaroni
⅔ cup chopped onions
10 oz. package frozen mixed vegetables
¾ cup low-fat cottage cheese
¼ cup low-fat yogurt
1½ tsp. Worcestershire sauce
¾ tsp. dry mustard
1 cup chopped carrots
½ cup chopped green peppers
¼ cup chopped red peppers
¼ cup chopped celery
⅛ cup chopped radishes

Cook macaroni and onion in boiling water according to package directions; drain and rinse with cold water. Cook vegetables and drain. Add cooked vegetables to macaroni and onion and chill for 15 minutes in freezer. Puree cottage cheese, yogurt, Worcestershire sauce, and mustard in blender until smooth. Add yogurt mixture and all remaining ingredients to chilled macaroni mixture. Toss until well blended.

**Per serving**
*180 calories*
*1.28 mg cholesterol*
*135 mg sodium*
*0.28 gm saturated fat*
*1.3 gm fat*

**Exchanges per serving**
*1 bread*
*1 meat*
*1 vegetable*

**On the side** Serve with fresh pears for a refreshing complement to this salad.

6 oz. rigatoni

2½ cups chopped tomatoes

⅓ cup feta cheese

⅓ cup low-cal Italian dressing

½ cup chopped green onions

⅛ cup sliced pitted black olives

6 cups torn, fresh spinach

⅛ tsp. pepper

Cook pasta according to directions on package; drain. Combine pasta and remaining ingredients. Toss to coat.

**Per serving**

*123 calories*

*6.25 mg cholesterol*

*196 mg sodium*

*1.17 gm saturated fat*

*2.87 gm fat*

**Exchanges per serving**

*1 bread*

*½ fat*

*1 vegetable*

**On the side** You can increase the nutritional content of this salad by adding more cheese, or serve with an 8 ounce glass of milk and a fresh fruit to complete the meal.

# 21   Potato Broccoli Salad

5 medium potatoes
1 bunch broccoli
¼ cup vegetable oil
¼ cup lime juice
½ tsp. garlic powder
1¼ tsp. basil
⅛ tsp. Tabasco sauce
⅛₄ cup onions, chopped

Peel and cook potatoes until tender; then dice them.
Wash broccoli and break into small florets. Steam
broccoli florets until tender-crisp. In a small
saucepan, combine oil, lime juice, garlic powder,
basil, Tabasco sauce and onions. Bring mixture to a
boil, stirring all the while. Put potatoes and broccoli
in serving bowl. Pour sauce over vegetables; toss
gently.

**Per serving**
*180 calories*
*0 mg cholesterol*
*53 mg sodium*
*1.2 gm saturated fat*
*9.5 gm fat*

**Exchanges per serving**
*1 bread*
*1 fat*
*1 vegetable*

**On the side** Serve with a glass of milk and a fresh fruit to have a
nutritionally complete meal.

*One Year of Healthy, Hearty & Simple One-Dish Meals*   ■   23

2 cups green beans, cut in half
1½ cups fresh peas
2 cups cooked rice
3 cups fresh tomatoes, cubed
½ cup sliced green onions
1 Tbsp. fresh basil
1 tsp. dried parsley flakes, crushed
1½ Tbsp. lemon juice
2½ Tbsp. vegetable oil
2 tsp. safflower oil
1 7 oz. can tuna fish

Steam beans until tender, then cool. Cook peas until tender, then cool. Mix together remaining ingredients. Mix in beans and peas. Toss.

### Per serving
*267 calories*
*19 mg cholesterol*
*469 mg sodium*
*1.4 gm saturated fat*
*9.7 gm fat*

### Exchanges per serving
*2 bread*
*1 fat*
*1 meat*
*1 vegetable*

**On the side** Serve with honeydew, ⅓ melon, or 1 cup per person. Add a glass of milk to complete the meal.

# 23   Shrimp and Pea Salad

1 8 oz. package frozen, cooked small shrimp
2 cups frozen peas, thawed
½ cup low-fat plain yogurt
¼ cup light mayonnaise
½ tsp. curry powder
½ tsp. lemon juice
½ tsp. celery seed
⅛ cup green onions, sliced
½ cup chopped celery
1 small tomato, chopped
4 lettuce leaves

Rinse and drain shrimp and peas. In a mixing bowl, stir together yogurt, mayonnaise, curry powder, lemon juice, and celery seed. Add shrimp, peas, onions, celery, and tomatoes. Toss until coated. To serve, line plates with lettuce leaves. Spoon shrimp mixture onto plates.

### Per serving
*201 calories*
*83 mg cholesterol*
*212 mg sodium*
*0.75 gm saturated fat*
*5.75 gm fat*

### Exchanges per serving
*½ bread*
*1 fat*
*2 meat*

**On the side** Add more vegetables to this recipe to enhance it nutritionally, or serve surrounded with fresh, crunchy vegetables of your choice. Finish off the meal with a refreshing cup of honeydew melon balls.

2 envelopes unflavored gelatin

2 cups skim milk

1 cup plain nonfat yogurt

3 Tbsp. vinegar

1 tsp. salt

1 tsp. prepared horseradish

2 4½ oz. cans shrimp, drained

½ cup diced celery

¼ cup chopped green pepper

½ cup diced part-skim American cheese

In 2-quart saucepan, add gelatin and ½ cup milk. Stir until dissolved over low heat. Add remaining milk and remove from heat. Chill until mixture begins to set. Add yogurt, vinegar, salt, and horseradish; mix well. Fold in shrimp, celery, green pepper, and cheese. Pour into 9 x 9-inch pan and chill 3 hours. Cut into 3-inch squares. 1 square = 1 serving.

**Per serving**
*102 calories*
*60.2 mg cholesterol*
*391 mg sodium*
*0.8 gm saturated fat*
*1.5 gm fat*

**Exchanges per serving**
*1 meat*
*½ skim milk*

**On the side** Serve with cantaloupe, a slice of bread, and a crunchy vegetable salad for a complete meal.

# 25  Spinach Fruit Salad

¼ cup vegetable oil
3 Tbsp. red wine vinegar
1 Tbsp. lemon juice
½ tsp. ground ginger
1 lb. fresh spinach
3 cups fresh strawberries, sliced
½ cup part-skim cheddar cheese, shredded

Blend oil, vinegar, lemon juice, and ginger in a large bowl. Add spinach, strawberries and cheese; toss.

**Per serving**
*119 calories*
*2.3 mg cholesterol*
*43 mg sodium*
*1.4 gm saturated fat*
*10.5 gm fat*

**Exchanges per serving**
*1 fat*
*1 fruit*
*1 vegetable*

**On the side** Serve with a slice of your favorite fresh bread and a cup of low-fat plain yogurt.

6 oz. fresh spinach
1 15¼ oz. can chunk pineapple in unsweetened juice
4 tsp. cornstarch
½ tsp. ginger
¼ tsp. allspice
⅛ tsp. lemon pepper
12 oz. cooked, smoked turkey sausage
1 Tbsp. lemon juice
2 cups broccoli florets
1 cup sliced red pepper

Clean spinach and tear into bite-size pieces. Drain pineapple and reserve juice. Add water to juice to equal one cup. In a bowl, combine juice mixture, cornstarch, ginger, allspice, and lemon pepper. Set aside. Cut turkey into thin slices. In a large skillet, cook and stir turkey sausage until browned. Stir in pineapple juice mixture, lemon juice, broccoli, and red pepper strips. Cook and stir until thickened; add pineapple and cook through. Cool and toss with spinach in a bowl.

**Per serving**
*218 calories*
*36 mg cholesterol*
*935 mg sodium*
*1.0 gm saturated fat*
*3.3 gm fat*

**Exchanges per serving**
*1 fruit*
*2 meat*
*1 vegetable*

**On the side** Serve with a slice of toasted bread and some crunchy fresh vegetables for a complete meal.

# 27  Tarragon Shrimp Salad

8 oz. medium-sized cooked shrimp, peeled and
   deveined
5 Tbsp. light mayonnaise
¼ cup sliced green onion
2 tsp. lemon juice
1½ tsp. skim milk
½ tsp. dried tarragon, crushed
⅛ tsp. lemon pepper
⅛ tsp. paprika
2 cups chopped lettuce

Cut shrimp in half lengthwise. In a bowl, combine
mayonnaise, green onions, lemon juice, milk,
tarragon, lemon pepper, and paprika. Stir shrimp
into mixture; cover and chill for 1 hour. Serve on
chopped lettuce.

### Per serving
*184 calories*
*178 mg cholesterol*
*221 mg sodium*
*1.4 gm saturated fat*
*7.2 gm fat*

### Exchanges per serving
*1 fat*
*3 meat*

**On the side** Serve with fresh cantaloupe, bread, and crunchy
vegetables for a nutritionally complete meal.

1½ cup shredded, cooked turkey
2 bananas, sliced and peeled
⅛ cup chopped celery
⅓ cup chopped carrots
⅛ cup green onions
⅓ cup raisins
⅓ cup light mayonnaise
¼ tsp. cumin
¼ tsp. dill
⅛ tsp. garlic powder
salad greens

Toss together turkey, bananas, celery, carrots, onions and raisins. Combine the mayonnaise, cumin, dill and garlic powder; blend well. Fold into turkey mixture. Refrigerate for one hour. Serve on top of salad greens.

**Per serving**
*370 calories*
*95 mg cholesterol*
*171 mg sodium*
*2.9 gm saturated fat*
*9.2 gm fat*

**Exchanges per serving**
*1 fat*
*1 fruit*
*3 meat*
*1 vegetable*

**On the side** Serve with fresh bread to complete the meal.

1 10 oz. can tuna in spring water
⅔ cup chopped celery
½ cup chopped green onions
1 chili pepper, chopped
1 tsp. minced garlic
4 tsp. lemon juice
½ tsp. celery seed
1 Tbsp. soy sauce
2 Tbsp. frozen apple juice concentrate, thawed
1 cup frozen peas, thawed
⅔ cup grated carrots
2 cups cooked rice
1½ tsp. sweet basil
1 tsp. prepared mustard
6 lettuce leaves

Mix all the ingredients except lettuce together in a mixing bowl. Serve on lettuce leaves.

### Per serving
*151 calories*
*1 mg cholesterol*
*497 mg sodium*
*0.1 gm saturated fat*
*0.22 gm fat*

### Exchanges per serving
*1 bread*
*1½ meat*

**On the side** Serve with cantaloupe and a glass of low-fat milk to complete the meal.

3 Tbsp. lemon juice
3 small red Delicious apples, diced
⅔ cup diced celery
⅓ cup raisins
½ cup shredded carrots
3 Tbsp. light mayonnaise
2 Tbsp. sunflower seeds

In a small bowl, sprinkle lemon juice over apples, toss. Add celery, raisins, carrots and mayonnaise; mix until coated. Cover and refrigerate 30 minutes. Before servings, sprinkle mixture with sunflower seeds.

### Per serving
*159 calories*
*1.5 mg cholesterol*
*33 mg sodium*
*0.62 gm saturated fat*
*5.7 gm fat*

### Exchanges per serving
*1½ fat*
*1 fruit*
*1 vegetable*

**On the side** Serve with a glass of milk or a cup of plain nonfat yogurt and a slice of bread.

# 31   Warm Chicken Salad

2 cups skinned and cooked chicken, cubed
⅔ cup low-fat plain yogurt
1 Tbsp. minced onion
½ tsp. curry
⅔ cup diced celery
½ cup water chestnuts, cut
1 cup fresh, sliced mushrooms
3 whole-wheat English muffins, toasted

Mix all ingredients except the muffins together in an 8-inch square baking dish. Bake at 450°F for 10 to 15 minutes. Cut English muffins in half. Divide mixture evenly on each half.

### Per serving
*266 calories*
*73 mg cholesterol*
*238 mg sodium*
*1.74 gm saturated fat*
*5.6 gm fat*

### Exchanges per serving
*1 bread*
*2 meat*
*½ skim milk*

**On the side** Serve with green, red and yellow peppers and a fresh fruit for a nutritionally complete meal.

½ cup plain low-fat yogurt

2 Tbsp. light mayonnaise

½ cup lemon juice

¼ cup grated Parmesan cheese

2 tsp. minced garlic

1 lb. boneless, skinned, cooked chicken, cubed

½ cup diced celery

¼ cup diced green onion

⅛ tsp. pepper

In a bowl, combine yogurt, mayonnaise, lemon juice, Parmesan cheese and garlic; blend well. Add chicken, celery, green onion and pepper. Toss well to coat.

**Per serving**
*234 calories*
*82 mg cholesterol*
*88 mg sodium*
*3.0 gm saturated fat*
*8.37 gm fat*

**Exchanges per serving**
*½ bread*
*1 fat*
*2 meat*

**On the side** Serve with a vegetable of your choice and top off with fresh honeydew melon slices for dessert.

Soups

# 33  Broccoli and Pasta Soup

½ cup finely chopped onion

4¼ cups water

1 tsp. minced garlic

2 Tbsp. tomato sauce

1½ Tbsp. soy sauce

1 tsp. Worcestershire sauce

½ tsp. black pepper

2 broccoli stalks, florets

2 cups elbow macaroni

In saucepan, cook onions with ¼ cup water until onion is soft. Add garlic and cook for one minute. Add tomato sauce, soy sauce and Worcestershire sauce. Stir well. Add 4 cups water and bring to a boil. Add pepper and broccoli; cook for 5 minutes. Add macaroni and cook for 10 to 15 minutes more.

### Per serving
*130 calories*
*0 mg cholesterol*
*257 mg sodium*
*0 gm saturated fat*
*1.02 gm fat*

### Exchanges per serving
*1½ bread*
*1 vegetable*

**On the side** To make this a nutritionally complete meal, serve with a glass of milk, and top off with a fresh fruit of your choice.

1 Tbsp. vegetable oil

⅔ cup finely chopped onions

⅔ cup chopped red peppers

½ cup chopped celery

½ cup bran

½ tsp. cayenne pepper

¾ tsp. garlic powder

6 cups low-sodium chicken broth

2 bay leaves

2 16 oz. cans red beans, drained

1½ lbs. boneless, skinless chicken breasts, cubed

In 8-quart saucepan, heat oil. Add onions, red pepper and celery; sauté and stir constantly. Add bran, cayenne pepper and garlic powder; continue to sauté until bran begins to fill bottom of saucepan and turn brown. Add broth; stir. Add bay leaves and beans; simmer for 30 minutes. Add chicken and cook until chicken is cooked through. Remove bay leaves.

**Per serving**
*287 calories*
*84 mg cholesterol*
*240 mg sodium*
*3.2 gm saturated fat*
*7.6 gm fat*

**Exchanges per serving**
*1 bread*
*½ fat*
*2 meat*
*1 vegetable*

**On the side** To complete this meal, serve fresh fruit for dessert.

# 35  Easy Gumbo Soup

1 8 oz. can stewed tomatoes
1 6 oz. can vegetable juice cocktail
½ cup chopped green pepper
1 tsp. minced onion
½ tsp. Worcestershire sauce
¼ tsp. ground red pepper
⅔ cup water
1 6 oz. package frozen, cooked, small shrimp
⅓ cup quick-cooking rice

In saucepan, combine stewed tomatoes, vegetable juice, green pepper, onion, Worcestershire sauce, red pepper, and ⅔ cup water. Bring to a boil. Stir in shrimp and rice. Return to a boil; remove from heat and let stand 5 minutes or until rice is done.

### Per serving
*176 calories*
*128 mg cholesterol*
*541 mg sodium*
*0 gm saturated fat*
*1 gm fat*

### Exchanges per serving
*1 bread*
*1 meat*
*1 vegetable*

**On the side** Complete this meal by serving a fruit compote as dessert.

1 cup chopped onions
1 cup shredded carrots
2 Tbsp. dried parsley flakes
1 tsp. dried tarragon
⅛ tsp. pepper
1 Tbsp. vegetable oil
2 8 oz. bottles clam juice
1¾ cup low-sodium tomato juice
½ cup water
⅓ cup small seashell pasta
1 lb. frozen white-flesh fish fillets, thawed

In saucepan, cook onions, carrots, parsley, tarragon, and pepper in oil, over medium heat. Stir often until onion is tender. Stir in clam and tomato juice, water, and pasta. Cover and simmer 10 minutes. Cut fish into 1-inch chunks. Add fish and cook for 5 to 10 minutes more.

**Per serving**
*205 calories*
*49 mg cholesterol*
*347 mg sodium*
*0.58 gm saturated fat*
*3.7 gm fat*

**Exchanges per serving**
*1 bread*
*2 meat*
*1 vegetable*

**On the side** Serve with cantaloupe melon slices as dessert for a nutritionally complete meal.

2 quarts water
1 tsp. salt
2 cups chopped carrots
2 cups diced potatoes
2 cups diced, fresh tomatoes
1 cup sliced green onions
1 cup frozen lima beans
2 cups fresh green beans, cut into 1 inch pieces
1 cup frozen corn
½ cup instant rice

In 6-quart pan, combine everything except corn and rice. Cover and bring to a boil. Reduce heat and simmer for 30 minutes. Add corn and rice; simmer for 15 minutes. Serve.

**Per serving**
*133 calories*
*0 mg cholesterol*
*237 mg sodium*
*0.07 gm saturated fat*
*0.36 gm fat*

**Exchanges per serving**
*1½ bread*
*1 vegetable*

**On the side** Serve this hearty soup with a glass of milk and top off the meal with baked apples (one apple per person) for dessert and nutritional balance.

15 oz. very lean beef for stew, cubed
1½ quarts water
1 cup vegetable juice
1 cup chopped cabbage
½ cup chopped celery
¾ cup chopped green onions
2 oz. uncooked lentils
1 cup chopped carrots
1 cup peeled, chopped potatoes
1 tsp. minced garlic
½ cup sliced, fresh mushrooms
⅛ tsp. pepper
⅛ tsp. salt

On broiling pan, place beef and broil until browned on each side. Transfer beef to a 4-quart saucepan and add all of the ingredients. Bring to a boil. Reduce heat and simmer for 50 minutes.

**Per serving**
*428 calories*
*103 mg cholesterol*
*287 mg sodium*
*6.1 gm saturated fat*
*16 gm fat*

**Exchanges per serving**
*1½ bread*
*3½ meat*
*1 vegetable*

**On the side** Finish this meal with fresh fruit for nutritional balance.

3 lbs. potatoes, peeled and cubed

3 cups carrots, cubed

2 cups chopped onions

3 cups skim milk

1 cup evaporated skim milk

¼ cup chopped parsley

⅛ tsp. pepper

¼ tsp. salt

In a large saucepan, place potatoes, carrots and onions in boiling water. Cover and cook 15 minutes. Drain. Stir in milk and evaporated milk. Heat soup just to boiling. Sprinkle with chopped parsley and season with salt and pepper.

**Per serving**

*410 calories*

*76 mg cholesterol*

*352 mg sodium*

*9.8 gm saturated fat*

*15 gm fat*

**Exchanges per serving**

*2 bread*

*2 fat*

*1 milk*

*2 vegetable*

**On the side** Finish this meal off with a compote of your favorite fresh fruits.

1 fresh jalapeño chili pepper

1 Tbsp. vegetable oil

1 cup chopped onion

1 tsp. minced garlic

¾ tsp. cumin seed

6 cups low-sodium chicken broth

¾ cup rice

2 cups tomatoes, diced

1 10 oz. package frozen peas, thawed

¾ lb. tiny cooked shrimp

Cut jalapeño chili in half. In a 6-quart saucepan, combine oil, onion, garlic, cumin seed, and half of a jalapeño chili. Stir over medium heat until onion is tender. Add broth and rice; bring to a boil. Reduce heat and simmer for 30 minutes. Add tomatoes, peas, and shrimp. Remove and discard chili half. Cut remaining chili into slices. Serve and sprinkle chili slices on top.

**Per serving**
*200 calories*
*85 mg cholesterol*
*277 mg sodium*
*0.33 gm saturated fat*
*3.6 gm fat*

**Exchanges per serving**
*1 bread*
*1 meat*
*1 vegetable*

**On the side** Chilled pears offer a refreshing taste as a dessert and to round out this complete meal.

½ lb. green split peas
½ tsp. minced garlic
½ tsp. ground cumin
¼ tsp. curry powder
½ tsp. ground ginger
6 cups water
1½ cups diced carrots
1 lb. boneless, skinless chicken breasts, cubed
¾ cup chopped onions
⅛ tsp. black pepper

Put peas, garlic, cumin, curry powder, and ginger in saucepan; add 6 cups water and slowly bring to a boil. Reduce heat and simmer for 40 minutes. Add carrots, chicken and onions; cook 15 to 20 minutes longer or until chicken is cooked through. Season with pepper.

### Per serving
*212 calories*
*71 mg cholesterol*
*76 mg sodium*
*2.3 gm saturated fat*
*4.2 gm fat*

### Exchanges per serving
*1 bread*
*1 meat*
*1 vegetable*

**On the side** Serve pears and apples with blueberries in a compote as a tasty follow-on to this spicy soup.

Sandwiches

6⅛ oz. tuna in spring water, drained and flaked
1 cup chopped avocado, very ripe
¼ cup chopped tomatoes
¼ cup diced onions
1 tsp. lemon juice
1 tsp. dried parsley flakes
1 Tbsp. apple cider vinegar
¼ tsp. horseradish
2 6-inch whole-wheat pita bread rounds, halved

Combine ingredients in a bowl and blend thoroughly with a fork. Fill each pita half with ¼ of the tuna mixture.

**Per serving**
*288 calories*
*10 mg cholesterol*
*73 mg sodium*
*1.3 gm saturated fat*
*5.6 gm fat*

**Exchanges per serving**
*1 bread*
*1 fat*
*2 meat*

**On the side** Cantaloupe melon provides a refreshing and nutritious completer for this meal.

## 43 Grilled Tomato and Cheese Sandwiches

2 slices part-skim American cheese
1 tomato, thinly sliced
4 slices whole-wheat bread
nonstick cooking spray

Put cheese and tomato slices on two of the bread slices; cover with remaining 2 slices of bread. Spray skillet with nonstick cooking spray and toast each side of sandwiches until golden brown.

**Per serving**
*221 calories*
*15.9 mg cholesterol*
*493 mg sodium*
*2.8 gm saturated fat*
*7 gm fat*

**Exchanges per serving**
*2 bread*
*1 meat*

**On the side** Cottage cheese (¼ cup per person) , a fresh fruit, or a glass of milk will complete this meal.

# 44　Pepper Steak Pita Pockets

*Serves 4*

2 6-inch whole-wheat pita pockets, halved
½ lb. sliced, cooked roast beef
1 cup fresh bean sprouts, rinsed and drained
¼ cup chopped celery
¼ cup chopped green peppers
¼ cup chopped tomato

Dressing:
¼ cup vegetable oil
2 Tbsp. vinegar
2 Tbsp. Dijon-style mustard
1 tsp. soy sauce
½ tsp. ginger
⅛ tsp. black pepper
¼ tsp. minced garlic

In small bowl, mix all dressing ingredients; blend well. Fill each pocket with ¼ of the beef and vegetables. Drizzle dressing inside each pocket.

**Per serving**
*286 calories*
*58 mg cholesterol*
*247 mg sodium*
*3.3 gm saturated fat*
*18.0 gm fat*

**Exchanges per serving**
*½ bread*
*2 fat*
*1½ meat*
*1 vegetable*

**On the side** Fresh cucumbers make a nice accompaniment to this sandwich. A fresh fruit and a glass of milk make it a complete meal.

*One Year of Healthy, Hearty & Simple One-Dish Meals*　■　51

¼ cup plain low-fat yogurt

1½ Tbsp. light mayonnaise

1½ tsp. Dijon-style mustard

1 tsp. dried dillweed

⅛ tsp. black pepper

14¾ oz. can salmon in spring water, drained

½ cup finely chopped green pepper

¼ cup chopped onions

3 whole-wheat English muffins, halved and toasted

In a bowl, mix yogurt, mayonnaise, mustard, dillweed and pepper; blend well. In another bowl, mix salmon, green pepper and onion. Spoon over dressing, toss to coat. Refrigerate covered for 30 minutes. Divide evenly over muffins.

**Per serving**
*220 calories*
*2.3 mg cholesterol*
*73 mg sodium*
*0.78 gm saturated fat*
*3.3 gm fat*

**Exchanges per serving**
*½ bread*
*1 fat*
*2 meat*

**On the side** Honeydew melon adds a refreshing taste to this delicious sandwich. A glass of milk and a tossed salad nutritionally round out this meal.

# 46 Sauced Tuna Pita

1 6⅛ oz. can tuna
¼ cup shredded carrots
½ cup alfalfa sprouts
4 lettuce leaves
⅓ cup plain low-fat yogurt
½ cup chopped and peeled cucumber
2 Tbsp. sliced green onions
1 tsp. lemon juice
¾ tsp. dried dillweed
⅛ tsp. paprika
⅛ tsp. celery seed
2 6-inch pita bread rounds

In a bowl, combine all ingredients except lettuce leaves and alfalfa sprouts; toss gently. Line each pita half with lettuce leaves and alfalfa sprouts. Spoon tuna mixture evenly into each pita pocket half.

**Per serving**
*169 calories*
*27 mg cholesterol*
*489 mg sodium*
*1.1 gm saturated fat*
*4.3 gm fat*

**Exchanges per serving**
*1 bread*
*1 meat*
*1 vegetable*

**On the side** A cup of plain, low-fat yogurt adds 1½ milk and ½ fat exchanges or 144 calories to this meal. A piece of fruit makes the meal complete.

# 47 Shrimp Salad Pocket

2 cups frozen, cooked small shrimp, thawed
½ cup frozen peas, thawed
½ cup chopped red pepper
⅓ cup low-cal creamy cucumber salad dressing
1 tsp. lime juice
1 tsp. dried thyme, crushed
2 cups shredded lettuce
4 6-inch pita bread rounds

Coarsely chop shrimp. In a mixing bowl, combine shrimp, peas, red pepper, salad dressing, lime juice, and thyme. Stir until combined. Add shredded lettuce to the shrimp mixture. Toss to mix. Cut pita bread in half. Spoon the shrimp mixture into pita pockets.

**Per serving**
*190 calories*
*89 mg cholesterol*
*271 mg sodium*
*0.69 gm saturated fat*
*8.0 gm fat*

**Exchanges per serving**
*½ bread*
*1 fat*
*2 meat*

**On the side** Cottage cheese, in ¼ cup servings, some crunchy vegetables, and a piece of fruit complete this meal.

# 48   Shrimp Stuffed Pitas

¾ cup cracked wheat

1 Tbsp. light mayonnaise

1 cup chopped cucumber

1 cup chopped tomatoes

2 tsp. Dijon-style mustard

3 tsp. red wine vinegar

½ cup lime juice

1 lb. cooked shrimp, peeled and deveined

6 6-inch whole-wheat pita bread pockets

6 leaves of lettuce

Prepare cracked wheat according to package directions; soak in water for at least one hour. Combine
cracked wheat and all the other ingredients in mixing
bowl; toss and blend. Split open the pitas, insert a
lettuce leaf in each and stuff with salad mixture.

### Per serving
*225 calories*
*132 mg cholesterol*
*219 mg sodium*
*0.13 gm saturated fat*
*0.6 gm fat*

### Exchanges per serving
*2 bread*
*½ fat*
*½ meat*
*1 vegetable*

**On the side** Cottage cheese and fruit make this meal nutritionally balanced.

2 Tbsp. margarine
¾ cup sliced mushrooms
1 cup thinly sliced zucchini
1 tsp. minced garlic
⅛ tsp. pepper
½ cup shredded part-skim mozzarella cheese
¼ cup finely chopped tomato
½ cup alfalfa sprouts
1 Tbsp. grated Parmesan cheese
4 slices whole-wheat bread, toasted

In skillet, melt margarine. Sauté mushrooms, zucchini, garlic and pepper until crisp-tender; drain. Sprinkle ¼ cup shredded mozzarella cheese on 2 slices of toasted bread, arrange sautéed vegetables over cheese. Top with tomato and sprouts. Sprinkle with remaining mozzarella cheese and Parmesan cheese on top. Broil until cheeses melt. Top each with slices of bread. Cut in half diagonally.

**Per serving**
*286 calories*
*11 mg cholesterol*
*109 mg sodium*
*2.3 gm saturated fat*
*6.83 gm fat*

**Exchanges per serving**
*2 bread*
*1 fat*
*½ meat*
*1 vegetable*

**On the side** Adding some fresh tomatoes, arranged attractively on the plate around this sandwich, round out this meal.

1 8 oz. can pineapple slices in unsweetened juice
1 tsp. vegetable oil
2 8 oz. boneless, skinless chicken breast halves
2 tsp. pineapple juice
2 Tbsp. Dijon-style mustard
2 Tbsp. light mayonnaise
3 tsp. soy sauce
2 tsp. honey
2 slices onion
¼ cup part-skim shredded Swiss cheese
2 small whole-wheat rolls

Drain pineapple and reserve the two teaspoons of juice. In skillet, heat oil and brown the chicken; cook until done. Combine in a bowl, pineapple juice, mustard, mayonnaise, soy sauce and honey; spread wheat rolls with sauce. Top each sandwich with chicken, cheese, pineapple and onion.

**Per serving**
*423 calories*
*115 mg cholesterol*
*854 mg sodium*
*7 gm saturated fat*
*17.8 gm fat*

**Exchanges per serving**
*1 bread*
*1 fat*
*1 fruit*
*3 meat*

**On the side** Cottage cheese (¼ cup servings) or fresh crunchy vegetables complete this meal.

# 51 Toasted Mushroom Sandwiches

1 Tbsp. margarine
4 cups sliced, fresh mushrooms
½ cup chopped onions
½ tsp. minced garlic
1 cup light sour cream
¼ tsp. dried thyme
½ tsp. lemon juice
⅛ tsp. pepper
16 slices whole-wheat bread

In skillet, melt margarine. Add mushrooms, onions and garlic, and cook until liquid evaporates, stirring frequently. Remove from heat. Stir in sour cream, thyme, lemon juice and pepper. Spread ¼ cup mushroom mixture on each of 8 bread slices. Top with remaining 8 slices of bread. Lightly spread margarine on outside of sandwiches. Heat skillet over medium heat and toast sandwiches on both sides.

**Per serving**
*250 calories*
*12 mg cholesterol*
*317 mg sodium*
*0.5 gm saturated fat*
*4 gm fat*

**Exchanges per serving**
*2 bread*
*1 fat*
*1 vegetable*

**On the side** Tomatoes and cucumbers on the side of this tasty sandwich provide a good accompaniment. A glass of skim milk completes the meal.

# 52   Tuna 'n' Cheese Filled Pitas

*Serves 4*

1 9¼ oz. can tuna in spring water, drained
¾ cup part-skim shredded cheddar cheese
⅓ cup chopped celery
¼ cup chopped pecans
⅓ cup light sour cream
¼ cup light mayonnaise
2 6-inch pita bread rounds
1 cup shredded lettuce
½ cup alfalfa sprouts

In a mixing bowl, stir together tuna, shredded
cheddar cheese, celery, pecans, sour cream, and
mayonnaise. Cut pita bread in half to make a pocket.
Line each pita half with lettuce and alfalfa sprouts.
Spoon tuna mixture in each pocket half.

**Per serving**
*298 calories*
*23 mg cholesterol*
*512 mg sodium*
*5.5 gm saturated fat*
*14.8 gm fat*

**Exchanges per serving**
*1 bread*
*1 fat*
*3 meat*
*1 vegetable*

**On the side** Fresh pears, 1 per person, complete this meal and
give it nutritional balance.

# 53  Tuna Pitas

1 6⅛ oz. can tuna in spring water
⅓ cup low-fat plain yogurt
⅛ cup diced celery
1½ tsp. Dijon-style mustard
¼ tsp. dried dillweed
2 6-inch round pita breads, halved
4 lettuce leaves
1 tomato, sliced

Combine tuna, yogurt, celery, mustard and dillweed.
Line bread halves with lettuce leaves and tomatoes.
Divide tuna mixture among bread halves. Serve
immediately.

### Per serving
*270 calories*
*1.8 mg cholesterol*
*220 mg sodium*
*0.5 gm saturated fat*
*0.8 gm fat*

### Exchanges per serving
*1 bread*
*½ fat*
*3 meat*

**On the side** Cottage cheese (¼ cup per person) and fresh
peaches complete this meal.

8 slices rye bread
4 Tbsp. low-calorie thousand island dressing
1 lb. cooked fresh turkey tenderloin, sliced
2 cups sauerkraut
⅔ cup shredded part-skim Swiss cheese

Coat four slices of rye bread evenly with Thousand
Island dressing. Top each with ½ of turkey tenderloin,
¼ cup sauerkraut and ¼ of the cheese; top with
second slice of rye bread. Grill until cheese melts
and turkey is heated through

## Per serving
*475 calories*
*82 mg cholesterol*
*1790 mg sodium*
*9 gm saturated fat*
*17.6 gm fat*

## Exchanges per serving
*2 bread*
*1 fat*
*3 meat*
*1 vegetable*

**On the side** Cucumbers and tomatoes combine for a refreshing
addition to complete this meal.

1 10 oz. can mandarin oranges in water

3 cups torn salad greens

⅓ cup low-calorie buttermilk salad dressing

½ tsp. dried tarragon

1 6 oz. pkg. sliced, cooked turkey breast

2 6-inch whole-wheat pita bread rounds, halved

Drain mandarin orange sections. In a bowl, mix mandarin oranges, salad greens, buttermilk dressing, and tarragon. Toss well to coat. Place 2 slices of turkey breast into each pita half. Divide salad mixture among the 4 pocket halves.

**Per serving**
*184 calories*
*31 mg cholesterol*
*110 mg sodium*
*0.75 gm saturated fat*
*3.5 gm fat*

**Exchanges per serving**
*½ bread*
*½ fat*
*½ fruit*
*1½ meat*

**On the side** Cottage cheese and some crunchy fresh vegetables make this a complete meal.

# Pasta and Rice

# 56 Asparagus Spaghetti Toss

6 oz. spaghetti

8 oz. package frozen cut asparagus, thawed

¾ tsp. basil

¾ tsp. thyme

½ tsp. onion powder

1 cup chopped tomatoes

½ cup low-calorie Italian salad dressing

1 Tbsp. lemon juice

Cook spaghetti and asparagus separately according to package directions; drain. Toss spaghetti with basil, thyme, and onion powder. Add asparagus, tomatoes, salad dressing and lemon juice. Cover and chill in freezer for 10 to 15 minutes.

**Per serving**
*179 calories*
*0 mg cholesterol*
*239 mg sodium*
*0.25 gm saturated fat*
*2.3 gm fat*

**Exchanges per serving**
*1½ bread*
*½ fat*
*1 vegetable*

**On the side** Add a tossed salad and a fruit to make this meal nutritionally complete.

1⅓ cup water

½ cup cracked wheat

¼ cup long-grain rice

2 tsp. instant beef bouillon granules

¾ cup chopped carrots

½ cup chopped celery

¾ cup onions, chopped

⅛ tsp. salt

⅛ tsp. lemon pepper

½ tsp. celery seed

Combine all ingredients in a 2-quart saucepan. Bring to a boil. Reduce heat and simmer for 25 minutes.

**Per serving**
*54 calories*
*0 mg cholesterol*
*539 mg sodium*
*0 gm saturated fat*
*0.5 gm fat*

**Exchanges per serving**
*½ bread*
*1 vegetable*

**On the side** A glass of milk, a fresh vegetable salad and a piece of your favorite fruit for dessert round out this meal nutritionally.

# 58 Fettuccine with Mushrooms

4 oz. fettuccine

2 tsp. margarine

1½ cups sliced mushrooms

½ tsp. minced garlic

1 Tbsp. skim milk

⅓ cup grated Parmesan cheese

Cook fettuccine according to package directions. In a saucepan, heat margarine. Add mushrooms and garlic. Cook until tender. Add milk and Parmesan cheese. Toss gently until fettuccine is well coated.

### Per serving
*148 calories*
*28 mg cholesterol*
*51 mg sodium*
*0.57 gm saturated fat*
*4.6 gm fat*

### Exchanges per serving
*1½ bread*

**On the side** Add a salad of fresh, crunchy vegetables, a glass of milk and a fresh fruit to complete the meal.

# 59  Herbed Spinach Fettuccine

*Serves 4*

8 oz. spinach fettuccine

2 tsp. margarine

¼ cup finely chopped onions

¾ tsp. minced garlic

2 tsp. cornstarch

1½ tsp. dried basil

1 tsp. instant chicken bouillon granules

⅔ cup skim milk

⅔ cup water

¼ cup grated Parmesan cheese

Cook pasta according to directions on package. In saucepan, melt margarine and cook onions and garlic until tender. Stir cornstarch, basil, bouillon granules; blend. Add milk and water. Cook and stir until thickened and bubbly. Toss with pasta. Sprinkle with cheese.

**Per serving**
*231 calories*
*9.25 mg cholesterol*
*286 mg sodium*
*0.75 gm saturated fat*
*2.55 gm fat*

**Exchanges per serving**
*2 bread*
*1 fat*

**On the side** A tossed salad, a glass of milk, and a piece of fresh fruit makes this meal nutritionally complete.

# 60　Lasagna with Chickpeas

Serves 8

9 lasagna noodles
1 Tbsp. margarine
1 cup sliced onions
1½ cups sliced fresh mushrooms
2 19 oz. cans chickpeas, drained
1½ tsp. oregano
4 cups low-sodium tomato sauce
2 cups skim-milk ricotta cheese
5 Tbsp. grated Parmesan cheese

Preheat oven to 350°F. Cook lasagna according to package directions; drain. In skillet, heat margarine; add onions and mushrooms; sauté. Add chickpeas, oregano and 2 cups tomato sauce. Simmer for 15 minutes. In 9 x 13 inch baking dish, pour one cup tomato sauce on bottom. Place a layer of noodles. Spoon ⅓ of the chickpeas, mushrooms, and tomato sauce, ⅓ of the ricotta cheese, and one tablespoon of Parmesan cheese over the noodles. Repeat to create two more layers. Top with one cup of tomato sauce. Sprinkle a tablespoon of Parmesan over top and bake uncovered for 35 to 40 minutes.

**Per serving**
*425 calories*
*30.5 mg cholesterol*
*676 mg sodium*
*5.4 gm saturated fat*
*17.2 gm fat*

**Exchanges per serving**
*2 bread*
*1 fat*
*1.2 meat*
*1 vegetable*

**On the side** Cantaloupe melon, a fresh pear, or a baked apple complete the meal.

1½ cups elbow macaroni

⅔ cup chopped carrots

½ cup chopped celery

½ cup chopped onions

1 can cream of celery soup

¾ cup skim milk

2 6⅛ oz. cans tuna in spring water

¾ cup frozen peas, thawed

Cook macaroni according to package directions; drain. Cook carrots, celery and onion in a small amount of water and steam the vegetables; drain. In 2-quart casserole dish, combine macaroni, vegetables, soup and milk; blend. Fold in tuna and peas. Cover and bake at 375°F for 30 minutes.

**Per serving**
*290 calories*
*6.6 mg cholesterol*
*427 mg sodium*
*0.73 gm saturated fat*
*3.3 gm fat*

**Exchanges per serving**
*1½ bread*
*1 fat*
*2 meats*

**On the side** Accompany with a tossed salad and finish the meal with fresh fruit.

# 62   Noodles with Ginger-Sesame Sauce    *Serves 2*

4 oz. thin Italian noodles

½ cup green onions, chopped

1 Tbsp. coarsely grated ginger

2 tsp. soy sauce

2 tsp. red wine vinegar

½ tsp. sugar

1 tsp. sesame oil

Cook noodles according to directions on package. In large bowl, combine remaining ingredients; mix. Stir noodles into sauce.

### Per serving

*123 calories*

*0 mg cholesterol*

*1127 mg sodium*

*0.5 gm saturated fat*

*4.1 gm fat*

### Exchanges per serving

*1½ bread*

**On the side** Stir-fry your favorite vegetables and finish the meal off with fruit and yogurt for a nutritionally complete meal.

6 oz. vermicelli

3 tsp. sesame oil

½ tsp. Chinese five-spice powder (available in specialty stores or in Chinese markets)

2 Tbsp. soy sauce

1 tsp. sugar

¾ cup shredded cooked chicken

¼ cup green onions

1½ cups shredded red cabbage

1½ cups frozen peas, thawed

½ tsp. coriander

Cook pasta in boiling water; drain and rinse with cold water. Combine sesame oil, five-spice powder, soy sauce and sugar. Mix well. In large bowl, combine pasta with sesame oil mixture. Add chicken, green onions, cabbage, peas and coriander. Toss lightly.

**Per serving**
*304 calories*
*35 mg cholesterol*
*543 mg sodium*
*11.5 gm saturated fat*
*2.75 gm fat*

**Exchanges per serving**
*2 bread*
*1 fat*
*1 meat*

**On the side** Complete this meal nutritionally by adding a melange of cooked peppers and a fruit compote for dessert.

1 Tbsp. olive oil

1 Tbsp. minced garlic

2½ cups sliced mushrooms

1½ cups sliced carrots

2½ cups water

1¼ cups low-sodium beef broth

1¼ cups uncooked small pasta shells

1 tsp. dried basil

1 tsp. lemon pepper

½ tsp. dried tarragon

½ tsp. oregano

¼ tsp. ground pepper

½ cup chopped onions

½ cup canned chickpeas, rinsed and drained

1 cup frozen peas

1 cup red kidney beans, drained

In saucepan, heat oil over medium heat. Add garlic
and cook 1 minute. Add mushrooms and carrots;
cook until tender. Add water and broth; bring to a
boil. Stir in pasta and seasonings. Reduce heat and
simmer 10 minutes. Add onions, chickpeas, peas and
kidney beans. Simmer until vegetables are tender.

**Per serving**
*168 calories*
*0 mg cholesterol*
*68.3 mg sodium*
*0.33 gm saturated fat*
*2.9 gm fat*

**Exchanges per serving**
*1½ bread*
*1 vegetable*

**On the side** Fruit and yogurt make a perfect dessert.

2 small zucchinis, sliced

1 cup green beans, cut

1 cup shredded carrots

½ cup peas

⅔ cup olive oil

1 Tbsp. lemon juice

1 tsp. minced garlic

¾ tsp. oregano

¼ cup chopped green onions

1 lb. thin linguine

Steam zucchini, beans, carrots and peas over boiling water until peas are tender. Combine oil, lemon juice and garlic; mix well. Mix with steamed vegetables. Add oregano and green onions. Toss so that vegetables are well coated. Cook linguine according to package directions; drain. Place in serving dish. Pour vegetable mixture over linguine; toss to mix well and serve at once.

**Per serving**
*399 calories*
*0 mg cholesterol*
*14 mg sodium*
*1.7 gm saturated fat*
*15 gm fat*

**Exchanges per serving**
*3 bread*
*2 fat*
*1 vegetable*

**On the side** Mixed fruit compote with low-fat yogurt for dessert, and this meal is nutritionally complete.

Dressing:
3 Tbsp. vegetable oil
2 Tbsp. apple cider vinegar
½ tsp. ginger

Salad:
2 cups curly macaroni
¼ cup chopped green onions
1 mandarin orange, cut into pieces
¾ cup bean sprouts
1 6 oz. package frozen pea pods, thawed, rinsed, and drained

In small bowl, combine all dressing ingredients. Mix well. Cook macaroni according to directions. Drain and rinse with cold water. In large bowl, combine macaroni, onion, orange, been sprouts, and pea pods. Drizzle dressing over salad. Toss until combined.

**Per serving**
*166 calories*
*0 mg cholesterol*
*68.66 mg sodium*
*0.83 gm saturated fat*
*7.5 gm fat*

**Exchanges per serving**
*1 bread*
*1 fat*
*1 fruit*

**On the side** Serve this tasty salad with a glass of milk and your meal is nutritionally complete.

1 cup chopped carrots

¾ cup chopped onions

2 cups sliced, fresh mushrooms

½ cup diced celery

¼ cup margarine

½ tsp. salt

½ tsp. paprika

½ tsp. garlic powder

½ cup green pepper

1 diced tomato

½ cup water

2 cups uncooked rice

Melt margarine in large skillet. Sauté all vegetables, except tomatoes, until tender. Add seasonings, tomato and water; bring to a boil. Stir in rice. Cover and simmer for 10 minutes or until rice is tender.

**Per serving**
*235 calories*
*0 mg cholesterol*
*395 mg sodium*
*1.3 gm saturated fat*
*8 gm fat*

**Exchanges per serving**
*3 bread*
*1½ fat*
*1 vegetable*

**On the side** A dessert of fruit with low-fat yogurt rounds out this meal nutritionally.

1½ Tbsp. margarine
½ cup chopped onion
¼ cup chopped celery
¾ cup rice
¾ cup vermicelli, broken up
1½ cups low-sodium chicken broth
¾ cup water
3 Tbsp. dry white wine
¼ tsp. salt
½ tsp. thyme
⅛ tsp. ground pepper
¼ cup dried parsley flakes

In skillet, melt margarine. Add onion and celery; cook until soft. Add rice and vermicelli and cook until lightly browned. Add remaining ingredients and bring to a boil. Reduce heat and simmer 30 to 40 minutes or until rice is tender

**Per serving**
*135 calories*
*0 mg cholesterol*
*173 mg sodium*
*0.5 gm saturated fat*
*3.2 gm fat*

**Exchanges per serving**
*1 bread*
*1 fat*

**On the side** Serve this with a glass of nonfat milk and a compote of fresh fruit as dessert and your meal is complete.

# 69 Spaghetti with Peas and Tomato Sauce

1 Tbsp. vegetable oil

1½ tsp. minced garlic

⅓ cup chopped onions

6 cups diced tomatoes

2 Tbsp. tomato paste

⅛ tsp. pepper

½ tsp. oregano

¼ tsp. basil

1½ cups frozen peas, thawed

¾ lb. spaghetti

4 Tbsp. grated Parmesan cheese

Heat oil in a skillet over low heat and sauté garlic and onions for 2 minutes. Add tomatoes, tomato paste and cook over medium heat for 20 minutes. Add pepper, oregano, and basil. Stir in peas. Cook spaghetti according to package directions; drain. Toss with tomato-pea sauce. Serve with Parmesan cheese sprinkled on top.

### Per serving
*306 calories*
*8 mg cholesterol*
*127 mg sodium*
*1.5 gm saturated fat*
*7.15 gm fat*

### Exchanges per serving
*2½ bread*
*1 fat*
*1 vegetable*

**On the side** Serve with plain nonfat yogurt and fruit as dessert to complete this meal nutritionally.

*Serves 2 (4 shells each)*

8 uncooked jumbo macaroni shells
3 Tbsp. low-calorie Italian dressing
¾ cup cottage cheese, part-skim
⅔ cup part-skim ricotta cheese
¼ cup chopped green onions
2 Tbsp. grated Parmesan cheese
1½ tsp. lemon juice
1 Tbsp. finely chopped red pepper
⅛ tsp. black pepper

Cook macaroni according to package directions. In
a shallow glass bowl combine macaroni shells and
Italian dressing; toss to coat. Cover and marinate
in refrigerator for 1 hour. In a small bowl, combine
remaining ingredients; mix. Remove shells from bowl,
reserving dressing. Spoon ⅛ of cheese mixture into
each shell. Drizzle with reserved dressing.

**Per serving**
*262 calories*
*36 mg cholesterol*
*512 mg sodium*
*6.15 gm saturated fat*
*11.35 gm fat*

**Exchanges per serving**
*2 bread*
*2 fat*
*1 meat*

**On the side** Serve with a fresh tomato and vegetable salad and a
fruit for dessert to complete this meal nutritionally.

2 Tbsp. olive oil
1 cup finely grated onion
2 tsp. minced garlic
3 cups chopped tomatoes
⅛ tsp. salt
⅛ tsp. pepper
1 lb. spaghetti
2½ cups grated zucchini
2 Tbsp. fresh basil
1 Tbsp. margarine
¼ cup grated Parmesan cheese

In a skillet, heat oil. Add onions and garlic; cook until soft and golden. Add tomatoes, salt and pepper. Prepare spaghetti according to package directions. Just before spaghetti is ready, add zucchini and basil to the tomato mixture and simmer for 5 minutes. Drain spaghetti and toss with margarine. Top spaghetti with vegetable mixture. Serve with Parmesan cheese.

**Per serving**
*261 calories*
*5 mg cholesterol*
*111 mg sodium*
*1.7 gm saturated fat*
*9.3 gm fat*

**Exchanges per serving**
*2½ bread*
*1½ fat*
*2 vegetable*

**On the side** Start the meal with an antipasto of low-fat, thinly sliced meats of your choice. Finish off with a refreshing blend of mixed fruits.

1 can cream of celery soup
1 cup skim milk
1 cup water
½ tsp. dillweed
½ tsp. celery seed
¼ cup chopped onions
3 cups uncooked noodles
1 cup frozen peas
1 6⅛ oz. can tuna in spring water

In large skillet, combine soup, milk, water, dillweed, celery seed and onions. Bring to a boil. Add noodles and bring to a second boil. Reduce heat and simmer until noodles are tender. Stir in peas and tuna. Cook covered an additional 15 minutes.

**Per serving**
*352 calories*
*13.7 mg cholesterol*
*387 mg sodium*
*0.7 gm saturated fat*
*2.8 gm fat*

**Exchanges per serving**
*2½ breads*
*1 fat*
*1 meat*

**On the side** This easy one-dish meal needs only a tossed salad and a fruit to be a complete meal nutritionally.

8 oz. uncooked spaghetti

4 Tbsp. margarine

½ cup chopped green peppers

½ cup chopped onion

1 cup fresh sliced mushrooms

1½ Tbsp. flour

1½ cup skim milk

¼ tsp. salt

⅛ tsp. nutmeg

2½ cups hot cooked vegetables, any kind

½ cup grated Parmesan cheese

Cook spaghetti according to package directions; drain and rinse with hot water. In saucepan, melt margarine and sauté green pepper, onions and mushrooms until tender. Add flour, milk, salt and nutmeg. Blend and bring to a boil over medium heat. Remove and stir in cooked vegetables. Toss spaghetti and sauce in large bowl. Sprinkle with Parmesan cheese.

**Per serving**
*318 calories*
*12.5 mg cholesterol*
*357 mg sodium*
*3 gm saturated fat*
*11.5 gm fat*

**Exchanges per serving**
*2 bread*
*2 fat*
*½ skim milk*
*1 vegetable*

**On the side** Top this meal off with your favorite fruit and you have a nutritionally complete meal.

2 Tbsp. vegetable oil
1 medium eggplant, chopped
½ cup chopped onions
2 cups sliced fresh mushrooms
9 lasagna noodles
1 15½ oz. can low-sodium spaghetti sauce
1 cup part-skim mozzarella cheese, shredded
1 cup part-skim cheddar cheese, shredded
½ cup grated Parmesan cheese

In skillet, heat 1 tablespoon oil. Add eggplant and brown; set aside. In same skillet, heat 1 tablespoon oil. Add onions, mushrooms and cook until tender. Cook lasagna noodles according to package directions but without the salt. Preheat oven to 350°F. Spoon ½ cup sauce in 11 x 17 inch baking dish. Arrange three layers of noodles, mushroom mixture, mozzarella cheese, cheddar cheese, eggplant, sauce, and Parmesan cheese. Cover and bake 30 to 40 minutes.

**Per serving**
*288 calories*
*28 mg cholesterol*
*454 mg sodium*
*5.7 gm saturated fat*
*31.3 gm fat*

**Exchanges per serving**
*2 bread*
*4 fat*
*1 meat*
*1 vegetable*

**On the side** Complete this meal by serving fresh fruit for dessert.

# 75  Zucchini Lasagna

9 lasagna noodles
1 cup part-skim ricotta cheese
½ cup grated Parmesan cheese
1 Tbsp. dried parsley flakes
⅛ tsp. ground pepper
4 cups tomato sauce (low sodium)
½ cup chopped onion
1 tsp. oregano
1 tsp. basil
2½ cups chopped zucchini
1 cup part-skim shredded mozzarella cheese

Heat oven to 400°F. Cook noodles as directed on package; drain. In bowl, combine ricotta cheese, Parmesan cheese, parsley and ground pepper. Set aside. In saucepan, add tomato sauce, onions, oregano and basil. Bring to a boil stirring occasionally. Cover and simmer for 10 minutes. In a 13 x 9 inch pan, layer ¼ of the tomato sauce mixture, 3 lasagna noodles, ⅓ of the cheese mixture and ⅓ of the chopped zucchini. Repeat layers two more times. Spoon remaining sauce over top; sprinkle with mozzarella cheese. Bake for 35 to 40 minutes.

### Per serving
*190 calories*
*13.7 mg cholesterol*
*140.6 mg sodium*
*2.5 gm saturated fat*
*4.4 gm fat*

### Exchanges per serving
*1 bread*
*½ fat*
*1 meat*
*1 vegetable*

**On the side** Complete the meal with your favorite fresh fruit to round it out nutritionally.

# 76  Zippy Noodles

4 oz. noodles
½ cup chopped celery
1 Tbsp. margarine
1 10¾ oz. can cream of chicken soup
½ cup plain low-fat yogurt
1½ Tbsp. skim milk
½ tsp. Worcestershire sauce
3 Tbsp. wheat germ

Cook noodles according to package directions; drain.
In saucepan, cook celery in margarine. Stir in soup,
yogurt, milk, and Worcestershire sauce. Fold in
noodles. Place in casserole dish. Sprinkle wheat
germ on top. Bake at 350°F for 35 minutes..

**Per serving**
*135 calories*
*9.1 mg cholesterol*
*445 mg sodium*
*1.3 gm saturated fat*
*6 gm fat*

**Exchanges per serving**
*1½ bread*
*1 fat*

**On the side** Pick your favorite ingredients for a crunchy tossed
salad, and enjoy fruit and low-fat plain yogurt for dessert and
the meal is nutritionally complete.

Vegetables
and
Legumes

1 Tbsp. vegetable oil
1½ cups chopped red pepper
¼ cup chopped green onion
1 Tbsp. chili powder
1 Tbsp. ground cumin
¾ tsp. garlic powder
2 15 oz. cans black beans
⅓ cup ketchup
¼ cup low-fat yogurt
1 cup part-skim cheddar cheese, shredded

In saucepan, heat oil. Add red peppers and green onions; sauté. Stir in chili powder, cumin and garlic powder; sauté for 30 seconds. Add black beans with their liquid and simmer for 20 to 25 minutes. Add ketchup and simmer for 10 more minutes. Stir in yogurt and simmer until heated. Sprinkle with cheddar cheese. Simmer until cheese melts.

### Per serving
*255 calories*
*18.7 mg cholesterol*
*311 mg sodium*
*4.4 gm saturated fat*
*9.3 gm fat*

### Exchanges per serving
*1½ bread*
*1 fat*
*1 meat*
*1 vegetable*

**On the side** Serve this with a glass of milk and a fresh fruit for dessert and the meal is nutritionally complete.

1 cup dry noodles
2½ cups finely chopped cabbage
1 Tbsp. margarine
¾ tsp. caraway seeds
½ tsp. onion powder

Cook noodles according to package directions, omitting salt. In skillet, heat margarine. Add cabbage and stir-fry until cabbage is tender. Add drained noodles, caraway seed and onion powder. Stir together and heat through.

### Per serving
*104 calories*
*0 mg cholesterol*
*30.6 mg sodium*
*0.3 mg saturated fat*
*1.9 gm fat*

### Exchanges per serving
*1 bread*
*1 vegetable*

**On the side** Add a glass of milk and a baked apple and the meal is complete nutritionally.

2 cups chopped celery

1 cup chopped onion

1 Tbsp. minced garlic

1 cup chopped green pepper

½ cup chopped red pepper

1 cup chopped cucumber

1 cup low-sodium chicken broth

1 eggplant, peeled and cut into cubes

1 16 oz. can low-sodium tomato puree

⅛ tsp. cayenne

1½ Tbsp. soy sauce

1 cup whole-wheat bread crumbs

Sauté celery, onion, garlic, green and red pepper, and cucumber in broth until thoroughly cooked. Add the eggplant, tomato puree, cayenne and soy sauce. Place mixture in a casserole dish and cover with bread crumbs. Cover and bake for 30 minutes at 350°F. Uncover and bake an additional 10 to 15 minutes.

**Per serving**
*120 calories*
*0 mg cholesterol*
*63 mg sodium*
*0.16 gm saturated fat*
*0.9 gm fat*

**Exchanges per serving**
*½ bread*
*2 vegetables*

**On the side** Add a glass of low-fat milk and a fresh pear for a nutritionally complete meal.

1 large eggplant, sliced
1 Tbsp. vegetable oil
1 16 oz. jar marinara sauce
1 Tbsp. dried parsley flakes, crushed
4 Tbsp. grated Parmesan cheese
⅛ tsp. pepper
⅛ tsp. salt
½ cup shredded part-skim mozzarella cheese

Brush eggplant with oil and place on a nonstick backing sheet; broil until brown on both sides. In a 9-inch baking dish, place ¼ cup of marinara sauce on bottom. Add a layer of eggplant slices, top with some sauce, parsley, and 2 tablespoons Parmesan cheese. Repeat with a second layer. Season with salt and pepper. Sprinkle with mozzarella cheese. Bake at 375°F for 20 minutes.

**Per serving**
*160 calories*
*21.5 mg cholesterol*
*974 mg sodium*
*4.35 gm saturated fat*
*10.2 gm fat*

**Exchanges per serving**
*½ fat*
*1 meat*
*2 vegetables*

**On the side** Serve with New Potatoes , a glass of milk, and a fresh fruit for a nutritionally balanced meal.

# 81 Eggplant Mozzarella

1 lb. eggplant

1 medium tomato, chopped

⅔ cup low-sodium vegetable juice

1 tsp. dried basil

½ tsp. oregano

1 tsp. minced garlic

¾ cup part-skim mozzarella cheese, shredded

½ tsp. black pepper

Heat oven to 350°F. Peel and slice eggplant. Layer in 8-inch baking dish; top with tomatoes. In bowl, combine remaining ingredients except cheese; mix. Pour over eggplant and tomatoes. Sprinkle with cheese. Bake 35-40 minutes.

**Per serving**
*81 calories*
*14 mg. cholesterol*
*81 mg sodium*
*2.32 gm saturated fat*
*3.75 gm fat*

**Exchanges per serving**
*½ meat*
*1 vegetable*

**On the side** A glass of milk, a slice of your favorite bread, and fresh fruit for dessert makes this meal nutritionally complete.

1 lb lean ground beef

⅛ tsp. salt

⅛ tsp. pepper

½ cup chopped onions

¼ tsp. oregano

1 6 oz. can low-sodium tomato paste

1⅔ cups water

1 medium eggplant

¼ cup grated part-skim mozzarella cheese

In a skillet, brown beef; drain fat. Add salt, pepper, onions, and oregano. Add tomato paste and stir in water. Simmer for 15 minutes. Peel eggplant and slice. Spoon a thin layer of meat sauce into a baking dish. Arrange a single layer of eggplant slices over sauce. Repeat. Sprinkle with mozzarella cheese. Bake for 30 minutes at 350°F.

**Per serving**
*258 calories*
*68 mg cholesterol*
*142 mg sodium*
*5.8 gm saturated fat*
*13.9 gm fat*

**Exchanges per serving**
*3 meat*
*1 vegetable*

**On the side** A serving of white rice, a glass of milk, and a cup of melon balls, or your favorite fresh fruit for dessert, completes this meal nutritionally.

1½ cups dried lentils, washed and drained
1½ cups finely chopped onion
1 Tbsp. minced garlic
1 tsp. ground cumin
½ cup fresh tomatoes, diced
¼ tsp. black pepper
1 tsp. red wine vinegar

Simmer lentils in water for 1 hour or until they are tender; drain. In large saucepan, cook onions and garlic with ¼ cup water until onions are soft. Add cumin, tomatoes, and pepper. Cook a few minutes. Add lentils and heat through. Stir in vinegar. Serve.

**Per serving**
*90 calories*
*0 mg cholesterol*
*8 mg sodium*
*0 gm saturated fat*
*0 gm fat*

**Exchanges per serving:**
*1 bread*

**On the side** A glass of milk and a fresh fruit of your choice round out this meal.

2½ cups whole wheat flour

1 package active dry yeast

1 tsp. salt

¾ cup warm water

2 Tbsp. olive oil, divided

2½ cups sliced mushrooms

¼ cup chopped onions

1 small green pepper, chopped

1 8 oz. can low-sodium tomato sauce

½ cup chopped tomato

2 cups shredded part-skim mozzarella cheese

1 Tbsp. Parmesan cheese, grated

For crust mix: 1½ cups flour, yeast and salt. Stir in water and 1 tablespoon oil. With mixer on low speed, beat until flour is just moistened. Knead with enough remaining flour to make a moderately stiff dough that is smooth and elastic. Cover with towel and set aside to rise, about 30 to 45 minutes.

In a skillet, heat remaining oil. Add mushrooms, onions, green peppers, and cook until tender. Form dough to fit a 13 x 9 x 2-inch pan (spray pan with nonstick spray). Spread tomato sauce over dough. Sprinkle mushrooms, onions, peppers, and tomatoes evenly over dough. Sprinkle with cheeses. Bake at 375°F for 20 to 25 minutes.

**Per serving**
*240 calories*
*28.8 mg cholesterol*
*504 mg sodium*
*5.6 gm saturated fat*
*12 gm fat*

**Exchanges per serving**
*1 bread*
*1 fat*
*1 meat*
*2 vegetable*

**On the side** Serve with a glass of milk and top off the meal with a fresh fruit of your choice.

# 85 Red Cabbage with Apples

1 head cabbage, shredded
3 Granny Smith apples, peeled, cored, and sliced
½ tsp. ground clove
⅛ tsp. fennel seed
¼ cup cider vinegar
½ cup apple juice concentrate

Combine all ingredients in a skillet and cook over medium heat for 40 to 45 minutes.

**Per serving**
*85 calories*
*0 mg cholesterol*
*11 mg sodium*
*0 mg saturated fat*
*0.52 gm fat*

**Exchanges per serving**
*1 fruit*
*1 vegetable*

**On the side** Complete this meal nutritionally by serving a glass of milk and a slice of your favorite fresh bread.

6 red peppers, seeded and cored
1 Tbsp. olive oil
¾ cup chopped onions
1½ cups sliced mushrooms
3 cups cooked rice
1 Tbsp. dried parsley flakes, crushed
½ tsp. dried basil
2 cups vegetable juice
1 Tbsp. ketchup

Preheat oven to 350°F. Place peppers in a baking pan. In a skillet, heat oil and sauté onion. Add mushrooms and cook until soft. Add rice, parsley, basil; mix. Add vegetable juice and ketchup; mix. Stuff the pepper with the mixture. Bake for 50 to 60 minutes until tender.

**Per serving**
*202 calories*
*0 mg cholesterol*
*325 mg sodium*
*0.4 gm saturated fat*
*2.9 gm fat*

**Exchanges per serving**
*2 bread*
*½ fat*
*2 vegetable*

**On the side** Enjoy a glass of nonfat milk and choose your favorite fresh fruit for dessert and your meal is nutritionally complete.

# 87  Savory Peppers

1½ quarts water
2 green peppers, halved and seeded
¼ lb. lean ground beef
½ cup chopped onions
⅛ tsp. ground pepper
½ cup low-sodium tomato sauce
1 tsp. oregano
1 tsp. basil
1 tsp. garlic
1 cup part-skim shredded mozzarella cheese

Heat oven to 350°F. In saucepan, bring water to a
boil. Put green peppers in water and boil for 3 to 4
minutes; drain.

In skillet, brown beef; drain off fat. Add onions,
ground pepper, tomato sauce, oregano, basil and
garlic. Stir and heat thoroughly. Place green pepper
halves in baking dish. Fill with meat mixture.
Sprinkle with mozzarella cheese. Bake at 350°F for
20 minutes.

## Per serving
*161 calories*
*37 mg cholesterol*
*155 mg sodium*
*4 gm saturated fat*
*9 gm fat*

## Exchanges per serving
*2 meat*
*1 vegetable*

**On the side** A glass of milk, a slice of your favorite bread, and
fresh fruit for dessert make this a nutritionally complete
meal.

2 eggs

4 cups cooked spaghetti squash

1 10 oz. package frozen chopped spinach

1½ cups sliced, fresh mushrooms

¼ cup finely chopped red pepper

⅓ cup bean sprouts

1 packet low-calorie chicken gravy mix, prepared
   according to package directions

¾ cup part-skim shredded mozzarella cheese

Preheat oven to 375°F. In mixing bowl, beat eggs;
add squash, mix well. In a one-quart casserole dish,
spread squash mixture evenly in dish. Bake for 15
to 20 minutes. In mixing bowl, combine remaining
ingredients, except cheese; blend well. Spread
spinach mixture over squash. Sprinkle with cheese.
Bake until cheese is melted and browned, 20 to
25 minutes.

**Per serving**
*249 calories*
*306 mg cholesterol*
*539 mg sodium*
*5.6 gm saturated fat*
*11.65 gm fat*

**Exchanges per serving**
*2 bread*
*½ meat*
*1 vegetable*

**On the side** Serve this casserole with a glass of nonfat milk
and a compote of fresh fruits for dessert for a nutritionally
balanced meal.

# 89   Stuffed Green Peppers

1 Tbsp. vegetable oil
½ cup chopped onion
½ cup chopped carrots
½ cup chopped celery
1 Tbsp. minced garlic
½ cup water
2 cups low-sodium beef broth
½ tsp. dried oregano
¼ tsp. dried basil
⅛ tsp. ground pepper
1 16 oz. can low-sodium stewed tomatoes
½ cup uncooked rice
6 large green peppers
⅓ cup shredded part-skim mozzarella cheese

In a skillet, heat oil. Add onions, carrots, celery and garlic; cook until vegetables are tender-crisp. Add water, beef broth, oregano, basil and pepper; bring to a boil. Add undrained tomatoes and uncooked rice; reduce heat and simmer until rice is tender. Cut tops from green peppers; clean and discard seeds. Cook whole peppers in boiling water for 5 minutes. Drain and stuff with rice mixture. Top with cheese. Bake at 350°F for 30 to 35 minutes.

**Per serving**
*117 calories*
*7.1 mg cholesterol*
*168 mg sodium*
*1.58 gm saturated fat*
*4.85 gm fat*

**Exchanges per serving**
*1 bread*
*1 vegetable*

**On the side** Serve these tasty peppers with a glass of cold non-fat milk and top off the meal with some fresh fruit.

½ cup chopped green pepper

2 large tomatoes

½ cup sliced green onions

¼ cup bran cereal, uncooked

1 egg

⅛ tsp. dried basil

⅛ tsp. oregano

½ Tbsp. dried parsley flakes

Heat oven to 350°F. Simmer green pepper in sauce-pan of water on stove for about 2 minutes. Slice each tomato in half. Scoop out pulp; chop pulp. In a bowl, mix tomato pulp, green pepper and remaining ingredients except parsley. Place tomato halves in baking dish. Fill each half with green pepper mixture. Sprinkle with parsley. Bake for 30 minutes.

**Per serving**
*49 calories*
*53 mg cholesterol*
*50 mg sodium*
*0.5 gm saturated fat*
*1.7 gm fat*

**Exchanges per serving**
*1 vegetable*

**On the side** White rice on the side of this colorful main dish adds a bread course. A glass of milk and a fruit for dessert make the meal nutritionally complete.

# 91  Tuna-Stuffed Tomato

4 tomatoes (6 oz. each)
¼ cup diced onions
¼ cup diced celery
2 tsp. Worcestershire sauce
⅛ tsp. pepper
⅛ tsp. pepper
2 6⅛ oz. cans tuna in spring water, drained
5 Tbsp. herb-seasoned bread crumbs

Cut slice off top of tomatoes; save slice. Remove and discard core. Scoop out pulp. Chop pulp and transfer to skillet. Add onion, celery, Worcestershire sauce, and pepper; cook over medium heat until all liquid evaporates. Remove from heat and add tuna and bread crumbs; mix well. Spoon tuna mixture into tomato shell and top with reserved tomato slices. Bake at 350°F for 15 to 20 minutes.

### Per serving
*250 calories*
*10 mg cholesterol*
*194 mg sodium*
*0.25 gm saturated fat*
*1.3 gm fat*

### Exchanges per serving
*½ bread*
*2 meat*
*1 vegetable*

**On the side** White rice is an appropriate accompaniment to this main dish. Fruit and milk complete the meal nutritionally.

3 Tbsp. vegetable oil

¾ cup diced onion

1 tsp. minced garlic

2 cups sliced potatoes

½ cup sliced carrots

1 cup chopped zucchini

1 cup low-sodium tomato sauce

1½ tsp. oregano

1½ tsp. basil

¾ tsp. cumin

⅛ tsp. pepper

In a skillet, heat oil. Add onions and garlic; sauté. Add the remaining ingredients; mix. Simmer, covered, until potatoes are tender

**Per serving**

*242 calories*
*0 mg cholesterol*
*75 mg sodium*
*1.25 gm saturated fat*
*10 gm fat*

**Exchanges per serving**

*2 bread*
*1 fat*
*1 vegetable*

**On the side** A glass of cold, nonfat milk and a fresh fruit for dessert make this meal nutritionally complete.

# 93 Vegetable Medley

1 cup cauliflower
1 cup broccoli
1 cup chopped carrots
1 cup chopped onions
1 cup green peppers
1 cup green beans
1 Tbsp. cornstarch
⅛ tsp. salt
¾ cup skim milk
4 Tbsp. margarine
2 Tbsp. dried dillweed
2 Tbsp. dried parsley flakes
1 Tbsp. lemon juice
¾ cup whole wheat bread crumbs
2 Tbsp. Parmesan cheese, grated

Heat oven to 350°F. Steam all vegetables until crisp-tender. In saucepan, combine cornstarch and salt. Add milk and 2 tablespoons margarine; bring to a boil. Remove from heat. Stir in dillweed, parsley and lemon juice. Toss with vegetables; put into baking dish. In small bowl combine bread crumbs, Parmesan cheese and 2 tablespoons melted margarine; mix. Sprinkle bread crumb mixture over vegetables. Bake 20 minutes.

**Per serving**
*128 calories*
*1 mg cholesterol*
*266 mg sodium*
*2 gm saturated fat*
*8 gm fat*

**Exchanges per serving**
*½ bread*
*1 fat*
*2 vegetables*

**On the side** A serving of brown rice, a glass of milk, and fruit compote for dessert make this meal complete.

7 egg whites
½ cup chopped carrots
½ cup green beans, cut
½ cup chopped green pepper
½ cup corn
¼ cup chopped onion
1 tsp. celery seed
1 tsp. dillweed
1 tsp. dry mustard
½ cup skim milk
½ cup light mayonnaise
½ cup flour
⅛ tsp. black pepper
⅛ tsp. salt

Heat oven to 325°F. Beat egg whites until stiff. In soufflé dish, mix all other ingredients. Fold egg whites into vegetable mixture. Bake 40 minutes. Serves 8.

**Per serving**
*70 calories*
*2.6 mg cholesterol*
*110 mg sodium*
*0.37 gm saturated fat*
*2.1 gm fat*

**Exchanges per serving**
*1 fat*
*1 vegetable*

**On the side** Serve this tasty soufflé with a slice of your favorite bread, a glass of cold nonfat milk, and top off the meal with a blend of melon balls and fresh berries.

2 cups red kidney beans
2 cups fresh chopped tomatoes
1¼ cups chopped onion
1 cup chopped green pepper
1 Tbsp. minced garlic
1 6 oz. can low-sodium tomato paste
¾ cup water
1 Tbsp. chili powder
1 Tbsp. soy sauce
½ tsp. ground cumin
½ tsp. ground pepper
½ tsp. oregano
4 cups brown rice, cooked

Drain kidney beans and set aside. In saucepan add tomatoes, onions, green peppers, garlic, tomato paste, water, chili powder, soy sauce, cumin, black pepper and oregano. Bring to a boil. Reduce heat; cover and simmer, stirring occasionally until mixture is thick and well blended, about 1½ to 2 hours. Stir in kidney beans and cook 15 minutes. Serve on brown rice.

**Per serving**
*196 calories*
*0 mg cholesterol*
*531 mg sodium*
*0 gm saturated fat*
*2.4 gm fat*

**Exchanges per serving**
*2 bread*
*1 vegetable*

**On the side** A glass of nonfat milk and a fresh chilled pear complete this meal nutritionally.

6 small zucchini
1 cup herb-seasoned bread crumbs
¼ cup chopped onions
1 tsp. dried parsley flakes
⅛ tsp. salt
⅛ tsp. pepper
½ tsp. paprika
2 Tbsp. vegetable oil

Scrub zucchini and remove stem ends. Cook zucchini in boiling water for 4 minutes. Slice each zucchini lengthwise and hollow out the centers. Chop the pulp and in a bowl, mix pulp, ¼ cup bread crumbs, onions, parsley, salt, pepper and paprika. Fill the zucchini with the mixture. Mix ¾ cup bread crumbs and vegetable oil. Place zucchini in baking dish and sprinkle bread crumb mixture over zucchini. Bake 30 minutes at 350°F.

**Per serving**
*92 calories*
*0 mg cholesterol*
*64 mg sodium*
*0.5 gm saturated fat*
*4.6 gm fat*

**Exchanges per serving**
*½ bread*
*1 vegetable*

**On the side** A serving of new potatoes, a glass of milk, and a baked apple complete this meal nutritionally.

3 medium zucchinis
1 lemon, thinly sliced
1 lime, thinly sliced
2 Tbsp. mint leaves
1½ Tbsp. sugar
¼ cup vegetable oil
4 Tbsp. orange juice
1½ tsp. orange peel, grated

Cut zucchini into 2-inch long, ¼ inch thick sticks. In a 5-quart saucepan, cook zucchini in boiling water for 3 to 4 minutes. In a large bowl, combine lemon, lime, mint, sugar, oil, orange juice, and orange peel. Combine zucchini with dressing; toss and serve.

**Per serving**
*114 calories*
*0 mg cholesterol*
*35 mg sodium*
*1.2 gm saturated fat*
*9.61 gm fat*

**Exchanges per serving**
*1 fat*
*½ fruit*
*1 vegetable*

**On the side** Garnish the plates with sections of fresh oranges, serve with your favorite bread and a glass of milk for a nutritionally balanced meal.

## 98  Zucchini Casserole

½ Tbsp. vegetable oil
¼ cup chopped onions
1½ cups shredded zucchini
½ cup bran cereal, uncooked
¼ cup part-skim mozzarella cheese, shredded
1 egg
¼ tsp. basil
¼ tsp. oregano
⅛ tsp. black pepper
½ cup low-sodium tomato sauce

Heat oven to 375°F. In a skillet, heat oil; sauté onions until tender. In a bowl, mix onions, zucchini, and remaining ingredients except tomato sauce; mix well. Pour into 8-inch baking dish. Spread tomato sauce evenly over top. Bake 30 minutes.

**Per serving**
*83 calories*
*48 mg cholesterol*
*74 mg sodium*
*1.45 gm saturated fat*
*3.91 gm fat*

**Exchanges per serving**
*½ meat*
*1 vegetable*

**On the side** Serve with a slice of bread, a glass of milk, and some honeydew melon (or fruit of your choice) for a nutritionally balanced, low-calorie meal.

# 99 Zucchini Stir-Fry

2 Tbsp. vegetable oil
2 tsp. minced garlic
2 med. zucchinis, sliced
¼ cup chopped red pepper
2 cups pea pods
2 cups bean sprouts, rinsed
½ tsp. salt

In a skillet, heat oil on high. Stir-fry garlic until golden. Add zucchini, red pepper, pea pods; stir-fry 1 minute. Add bean sprouts and salt; stir-fry until crisp-tender.

**Per serving**
*85 calories*
*0 mg cholesterol*
*187 mg sodium*
*0.6 mg saturated fat*
*4.8 gm fat*

**Exchanges per serving**
*1 fat*
*1 vegetable*

**On the side** Brown rice, milk, and fresh fruit round out this meal nutritionally.

# Beef and Veal

# 100 Barbecued Flank Steak

12 oz. flank steak

1 tsp. sherry

2 Tbsp. ketchup

1 tsp. minced garlic

1 tsp. minced onion

1 Tbsp. hoisin sauce*

1 tsp. soy sauce

1 tsp. Worcestershire sauce

Cut steak into strips 2 inches wide. Combine remaining ingredients in bowl and add steak, stirring to coat. Place steak on broiling pan and broil to desired doneness. Brush frequently with marinade.

*\* Available in the Oriental food section of most grocery stores.*

### Per serving
*300 calories*
*77 mg cholesterol*
*724 mg sodium*
*4.43 gm saturated fat*
*7.6 gm fat*

### Exchanges per serving
*4 meat*

**On the side** Cook up some fresh corn on the cob, pour a glass of cold nonfat milk, and end the meal with a tasty mixture of fresh fruits for nutritional balance.

1 lb. extra lean ground beef
⅓ cup diced onions
¼ tsp. garlic powder
3 cups shredded cabbage
1 cup sliced carrots
½ cup low-sodium beef broth
¼ tsp. pepper
½ tsp. caraway seed

Combine beef, onion, and garlic powder in a casserole dish. Bake for 15 minutes at 450°F. Stir occasionally to break up meat. Drain fat. Turn oven down to 350°F and add cabbage, carrots, broth, pepper, and caraway seed. Blend well. Cover and bake 60 minutes.

**Per serving**
*225 calories*
*111 mg cholesterol*
*303 mg sodium*
*4.0 gm saturated fat*
*10.3 gm fat*

**Exchanges per serving**
*2½ meat*
*1 vegetable*

**On the side** Serve with a slice of your favorite fresh bread or a small dinner roll, a glass of milk, and end with baked apples for a meal that's delicious and nutritionally complete.

# 102 Beef Burgundy

2 lb. lean beef stew meat, cubed
¼ cup flour
1 cup chopped onion
¾ cup chopped celery
1½ cups chopped carrots
1 can condensed consommé
½ cup water
⅓ cup burgundy wine
⅛ tsp. pepper
⅛ tsp. salt
¼ tsp. celery seed
1½ Tbsp. vegetable oil

In a skillet, heat oil. Lightly flour meat and brown. Add remaining ingredients, cover, and simmer until meat is tender, about 1½ hours. Stir often.

## Per serving
*390 calories*
*111 mg cholesterol*
*350 mg sodium*
*7.8 gm saturated fat*
*19.3 gm fat*

## Exchanges per serving
*1 fat*
*3 meat*
*1 vegetable*

**On the side** Mix green beans and carrots, steam them, and serve them with a slice of bread and a glass of milk for a nutritionally complete meal.

# 103  Beef Casserole

Serves 4

1 lb. lean beef stew meat, cut into cubes
1 cup low-sodium beef broth
½ cup chopped onion
¼ cup chopped celery
⅛ tsp. pepper
¼ cup flour
½ cup whole-wheat bread crumbs
4 cups cooked rice

Preheat oven to 300°F. Put meat into casserole dish with broth, onions, celery and pepper. Mix flour and bread crumbs and stir into liquid. Cover and bake 2 ½ to 3 hours. Serve over rice.

**Per serving**
*490 calories*
*80 mg cholesterol*
*607.5 mg sodium*
*7.0 gm saturated fat*
*15.1 gm fat*

**Exchanges per serving**
*3 bread*
*3 meat*

**On the side** A mixed green salad, a glass of milk, and fresh fruit for dessert complete this meal nutritiously.

118 ▪

1½ lbs. lean beef, cut into 1-inch cubes
2 tsp. minced garlic
¼ cup minced onion
⅓ cup lemon juice
½ tsp. dry mustard
¾ tsp. chili powder
⅛ tsp. pepper
2 tsp. honey
¾ tsp. ginger
1 tsp. allspice

Place meat in mixing bowl. Combine remaining ingredients and pour over meat; mix thoroughly. Let stand for 1 hour. Thread meat on skewers. Broil, turning occasionally, until desired doneness.

**Per serving**
*254 calories*
*185 mg cholesterol*
*102 mg sodium*
*4.25 gm saturated fat*
*13.3 gm fat*

**Exchanges per serving**
*3 meat*

**On the side** Serve with fresh tomatoes, a slice of bread, a glass of milk, and mixed fruit dessert for a meal that's delicious and nutritious.

1 lb. ground beef
1½ cups sliced onions
1 can chicken noodle soup
1 can mushroom soup
⅛ tsp. pepper
2 cups water
1 cup uncooked rice

Brown meat and onions. Add soups, water, and rice; mix. Place in a casserole dish. Bake for 1 hour 45 minutes at 350°F.

### Per serving
*339 calories*
*50 mg cholesterol*
*689 mg sodium*
*4.8 gm saturated fat*
*13.8 gm fat*

### Exchanges per serving
*2 bread*
*1½ fat*
*2 meat*
*½ vegetable*

**On the side** Serve this yummy goulash with a glass of cold, non-fat milk, and finish off the meal with baked apples as dessert.

10 oz. round steak
1 cup water
¼ cup finely chopped onion
2 tsp. ground ginger
2 Tbsp. soy sauce
3 tsp. Worcestershire sauce
1 tsp. garlic

In a blender, combine all ingredients, except steak, and process until smooth. Place steak in shallow pan and pour sauce over steak. Marinate for 1½ hours. Broil steak until done to taste. Heat marinade and serve with steak.

**Per serving**
*338 calories*
*114 mg cholesterol*
*425 mg sodium*
*8.5 gm saturated fat*
*19.5 gm fat*

**Exchanges per serving**
4½ meat

**On the side** Get a half-bunch of broccoli florets and steam them until they are tender to serve beside this tangy beef dish. Some rice or a slice of bread, a glass of milk, and fresh pears for dessert complete the meal nutritionally.

1 lb. lean ground beef

¾ cup green pepper, chopped

¼ cup chopped red pepper

¼ cup chopped onions

1 cup tomato sauce

4 tsp. Dijon-style mustard

3 tsp. Worcestershire sauce

1 Tbsp. ketchup

3 hamburger buns, whole wheat

In a skillet, cook meat and drain fat. Add green peppers, red peppers, and onions and cook over medium heat until vegetables are tender. Stir in tomato sauce, mustard, Worcestershire sauce, and ketchup. Bring to a boil. Reduce heat and simmer 10 to 15 minutes. Split hamburger buns in half and toast under broiler. Divide meat mixture among buns for an open-face sandwich.

**Per serving**
*247 calories*
*68.3 mg cholesterol*
*371 mg sodium*
*3.6 gm saturated fat*
*9.8 gm fat*

**Exchanges per serving**
*1 bread*
*2 meat*
*1 vegetable*

**On the side** Add a glass of milk and a fruit of your choice.

1 lb. beef round steak
¾ cup water
⅔ cup sliced onions
2 tsp. lime juice
½ tsp. instant beef bouillon granules
½ tsp. garlic powder
½ tsp. dried dillweed
⅛ tsp. pepper
1 Tbsp. cornstarch mixed with 2 Tbsp. water

Cut meat into 4 servings. In nonstick skillet, brown meat on medium-high heat. Add water, onion, lime juice, bouillon granules, garlic powder, dillweed, and pepper to skillet. Bring to a boil, then reduce heat. Cover and simmer for 30 to 40 minutes. Stir cornstarch mixture into juices. Cook until thick and bubbly.

**Per serving**
*185 calories*
*72 mg cholesterol*
*271 mg sodium*
*1.9 gm saturated fat*
*5.3 gm fat*

**Exchanges per serving**
*4 meat*

**On the side** Steamed cauliflower florets, a slice of bread, a glass of milk and chilled peaches for dessert make this meal nutritionally balanced.

4 Tbsp. margarine

3 lbs. lean round beef steak, cubed

½ cup flour

1 cup chopped onions

2 cups fresh, sliced mushrooms

2 tsp. garlic, crushed

1 cup sour cream

⅛ tsp. pepper

6 cups cooked noodles

In large skillet, melt margarine. Lightly coat each piece of meat with flour. Sauté meat until all sides are brown; remove and set aside. Add onions, mushrooms, and garlic; sauté until tender. Add sour cream and stir. Put beef back into skillet. Heat thoroughly. Serve over noodles.

### Per serving

*422 calories*
*79 mg cholesterol*
*114 mg sodium*
*8.7 gm saturated fat*
*22.1 gm fat*

### Exchanges per serving

*2 bread*
*2½ fat*
*3 meat*
*½ vegetable*

**On the side** A glass of milk and a piece of fruit make this meal a standalone, nutritionally.

# 110  Fluffy Meat Loaf

1 lb. lean ground beef
1 egg
⅓ cup oat meal
⅓ cup water
1 small potato, grated
1 tsp. dried parsley flakes
⅛ tsp. pepper
1 Tbsp. minced onion

Combine all ingredients in bowl. Mix well. Shape into loaf on a shallow baking dish. Bake at 350°F for 1 hour.

### Per serving
*320 calories*
*156 mg cholesterol*
*116 mg sodium*
*7.7 gm saturated fat*
*13.3 gm fat*

### Exchanges per serving
*1 bread*
*3 meat*

**On the side** Steamed fresh spinach, a glass of milk, and melon balls for dessert make this meal nutritionally complete.

# 111 Garden Burgers

1 egg white
2½ Tbsp. water
3 Tbsp. herb-seasoned bread crumbs
¾ tsp. dried oregano
⅛ tsp. salt
⅛ tsp. pepper
1 lb. lean ground beef
1 small cucumber, chopped
⅔ cup tomato sauce
1 tsp. minced onion

Preheat broiler. In a mixing bowl, beat egg white and water together until combined. Add bread crumbs. Stir in ½ tsp. oregano, salt, and pepper. Add beef, then mix well. Shape meat mixture into four patties. Place patties on broiling pan and broil until desired doneness. While meat is broiling, combine cucumber, tomato sauce, onion, and ¼ tsp. oregano. Heat mixture until bubbly, stirring all the while. Serve meat patties topped with tomato sauce mixture.

### Per serving
*290 calories*
*165 mg cholesterol*
*156 mg sodium*
*5.75 gm saturated fat*
*15.0 gm fat*

### Exchanges per serving
*3 meat*
*1 vegetable*

**On the side** Fresh tomatoes and lettuce leaves are delicious with these burgers, either on top or on the side. Add a glass of milk and a fruit for dessert to make the meal nutritionally balanced.

1 14 oz. can sauerkraut and juice
½ cup water
½ cup uncooked rice
¾ cup chopped onion
1 lb. lean ground beef
¼ cup finely diced green pepper
¼ cup low-sodium beef broth
1 8 oz. can low-sodium tomato sauce
¼ tsp. black pepper

In a casserole dish, pour in sauerkraut and its juices and add water. Sprinkle with rice, onion, beef and green pepper. Pour broth over mixture, then pour tomato sauce over the top. Sprinkle with black pepper. Bake uncovered for 1½ hours at 350°F.

**Per serving**
*200 calories*
*68 mg cholesterol*
*597 mg sodium*
*3.31 gm saturated fat*
*8.8 gm fat*

**Exchanges per serving**
*2½ meat*
*1 vegetable*

**On the side** A slice of rye bread, a glass of milk, and a fresh pear make this meal nutritionally complete.

1 lb. lean ground beef

2 eggs, beaten

1 cup plain bread crumbs

4 Tbsp. minced onion

4 Tbsp. pickle relish

2 tsp. Worcestershire sauce

1 cup sauerkraut, drained and chopped

½ cup part-skim Swiss cheese, shredded

Preheat oven to 350°F. In a bowl, combine all ingredients, except sauerkraut and cheese; mix thoroughly. Spread mixture to form a 6 x 8-inch rectangle. Spread sauerkraut over meat. Sprinkle half the cheese over the sauerkraut. Start at the short end and roll up meat like a jelly roll. Transfer to a pan and bake for 30 to 40 minutes. Sprinkle remaining cheese on top and bake until cheese is melted.

**Per serving**
*344 calories*
*169 mg cholesterol*
*796 mg sodium*
*7.28 gm saturated fat*
*16.45 gm fat*

**Exchanges per serving**
*1 bread*
*3 meat*
*4 vegetable*

**On the side** Boiled spaghetti squash, a glass of nonfat milk, and cantaloupe melon balls, 1 cup per person, complete this meal nutritionally.

1 lb. lean ground beef
1 8 oz. can low-sodium tomato sauce
2 Tbsp. ketchup
¼ tsp. pepper
¼ tsp. salt
1 7 oz. package Creamettes macaroni

In skillet, brown beef; pour off fat. Add tomato sauce, ketchup, salt and pepper. Mix. Cook noodles according to package directions; drain. Stir noodles into beef mixture. Heat thoroughly.

**Per serving**
*201 calories*
*68 mg cholesterol*
*140 mg sodium*
*3.5 gm saturated fat*
*9.0 gm fat*

**Exchanges per serving**
*1 bread*
*2 meat*

**On the side** Cabbage salad with carrots, a glass of nonfat milk, and a fresh pear complete this meal nutritionally.

½ lb. lean round beef steak

⅛ cup soy sauce

1 tsp. minced garlic

⅛ tsp. ground ginger

2 Tbsp. vegetable oil

½ cup chopped green onions

½ cup chopped red pepper

½ cup chopped green pepper

½ cup chopped celery

1 tsp. cornstarch

½ cup water

2 cups cooked rice

Cut beef into thin strips. Combine soy sauce, garlic, and ginger; mix. Add beef and toss. Heat oil in skillet. Add beef mixture and stir-fry over high heat until brown. Cover and simmer until meat is tender. Turn up heat and add vegetables and stir-fry until crisp-tender. Mix cornstarch with water; add to skillet. Stir and cook until thickened. Serve with rice.

**Per serving**
*260 calories*
*38.5 mg cholesterol*
*675 mg sodium*
*2.75 gm saturated fat*
*12.1 gm fat*

**Exchanges per serving**
*1 bread*
*2 meat*
*1 vegetable*

**On the side** Combine this zesty steak with a glass of milk and a serving of your favorite fruit and you have a meal that is delicious and nutritionally complete.

1 lb. lean ground beef
1 cup chopped onions
1 28 oz. can tomato puree
1 tsp. garlic
1½ tsp. dried basil
½ tsp. sugar
8 oz. package of macaroni, cooked
¼ cup grated Parmesan cheese

In a large saucepan, cook beef and onions until beef is browned, stirring frequently. Drain. Add tomato puree, garlic, basil, and sugar. Simmer for 20 minutes. Add macaroni to mixture and sprinkle with Parmesan cheese.

**Per serving**
*341 calories*
*110 mg cholesterol*
*124 mg sodium*
*6.1 gm saturated fat*
*15.7 gm fat*

**Exchanges per serving**
*1 bread*
*3 meat*
*1 vegetable*

**On the side** You need only drink a glass of nonfat milk and choose your favorite fruit as dessert for this meal to be nutritionally complete.

Nonstick cooking spray
1 lb. lean round steak
1 cup chopped onions
½ tsp. garlic, crushed
2½ cups low-sodium beef broth
2½ Tbsp. flour
¾ cup dry red wine
2 cups sliced mushrooms
1 cup light sour cream

Spray skillet with nonstick cooking spray. Brown meat, onions, and garlic. Add beef broth; cover and simmer for 1 to 1½ hours. Dissolve flour in wine, then whisk into meat juices until thickened. Add mushrooms and simmer for 5 to 10 minutes. Add sour cream and simmer an additional 5 to 10 minutes.

**Per serving**
*316 calories*
*63 mg cholesterol*
*90 mg sodium*
*9.8 gm saturated fat*
*17.7 gm fat*

**Exchanges per serving**
*2 fat*
*3 meat*

**On the side** This tasty Stroganoff is delicious over fettucine noodles (½ cup per serving). A side salad, a glass of milk, and fruit for dessert make the meal complete nutritionally.

# 118  Lemon Veal with Spinach

1 Tbsp. vegetable oil
1½ lb. lean veal shoulder, cut into cubes
1 cup chopped onions
¼ cup water
1 Tbsp. lemon juice
⅛ tsp. pepper
⅛ tsp. crushed fennel seed
¼ cup chopped green onions
1 10 oz. package frozen spinach

In skillet, heat oil; brown veal. Add onion, cook until tender. Pour off fat. Add water, lemon juice, pepper, and crushed fennel seed. Cover and simmer until veal is tender. Add green onions and spinach. More water may be added if needed. Simmer until spinach is tender.

### Per serving
*230 calories*
*124 mg cholesterol*
*145 mg sodium*
*2.9 gm saturated fat*
*9.0 gm fat*

### Exchanges per serving
*4 meat*
*½ fat*
*1 vegetable*

**On the side** Complete this meal nutritionally by serving each person a slice of bread, a glass of milk, and a fresh pear.

1 lb. lean ground beef
½ cup chopped onions
½ cup chopped celery
½ cup whole wheat bread crumbs
1 egg
2 tsp. Worcestershire sauce
⅛ tsp. black pepper
1 Tbsp. ketchup
1 tsp. minced garlic

Mix all ingredients together; blend well. Form into loaf. Place in loaf pan and bake at 325°F for 60 minutes.

### Per serving
*219 calories*
*110 mg cholesterol*
*170 mg sodium*
*4.0 gm saturated fat*
*10.33 gm fat*

### Exchanges per serving
*½ bread*
*2½ meat*

**On the side** Serve this wholesome meat loaf with roasted new potatoes, steamed green beans and carrots, a glass of milk, and mixed fruit compote for dessert for a well balanced and nutritionally complete meal.

# 120 Mini Meat Loaves

*Serves 6*

1 lb. lean ground beef
½ lb. lean ground pork
½ lb. lean ground veal
⅔ cup chopped onion
1 tsp. garlic
½ cup grated carrots
1 cup grated, peeled potato
½ cup chopped green pepper
1 Tbsp. finely chopped red pepper
½ Tbsp. chopped basil
2 eggs, beaten
⅛ tsp. salt
⅛ tsp. pepper
¼ cup ketchup
6 1-inch cubes part-skim cheddar cheese

Place all ingredients, except cheese, in a large bowl. Mix thoroughly. Shape into 6 small loaves. Place loaves on baking pan. Press a piece of cheese into the top of each loaf. Bake at 375°F for 30 minutes.

**Per serving**
*480 calories*
*108 mg cholesterol*
*719 mg sodium*
*9.6 gm saturated fat*
*27.9 gm fat*

**Exchanges per serving**
*1 bread*
*1 fat*
*4 meat*
*1 vegetable*

**On the side** Baby carrots cooked with gingerroot, a glass of milk, and mixed melon balls, 1 cup per serving, complete this meal nutritionally.

# 121  Moist Meat Loaf

1 lb. lean ground beef

⅔ cup oatmeal

½ cup skim milk

1 egg

⅓ cup chopped onions

1 Tbsp. mustard

1 Tbsp. Worcestershire sauce

½ tsp. black pepper

¼ cup ketchup

In a large bowl, mix all the ingredients together; blend well. Shape into a loaf and place in a loaf pan. Bake at 350°F for 1½ hours.

### Per serving
*229 calories*
*109 mg cholesterol*
*391 mg sodium*
*5.3 gm saturated fat*
*11.3 gm fat*

### Exchanges per serving
*1 bread*
*2 meat*

**On the side** Onions, mushrooms, and green peppers, sautéed in a little margarine, a glass of milk, and baked apple dessert complete this meal nutritionally.

Nonstick cooking spray
1 lb. veal steak, ¾ inch thick
1 Tbsp. flour
⅔ cup water
1 cup sliced, fresh mushrooms
¼ cup chopped onions
1 Tbsp. lemon juice

Spray skillet with cooking spray. Add steak and brown on both sides. Cover and simmer 30 to 35 minutes or until tender. Remove veal and keep warm. Stir flour into meat juices. Increase heat and gradually add water until smooth and thickened. Add mushrooms, onions, and lemon juice. Cook 5 minutes, stirring frequently. Spoon over veal.

**Per serving**
*209 calories*
*119 mg cholesterol*
*98 mg sodium*
*2.7 gm saturated fat*
*7.2 gm fat*

**Exchanges per serving**
*4 meat*

**On the side** Green beans, simply steamed, a slice of your favorite bread, a glass of nonfat milk, and fresh fruit as dessert complete this meal nutritionally.

# 123 Oven Porcupines

1 lb. lean ground beef
½ cup uncooked rice
1½ cups water
½ cup chopped onion
½ tsp. celery salt
⅛ tsp. garlic powder
⅛ tsp. pepper
1 15 oz. can low-sodium tomato sauce
1 Tbsp. Worcestershire sauce

In bowl, mix beef, rice, ½ cup water, onion, celery salt, garlic powder, and pepper. Shape mixture into 10 balls. Cook in skillet until brown on all sides. Drain. Place meatballs in 8 x 8-inch dish. Mix remaining ingredients; pour over meatballs. Cover and cook for 50 to 55 minutes at 350°F.

**Per serving**
*277 calories*
*103 mg cholesterol*
*414 mg sodium*
*5.3 gm saturated fat*
*13.3 gm fat*

**Exchanges per serving**
*1 bread*
*1 fat*
*2 meat*

**On the side** Choose green beans, carrots, or mixed vegetables, a glass of milk, and fruit to make this meal a nutritionally balanced one.

¾ lb. boneless beef round steak

¼ tsp. pepper

1½ cups low-sodium beef broth

1 tsp. beef bouillon

1 9 oz. package frozen green beans

2 cups frozen hash brown potatoes with onions and peppers

1 cup tomato sauce

¾ tsp. sugar

1 Tbsp. cornstarch

Trim fat from beef and cut into bite size pieces. Sprinkle with pepper. In a skillet, brown meat over medium heat. Add beef broth. Bring to a boil and reduce heat. Add beef bouillon; cover and simmer for 15 minutes. Rinse and drain beans and potatoes. Add beans and potatoes to skillet; simmer for 10 minutes. Stir together tomato sauce, sugar, and cornstarch and add to meat mixture. Cook and stir until bubbly and thickened.

**Per serving**
*302 calories*
*93 mg cholesterol*
*583 mg sodium*
*4.5 gm saturated fat*
*10.0 gm fat*

**Exchanges per serving**
*1 bread*
*2½ meat*
*1 vegetable*

**On the side** Serve this with a glass of milk and a single-cup serving of mixed melon balls for dessert for a healthful and nutritionally balanced meal.

# 125  Rolled Veal Loaf

2 lbs. ground veal
¾ cup plain bread crumbs
¾ cup chopped onions
1 egg, beaten
1 Tbsp. minced garlic
1 tsp. dried parsley flakes
1 Tbsp. low-cal Thousand Island dressing
1 tsp. oregano
1½ tsp. chili powder
⅛ tsp. salt
⅛ tsp. pepper
1 cup fresh, chopped mushrooms
½ cup part-skim mozzarella cheese

In a mixing bowl, combine all ingredients, except cheese and mushrooms; mix well. Shape meat mixture into a 20 x 9-inch rectangle. Sprinkle with cheese and mushrooms. Roll meat jelly-roll style, starting from 9-inch end. Transfer to a loaf pan. Bake for 1 hour at 350°F.

**Per serving**
*365 calories*
*41 mg cholesterol*
*237 mg sodium*
*8.82 gm saturated fat*
*18.5 gm fat*

**Exchanges per serving:**
*½ bread*
*½ fat*
*4 meat*

**On the side** Serve this with corn on the cob, and mix up your favorite fresh fruits for dessert for a nutritionally balanced meal.

# 126  Saucy Cubed Steaks

4 3 oz. cubed steaks
1 onion, sliced, separated into rings
2 Tbsp. vegetable oil
1 7½ oz. can cream of mushroom soup
1 cup fresh sliced mushrooms
2 Tbsp. dry white wine

In skillet, cook cubed steak and onions in oil until meat is browned. Drain off fat. Stir together cream of mushroom soup, mushrooms, and wine. Add to steaks. Simmer, covered, for 25 minutes.

### Per serving
*360 calories*
*84 mg cholesterol*
*689 mg sodium*
*11.0 gm saturated fat*
*20.0 gm fat*

### Exchanges per serving
*1 fat*
*3 meat*

**On the side** Serve with baked potatos, a side salad, a glass of nonfat milk, and fresh fruit to complete the meal nutritionally.

1 Tbsp. margarine
1 cup sliced, fresh mushrooms
1 tsp. minced garlic
3 Tbsp. red table wine
4 Tbsp. sour cream
2 5 oz. boneless beef steaks

In a skillet, heat margarine; add mushrooms and garlic and sauté until light brown. Reduce heat and add wine. Heat, stirring constantly. Stir in sour cream until heated through; set aside and keep warm. Place steaks on a broiling pan and broil steaks until done to desired taste. Remove steaks and pour sauce over.

**Per serving**
*429 calories*
*208 mg cholesterol*
*168 mg sodium*
*8.7 gm saturated fat*
*22.0 gm fat*

**Exchanges per serving**
*2 fat*
*4 meat*
*1 vegetable*

**On the side** Brussel sprouts, steamed and tossed lightly in a small amount of margarine, a glass of nonfat milk, and fruit for dessert make this meal nutritionally complete.

# 128 Tabbouleh with Beef

*Serves 4*

2 cups boiling water
⅓ cup cracked wheat
¾ cup ground lean beef
¾ cup chopped cucumber
⅓ cup finely chopped, fresh parsley
½ cup sliced green onion
2 tomatoes finely chopped
⅛ tsp. salt
⅛ tsp. black pepper
3 Tbsp. lemon juice

In medium bowl, pour boiling water over cracked wheat. Let stand until water is absorbed—about one hour. Drain. Cook beef and drain fat. Combine all ingredients together and mix with a spoon.

**Per serving**
*194 calories*
*24 mg cholesterol*
*20.5 mg sodium*
*1.25 gm saturated fat*
*3.36 gm fat*

**Exchanges per serving**
*1 bread*
*1 meat*
*1 vegetable*

**On the side** Fresh peaches with yogurt for dessert make this meal nutritionally complete.

1 16 oz. package frozen broccoli, baby carrots, and
  water chestnuts
1 lb. beef cubed steak
½ cup water
3 Tbsp. teriyaki sauce
2 tsp. soy sauce
½ tsp. five spice powder
½ tsp. minced garlic
2 cups cooked rice

Rinse and drain vegetables. Cut beef into bite-size
strips. In a bowl, combine water, teriyaki sauce, soy
sauce, five spice powder, and garlic.

In a skillet, stir-fry beef on high until browned. Add
vegetables and stir-fry for 3 to 4 minutes. Reduce
heat. Stir in sauce and cook until thick and bubbly.
Serve over rice.

**Per serving**
*331 calories*
*123 mg cholesterol*
*1229 mg sodium*
*2.8 gm saturated fat*
*7.0 gm fat*

**Exchanges per serving**
*1 bread*
*3 meat*
*1 vegetable*

**On the side** A glass of nonfat milk and some fresh fruit for
dessert round out this meal nutritionally.

1 lb. lean ground beef
1 Tbsp. minced onion
2 tsp. parsley flakes
1 6 oz. can low-sodium tomato paste
3 cups water
1 tsp. chili powder
½ cup sliced, fresh mushrooms
7 oz. package macaroni

Brown beef in skillet; drain fat. Add onions, parsley flakes, tomato paste, water, chili powder, mushrooms and macaroni. Bring to a boil. Cover and simmer until macaroni is tender.

### Per serving
*273 calories*
*63.4 mg cholesterol*
*68.4 mg sodium*
*1.7 gm saturated fat*
*5.4 gm fat*

### Exchanges per serving
*1 bread*
*2 meat*
*1 vegetable*

**On the side** Mixed fruit with a dollop of nonfat yogurt offers a refreshing dessert for this meal and completes it nutritionally.

# 131 Veal Barley Stew

Nonstick cooking spray
1 lb. lean boneless veal, cubed
3 cups sliced fresh mushrooms
1 cup chopped onions
1 tsp. minced garlic
2 12 oz. cans vegetable juice
1 cup sliced carrots
1 cup sliced celery
2 cups potatoes, cubed
½ cup pearl barley
1 bay leaf
¾ tsp. dried basil

Spray a skillet with nonstick spray. Brown veal and remove from skillet. Cook mushrooms, onion, and garlic until mushrooms are tender. Drain off any fat. Stir in meat, vegetable juice, carrots, celery, potatoes, barley, bay leaf, and basil. Bring to a boil. Reduce heat and simmer for 45 minutes. Discard bay leaf.

## Per serving
*359 calories*
*77 mg cholesterol*
*331 mg sodium*
*5.0 gm saturated fat*
*19.0 gm fat*

## Exchanges per serving
*1 bread*
*3 meat*
*1 vegetable*

**On the side** A glass of milk and a serving of fresh fruit complete this meal nutritionally.

Nonstick cooking spray
4 veal rib chops
1 Tbsp. margarine
½ cup chopped onion
1 tsp. minced garlic
4 cups sliced, fresh mushrooms
1 16 oz. can low-sodium stewed tomatoes
⅛ tsp. ground pepper
¼ tsp. sage
1 Tbsp. dry red wine

Spray skillet with nonstick cooking spray. Brown chops on both sides. Remove from skillet. Add margarine, onion, and garlic to skillet and cook until soft. Add mushrooms and cook until soft. Add tomatoes and their juice, pepper, sage, and wine; bring to a boil. Reduce heat. Return chops to skillet and simmer, turning occasionally, until veal is tender. Spoon sauce over veal.

**Per serving**
*310 calories*
*87 mg cholesterol*
*122 mg sodium*
*6.5 gm saturated fat*
*14.0 gm fats*

**Exchanges per serving**
*1 fat*
*3 meat*
*1 vegetable*

**On the side** A side dish of boiled spaghetti squash is delicious with this veal dish. A glass of milk and your pick of fresh fruits complete the meal nutritionally.

# 133 Veal with Peppers

2 Tbsp. vegetable oil
4 veal cutlets
1 large red pepper cut into strips
1 large green pepper cut into strips
¾ cup chopped onions
1 tsp. minced garlic
¼ tsp. ground pepper
½ tsp. sage
¼ cup water

In skillet, heat oil. Brown veal; remove from skillet. Reduce heat and add red peppers, green peppers, onion, garlic, sage, ground pepper. Cook until peppers are soft. Return veal to skillet. Add water and cook until veal is tender.

**Per serving**
*265 calories*
*87 mg cholesterol*
*76 mg sodium*
*4.7 gm saturated fat*
*16.0 gm fat*

**Exchanges per serving**
*1 fat*
*3 meat*
*1 vegetable*

**On the side** Add a serving of white rice and offer fresh fruit for dessert to make this meal nutritionally complete.

1 breast of veal, about 4 lbs. (3 lbs. cooked weight)
2 cups cooked rice
1 tsp. dried parsley flakes
½ tsp. grated lime rind
1 tsp. basil
⅛ tsp. salt
⅛ tsp. pepper
⅛ tsp. paprika
½ tsp. garlic powder

Split breast of veal to form pocket for stuffing. Trim off all fat. Combine rice, parsley, lime rind, basil, salt, and pepper. Stuff into veal pocket. Place veal in a roasting pan. Sprinkle with paprika and garlic powder. Roast in 350°F oven for 2½ hours or until browned and tender.

**Per serving**
*265 calories*
*133 mg cholesterol*
*545 mg sodium*
*2.1 gm saturated fat*
*7.6 gm fat*

**Exchanges per serving**
*½ bread*
*5 meat*

**On the side** Asparagus, steamed gently over boiling water, and a dessert of fresh pears complete this meal nutritionally.

6 veal cutlets
¾ cup skim milk
⅓ cup whole-wheat bread crumbs
1 cup chopped tomatoes
¼ tsp. oregano
¼ tsp. sage
2 medium zucchinis, sliced

Dip cutlets in milk, then in bread crumbs. Brown in nonstick pan. Add tomatoes, oregano, and sage. Cover and simmer for 30 minutes. Add zucchini and simmer for another 15 minutes.

**Per serving**
*276 calories*
*88 mg cholesterol*
*208 mg sodium*
*4.16 gm saturated fat*
*10.0 gm fat*

**Exchanges per serving**
*3 meat*
*1 vegetable*

**On the side** A side dish of brown rice, or a slice of your favorite bread, a glass of nonfat milk, and fresh fruit make this meal a complete and nutritionally balanced one.

# 136 Vegetable Beef Stir-Fry

1 Tbsp. vegetable oil

3 cups broccoli florets

1 cup sliced carrots

½ cup sliced onions

1 cup green pepper, chopped

1 cup sliced zucchini

12 oz. broiled sirloin steak, cut into strips

2 Tbsp. soy sauce

1 tsp. cornstarch

½ tsp. sugar

In large skillet, heat oil; add broccoli, carrots, onions, green pepper, and zucchini. Stir frequently and quickly until vegetables are tender-crisp. Stir in beef strips. In small bowl, combine soy sauce, sugar, and cornstarch; add to beef mixture and cook until sauce is thickened, stirring frequently.

**Per serving**
*274 calories*
*76 mg cholesterol*
*617 mg sodium*
*3.5 gm saturated fat*
*11.6 gm fat*

**Exchanges per serving**
*1 fat*
*3½ meat*
*2 vegetable*

**On the side** A serving of white rice (½ cup per person), a glass of milk, and fresh fruit for dessert, and you have a nutritionally complete meal.

1 Tbsp. tomato sauce

½ cup water

1 lb. lean ground beef

1 egg

⅓ cup grated zucchini

⅓ cup grated carrots

½ tsp. thyme

⅓ cup bran

⅛ tsp. pepper

1 tsp. Worcestershire sauce

¼ cup grated part-skim Swiss cheese

In a bowl, mix tomato paste with water. Add remaining ingredients. Mix well. Shape into loaf and place in loaf pan. Bake at 350°F for 1 hour.

**Per serving**
*355 calories*
*177 mg cholesterol*
*513 mg sodium*
*10.0 gm saturated fat*
*18.3 gm fat*

**Exchanges per serving**
*3 meat*
*1 vegetable*

**On the side** Serve this hearty meat loaf with a baked potato, a glass of milk, and a serving of your favorite fruit for dessert for a nutritionally balanced meal.

# Seafood
# and Fish

1 (4 lb.) whole bass

3½ quarts water

1 cup sliced carrots

1 cup sliced celery

1 tsp. salt

6 peppercorns

1 bay leaf

⅛ tsp. thyme

1 tsp. lemon pepper

Thoroughly clean and scale fish. Wrap fish loosely in foil; do not seal. In 5-quart saucepan, place foil-wrapped fish in the water and add remaining ingredients. Bring to a boil and reduce heat. Cook fish 15 minutes. Let stand in cooking liquid until ready to serve.

**Per serving**
_226 calories_
_128 mg cholesterol_
_533 mg sodium_
_1.5 gm saturated fat_
_6.87 gm fat_

**Exchanges per serving**
_3 meat_
_1 vegetable_

**On the side** Serve this tasty fish with a side dish of brown rice, and create a fresh fruit dessert using yogurt and peaches, and you'll have a meal that's delicious and nutritious.

# 139 Baked Cod

2 lbs. cod

½ cup sliced green onions

¾ cup sliced celery

1 tsp. minced garlic

1 tomato, sliced

⅛ tsp. lemon pepper

¾ tsp. dried thyme

½ tsp. dried basil

½ cup low-sodium tomato sauce

Preheat oven to 350°F. In baking dish, place a layer of onions, celery, garlic, and tomato slices. Place cod on top of layer, and cover fish with a repeat layer. Sprinkle with lemon pepper, thyme, and basil. Pour tomato sauce over top of fish. Cover and bake for 25 minutes or until fish is done.

**Per serving**
*211 calories*
*82 mg cholesterol*
*176 mg sodium*
*0.26 gm saturated fat*
*1.3 gm fat*

**Exchanges per serving**
*4 meat*

**On the side** A side dish of broccoli and cauliflower, steamed just until tender, and a dessert of fresh fruit with yogurt complete this meal nutritionally.

4 oz. frozen crab meat, thawed, drained

⅔ cup part-skim cheddar cheese, shredded

⅓ cup chopped green onions

4 eggs

¾ cup evaporated skim milk

½ tsp. dry mustard

⅛ tsp. black pepper

½ tsp. lemon juice

⅛ tsp. paprika

Preheat oven to 400°F. In medium bowl, combine crab meat, cheese and green onions. Pour crab meat in an 8-inch glass pie plate; press mixture over bottom and up sides. In mixing bowl, beat, using a wire whisk, eggs, milk, mustard, pepper, and lemon juice together. Pour over crab meat mixture. Sprinkle with paprika and bake for 30 to 35 minutes.

**Per serving**
*158 calories*
*266 mg cholesterol*
*376 mg sodium*
*2.42 gm saturated fat*
*7.48 gm fat*

**Exchanges per serving**
*2 meat*

**On the side** Serve this elegant quiche on a plate surrounded by alternating points of honeydew melon slices and fresh strawberries. A freshly baked muffin, bread, or a roll, and a glass of milk make this meal nutritionally complete.

# 141 Baked Ratatouille and Fish

*Serves 4*

1 medium size zucchini, sliced

1 small eggplant, cut into chunks

1 cup yellow pepper, chopped

1 cup red pepper, chopped

3 tsp. dry basil leaves

1 tsp. oregano

1 Tbsp. vegetable oil

1 lb. white-flesh fish fillets

⅓ cup part-skim Havarti cheese, shredded

In shallow 3-quart baking dish, combine zucchini, eggplant, yellow and red peppers, basil, oregano, and oil. Cover and bake in 425°F oven for 40 minutes. Push vegetables to sides of the dish and lay fish in the center. Cover and bake for 20 to 25 minutes. Sprinkle with cheese and bake until cheese melts.

**Per serving**
*226 calories*
*22 mg cholesterol*
*177 mg sodium*
*4.6 gm saturated fat*
*11.1 gm fat*

**Exchanges per serving**
*3 meat*
*1 vegetable*

**On the side** Serve this with a ½ cup of white rice per person, and finish the meal with slices of juicy, ripe oranges. A glass of milk with this meal makes it nutritionally complete.

158

1 pkg. (11½ oz.) frozen fish, thawed

2 Tbsp. lemon juice

⅛ tsp. salt

⅛ tsp. lemon pepper

⅛ tsp. paprika

2 Tbsp. light mayonnaise

2 Tbsp. plain low-fat yogurt

1 tsp. dried dillweed

1 tomato, sliced

½ tsp. dried parsley flakes, crushed

Preheat oven to 450°F. Place fish in a shallow baking dish. Brush fish with lemon juice; sprinkle with salt, lemon pepper, and paprika. Bake for 10 minutes or until fish flakes easily. Meanwhile, in a mixing bowl, stir together mayonnaise, yogurt, dillweed, and parsley. Spoon over fish. Serve with tomatoes.

**Per serving**
*168 calories*
*1.2 mg cholesterol*
*271 mg sodium*
*0.25 gm saturated fat*
*11.2 gm fat*

**Exchanges per serving**
*1 fat*
*2 lean meat*

**On the side** Serve this tangy fish dish with green noodles. Add a tossed salad, some fruit and yogurt for dessert, and the meal is nutritionally complete.

1 tsp. grated orange peel

1 cup orange juice

¼ cup soy sauce

1 tsp. ground ginger

3 medium carrots, cut in julienne strips

1 pkg. (11½ oz.) frozen fish portions, thawed

1 cup sliced zucchini

2 tsp. cornstarch

4 Tbsp. water

In a skillet, combine orange peel, orange juice, soy sauce, and ginger. Add carrot strips and bring to a boil. Reduce heat and simmer for 5 minutes. Push carrots to the side of the skillet and add fish. Arrange sliced zucchini around fish. Bring to a boil. Reduce heat, cover and simmer until fish flakes easily. Remove vegetables and fish from skillet. Stir together cornstarch and water. Add to orange juice mixture; cook and stir until thickened and bubbly. Return fish and vegetables to skillet. Heat through. Spoon glaze atop. Serve.

**Per serving**
*216 calories*
*0 mg cholesterol*
*1036 mg sodium*
*0 gm saturated fat*
*10 gm fat*

**Exchanges per serving**
*3 meat*
*1 vegetable*

**On the side** The oriental-style flavor of this dish recommends white rice as an accompaniment. Fresh fruit with yogurt completes the meal.

# 144 Parmesan Fillets

1 lb. fresh fish
½ cup herb-seasoned bread crumbs
⅓ cup grated Parmesan cheese
1 Tbsp. margarine, melted
⅛ tsp. pepper

Cut fish into four portions. Combine bread crumbs, Parmesan cheese, margarine, and pepper. Place fish in a nonstick shallow baking pan. Sprinkle with bread crumb mixture. Bake at 450°F for 25 to 30 minutes.

**Per serving**
*230 calories*
*10 mg cholesterol*
*262 mg sodium*
*2.25 gm saturated fat*
*6.7 gm fat*

**Exchanges per serving**
*½ bread*
*½ fat*
*3 meat*

**On the side** Boiled squash makes a nice addition to these cheesy fillets. Serve some fruit as dessert with a glass of non-fat milk and the meal is nutritionally balanced.

# 145 Wine Baked Fillets

1 lb. frozen or fresh fish fillets

dash of salt (to taste)

dash of pepper (to taste)

⅛ tsp. paprika

⅓ cup dry white wine

⅛ tsp. dried oregano, crushed

⅔ cup part-skim shredded Swiss cheese

Place fish in nonstick baking dish. Season with salt, pepper, and paprika. Pour wine over fish. Sprinkle with oregano. Bake at 350°F for 35 minutes. Sprinkle fish with cheese and bake for 10 minutes more.

**Per serving**
*160 calories*
*39 mg cholesterol*
*565 mg sodium*
*2.1 gm saturated fat*
*9.2 gm fat*

**Exchanges per serving**
*3 meat*

**On the side** Boiled spaghetti squash or a mixed broccoli and cauliflower side dish make nice accompaniments to Wine-Baked Fillets. A glass of milk and a fresh fruit of your choice as dessert complete the meal nutritionally.

Nonstick cooking spray

1 lb. haddock

¼ tsp. salt

¼ cup margarine, melted

⅛ tsp. black pepper

⅛ tsp. paprika

2 Tbsp. lemon juice

Heat oven to 350°F. Spray roasting pan with non-stick spray. Place fish in pan. Sprinkle with salt and melted margarine. Season with pepper and paprika. Bake 20 minutes or until fish flakes easily. Pour lemon juice over fish.

**Per serving**
*200 calories*
*65.29 mg cholesterol*
*215 mg sodium*
*2.1 gm saturated fat*
*12.07 gm fat*

**Exchanges per serving**
*1 fat*
*3 meat*

**On the side** Eggplant squares, a cabbage salad, fruit, and milk make this meal nutritionally complete.

1 lb. haddock fillets

½ chili pepper, chopped

⅔ cup chopped onion

⅓ cup chopped green pepper

⅓ cup chopped red pepper

1 lb. can low-sodium tomato puree

1½ tsp. basil

½ cup chopped carrots

4 tsp. lemon juice

Mix all the ingredients together, except fish, in a bowl. Pour half the mixture into a baking dish and place fish on top. Pour the remainder of the sauce over the fish. Bake at 350°F for 25 to 30 minutes.

**Per serving**
*117 calories*
*43.28 mg cholesterol*
*79.5 mg sodium*
*0.08 gm saturated fat*
*0.63 gm fat*

**Exchanges per serving**
*2 meat*
*1 vegetable*

**On the side** Rice makes a nice side dish with this flavorful fish dish. Some fruit with yogurt as dessert rounds out the meal nutritionally.

2 Tbsp. margarine

¼ cup slivered almonds

4 tsp. flour

⅛ tsp. pepper

2 haddock fillets

1 tsp. lime juice

In a skillet, melt 1 tablespoon margarine. Add almonds and sauté until golden; remove and set aside. In a bowl, combine flour and pepper. Sprinkle both sides of fillets with flour and pepper. In same skillet, heat 1 tablespoon margarine; add fillets and cook on both sides until brown. Remove. Reduce heat to low. Add lime juice and sautéed almonds to skillet and cook until heated. Top fillets with almond mixture.

**Per serving**
*292 calories*
*49 mg cholesterol*
*197 mg sodium*
*2.7 gm saturated fat*
*20.3 gm fat*

**Exchanges per serving**
*1½ fat*
*3 meat*

**On the side** A serving of white rice, some steamed green beans, and a fruit for dessert round out this meal nutritionally.

1 Tbsp. vegetable oil

1 cup chopped onions

¼ cup green onions, sliced

2 lbs. haddock fillets

1 cup diced tomatoes

1 tsp. dried parsley flakes, crushed

⅛ tsp. pepper

½ tsp. garlic powder

3 Tbsp. dry white wine

1 tsp. Italian herb blend

In a skillet, heat oil. Add onions and green onions. Sauté for 3 to 4 minutes. Place onions in an 8-inch square baking dish. Cut fish fillets into 6 portions and place atop of onions. Season fish with pepper and garlic powder. Place tomatoes on top of fish; sprinkle with Italian herbs, parsley flakes and wine. Cover and bake in preheated 375°F oven for
20 minutes.

**Per serving**
*216 calories*
*47.7 mg cholesterol*
*86 mg sodium*
*0.86 gm saturated fat*
*5.86 gm fat*

**Exchanges per serving**
*½ fat*
*4 meat*
*1 vegetable*

**On the side** Rice is really nice with this spicy Italian seafood dish. Milk and fruit are all you need to make the meal nutritionally complete.

# 150 Kettle of Fish

2 Tbsp. margarine, melted

3 large potatoes, thinly sliced

½ tsp. ginger

1 small zucchini, thinly sliced

2 cups tomato, peeled, seeded and sliced

½ cup green onions, sliced

1½ lb. haddock

¼ tsp. thyme

½ tsp. oregano

⅛ tsp. pepper

1 tsp. dried parsley flakes

Put melted margarine in oblong baking dish. Arrange sliced potatoes on bottom and sprinkle with ¼ of ginger. Cover and bake at 350°F for 15 minutes. Place other vegetables on top of potatoes and layer the fish fillets on top. Sprinkle with seasonings and remaining ginger. Return to oven and bake for 20 minutes or until fish flakes easily.

### Per serving
*246 calories*
*33 mg cholesterol*
*47.6 mg sodium*
*0.75 gm saturated fat*
*6 gm fat*

### Exchanges per serving
*½ bread*
*2 meat*
*1 vegetable*

**On the side** This tasty fish stew is a complete meal in itself and needs only a glass of milk and an apple to make it nutritionally balanced.

2 lb. haddock fillets

⅛ tsp. salt

⅛ tsp. pepper

½ cup margarine

2 cups herb-seasoned bread crumbs

¼ tsp. oregano

¼ tsp. marjoram

1 tsp. grated lemon rind

Preheat oven to 350°F. Cut fish into 6 servings. Arrange fish on a nonstick baking pan. Sprinkle with salt and pepper and pour ¼ of margarine over fish. Mix bread crumbs, oregano, marjoram, and lemon rind together and sprinkle over top of fish. Bake for 20 to 25 minutes.

**Per serving**
*396 calories*
*87.1 mg cholesterol*
*594 mg sodium*
*3.1 gm saturated fat*
*17.8 gm fat*

**Exchanges per serving**
*1½ bread*
*3½ fat*
*4 meat*

**On the side** Steamed carrot rounds make a colorful and healthful side dish to this seafood main course. A dessert of fruit and yogurt complete the meal nutritionally.

¼ cup finely chopped onions

½ tsp. minced garlic

1 cup chopped carrots

⅔ cup sliced fresh mushrooms

½ cup chopped tomatoes

1 tsp. dried parsley flakes

1 tsp. basil

⅛ tsp. pepper

1 lb. haddock

3 Tbsp. lime juice

In skillet, simmer all ingredients, except fish and lime juice. Cook until carrots are tender. Add fish and lime juice, spooning vegetables over fish. Cover and cook until fish is flaky; about 15 minutes.

**Per serving**
*163 calories*
*24 mg cholesterol*
*135 mg sodium*
*0.18 gm saturated fat*
*2.1 gm fat*

**Exchanges per serving**
*2 meat*
*1 vegetable*

**On the side** Serve this fish, which is a little heavier than a sole fillet, with a ½ cup of white rice, and choose a refreshing light-tasting fruit or combination of fruits for dessert. A glass of milk or some yogurt as a fruit topping make this meal nutritionally complete.

# 153 Baked Halibut with Sauce

*Serves 4*

4 halibut steaks

1 Tbsp. vegetable oil

1 cup chopped onions

1 cup chopped green onions

1 tsp. dried parsley flakes

1 tsp. garlic, minced

1 8 oz. can low-sodium tomato sauce

⅛ tsp. pepper

Preheat oven to 375°F. Place halibut in 9 x 13-inch baking dish. In skillet, heat oil and sauté onions until tender. Add remaining ingredients and simmer for 10 minutes. Pour onion mixture over halibut. Bake 20 to 25 minutes.

**Per serving**
*155 calories*
*27 mg cholesterol*
*58 mg sodium*
*0.5 gm saturated fat*
*3.5 gm fat*

**Exchanges per serving**
*3 meat*

**On the side** A serving of long-grain wild rice is a delicious addition to this seafood main dish. A side salad, and some fruit for dessert make the meal complete nutritionally.

1 lb. halibut

½ cup lemon juice

¾ cup water

¼ cup skim milk

1 Tbsp. flour

½ tsp. dried tarragon

1 tsp. minced onion

⅛ tsp. basil

⅛ black pepper

½ tsp. sage

⅛ tsp. Tabasco sauce

Marinate fish in lemon juice for about 1 hour. Broil fish until done; keep fish warm. In saucepan, add water, milk, and flour; stir until smooth. Cook over low heat until slightly thickened. Add seasonings; cook 5 minutes longer. Pour sauce over fish portions.

**Per serving**
*150 calories*
*37.6 mg cholesterol*
*70 mg sodium*
*0.4 gm saturated fat*
*2.7 gm fat*

**Exchanges per serving**
*3 meat*

**On the side** A serving of colorful and healthful sliced beets provide a ½ bread exchange and only 75 calories as an accompaniment to this broiled fish dish. A glass of nonfat milk and a fresh fruit compliment the tastes and complete the meal nutritionally.

# 155 Citrus Halibut

1 lb. halibut steaks

1 Tbsp. margarine

½ cup sliced green onions

1 tsp. minced garlic

1 tsp. grated orange peel

⅛ tsp. pepper

⅓ cup orange juice

4 tsp. lemon juice

Arrange fish in baking dish. In skillet, heat margarine and cook onion and garlic. Stir in orange peel and pepper. Spread over fish. Sprinkle orange juice and lemon juice over fish. Bake, covered, at 400°F for 20 minutes or until fish flakes easily. Pour juice over fish.

### Per serving
*168 calories*
*36 mg cholesterol*
*98 mg sodium*
*0.89 gm saturated fat*
*5.6 gm fat*

### Exchanges per serving
*3 meat*

**On the side** Baked squash on the side, a mixed vegetable of your choice, or a side salad, some fruit and a glass of milk make this meal nutritionally complete.

2 Tbsp. margarine

1 cup sliced fresh mushrooms

⅓ cup chopped green onions

1½ lbs. halibut

1 tsp. cornstarch

⅓ cup water

2 Tbsp. skim milk

¼ cup sherry

1 Tbsp. soy sauce

1 tsp. garlic

½ tsp. ground ginger

In skillet, heat margarine and sauté mushrooms and green onions. Remove and set aside. Add fish to skillet; cover and cook until fish is white in the center. Remove fish and set aside. Stir cornstarch, water, milk, sherry, soy sauce, garlic and ginger; pour into pan and add mushrooms and onions. Bring mixture to a boil. Pour sauce over fish.

**Per serving**
*208 calories*
*43 mg cholesterol*
*281 mg sodium*
*0.85 gm saturated fat*
*8.0 gm fat*

**Exchanges per serving**
*1 fat*
*3 meat*

**On the side** Long-grain wild rice tastes great with this sherry-flavored seafood entree. A tossed salad on the side and a fruit compote topped with a dollop of yogurt complete the meal nutritionally.

2 lbs. halibut fillets

⅔ cup green onions, chopped

1½ Tbsp. fresh ginger, crushed

½ cup soy sauce

1½ Tbsp. sugar

1 Tbsp. sesame oil

½ tsp. ground cinnamon

½ tsp. allspice

¼ tsp. ground cloves

⅛ tsp. anise seed

Cut fish in 2-inch x 2-inch long slices. Mix fish with onions, ginger, soy sauce, sugar, oil, and spices. Cover and chill for several hours. Broil on both sides until fish is opaque.

**Per serving**
*158 calories*
*0 mg cholesterol*
*886.6 mg sodium*
*0.237 gm saturated fat*
*4.42 gm fat*

**Exchanges per serving**
*3 meat*

**On the side** Stir-fried cabbage adds a complimentary flavor to this eastern-style fish dish. Add a slice of your favorite bread or a ½ cup serving of white rice, a glass of milk, and a serving of fruit for a nutritionally complete meal.

# 158 Halibut Steaks a la Citrus

1 lb. halibut steaks

2 tsp. finely shredded orange peel

⅔ cup orange juice

1 tsp. cooking oil

½ tsp. dried dillweed

⅛ tsp. pepper

Cut fish into four portions and place in a shallow baking dish. Combine orange peel, orange juice, oil, dillweed, and pepper; pour over fish. Cover and marinate in refrigerator for 1 hour. Place fish on broiling pan and brush with marinade. Broil until fish is flaky. Brush often with marinade.

**Per serving**
*123 calories*
*27 mg cholesterol*
*46 mg sodium*
*1.0 gm saturated fat*
*3.0 gm fat*

**Exchanges per serving**
*2 meat*

**On the side** Zucchini cooked al dente is a delicious side offering to this zesty fish entree. A dinner roll or slice of your favorite bread, some fruit and yogurt as dessert, and you have a meal that's nutritionally complete.

1 lb. fresh skinless Orange Roughy

1½ Tbsp. margarine

3 Tbsp. herb-seasoned bread crumbs

⅔ cup skim milk

1 Tbsp. flour

⅔ cup part-skim cheddar cheese, shredded

2 tsp. Dijon-style mustard

1 tsp. dried dillweed

Preheat oven to 400°F. Place fish in a nonstick shallow baking dish. Melt margarine and brush on top of fish. Top with bread crumbs and bake for 15 minutes or until fish is flaky. In a saucepan, stir together milk and flour. Cook until thickened. Add cheese and mustard. Stir until cheese melts. Divide sauce among four serving plates. Place one portion of fish on each plate, atop of sauce. Sprinkle with dillweed.

**Per serving**
*295 calories*
*169 mg cholesterol*
*313 mg sodium*
*4.87 gm saturated fat*
*19 gm fat*

**Exchanges per serving**
*½ bread*
*2 fat*
*3 meat*

**On the side** Steamed brussel sprouts provide a vegetable exchange and a nice contrasting flavor to this cheesy fish entree. Choose some fruit and maybe a glass of nonfat milk to round out the meal nutritionally and you're all set.

1 lb. Orange Roughy fillets

⅛ tsp. pepper

⅛ tsp. salt

⅔ cup lemon yogurt, low-fat

⅓ cup green onions, sliced

Arrange fillets in a 9 x 13-inch pan and sprinkle with salt and pepper. Evenly spread yogurt over fish. Sprinkle with green onions. Bake, uncovered, for 18 to 20 minutes, or until fish is opaque in center at 350°F.

**Per serving**
*170 calories*
*25 mg cholesterol*
*171 mg sodium*
*0.5 gm saturated fat*
*8.5 gm fat*

**Exchanges per serving**
*3 meat*

**On the side** A side of brussel sprouts, steamed until tender, or a tossed salad, a slice of bread, a glass of milk, and some fruit make this meal nutritionally complete.

1 Tbsp. vegetable oil

1 garlic clove, pressed

2 tsp. dried dillweed

4 Tbsp. lime juice

⅛ cup chopped peanuts

1 lb. Orange Roughy

⅛ tsp. pepper

In a skillet, heat oil and add dill, garlic, lime juice, and peanuts. Sauté for 1 to 2 minutes. Sprinkle fish with pepper and add fish to skillet. Cover and cook fish until done.

**Per serving**
*212 calories*
*45 mg cholesterol*
*24 mg sodium*
*1.4 gm saturated fat*
*11.2 gm fat*

**Exchanges per serving**
*1 fat*
*3 meat*

**On the side** Eggplant offers a tempting side dish to this nutty-flavored fish dish. A side salad of your favorite raw vegetables, and strawberries and milk, mixed in the blender, make this meal balanced nutritionally.

2 lbs. sole

½ cup margarine, melted

¼ tsp. salt

¼ tsp. black pepper

8 oz. package frozen broccoli

⅓ cup light sour cream

½ cup chopped green onions

⅛ tsp. paprika

Heat oven to 450°F. Divide fish into 8 portions, cutting fillets if necessary. Arrange in a 13 x 9-inch baking dish. Baste with melted margarine. Sprinkle with salt and pepper. Bake for 15 minutes. Steam broccoli until crisp-tender. Evenly distribute broccoli on fish. In bowl, combine sour cream and onions. Top each portion of fish with sour cream mixture. Sprinkle a dash of paprika on each portion. Bake an additional 5 minutes.

**Per serving**
*180 calories*
*4 mg cholesterol*
*83.1 mg sodium*
*1.7 gm saturated fat*
*7.2 gm fat*

**Exchanges per serving**
*1 fat*
*2 meat*
*1 vegetable*

**On the side** How about fresh corn on the cob for the starch course in this meal? The vegetables are already there. Add some fresh fruit and a glass of icy cold nonfat milk and the meal is nutritionally

1½ lb. flounder

1½ cups vegetable juice

1¼ tsp. lemon juice

½ cup diced onions

½ tsp. garlic, minced

⅛ tsp. pepper

Rinse fillets and pat dry; place in a shallow baking dish. In a saucepan, combine remaining ingredients and bring to a boil. Pour sauce over fish and bake at 375°F for 20 to 25 minutes. Occasionally baste.

**Per serving**
*125 calories*
*8 mg cholesterol*
*300 mg sodium*
*0.012 gm saturated fat*
*0.03 gm fat*

**Exchanges per serving**
*2 meat*
*1 vegetable*

**On the side** Cherry tomatoes with basil are really tasty with this pleasant seafood main dish. A ½ cup serving of white rice, or a slice of your favorite bread, a glass of nonfat milk, and a fresh fruit as dessert make the meal complete nutritionally.

1 (2 lb.) whole fish flounder

2½ Tbsp. vegetable oil

⅛ tsp. salt

⅛ tsp. paprika

½ tsp. lemon pepper

1 tsp. dried parsley flakes, crushed

¼ cup chopped green onions

2 Tbsp. margarine

1½ Tbsp. lemon juice

Preheat oven to 350°F. Wash and dry fish. Coat with the oil and season with salt, paprika, and lemon pepper. Bake 10 to 15 minutes. Combine parsley, onions, margarine, and lemon juice and spread over cooked fish. Place fish under broiler and broil until lightly brown.

**Per serving**
*285 calories*
*10 mg cholesterol*
*269 mg sodium*
*2.0 gm saturated fat*
*15.0 gm fat*

**Exchanges per serving**
*1 fat*
*3 meat*

**On the side** Long-grain wild rice, mixed vegetable of broccoli and cauliflower, steamed just until tender, and fresh berries, a half banana and a ½ cup of yogurt, well mixed in a blender, for a frothy dessert mousse make this meal nutritionally balanced.

¾ sole fillets

⅛ tsp. salt

⅛ tsp. lemon pepper

⅛ tsp. lemon juice

2 Tbsp. dry white wine

1 tsp. margarine

1 tsp. minced garlic

3 Tbsp. herb-seasoned bread crumbs

1 tsp. dried parsley flakes

Lay fillets in a baking dish. Season with salt, lemon pepper, and lemon juice. Add wine. Place fish under broiler while preparing the bread crumbs. In skillet, melt margarine. Stir in the garlic and heat for about one minute. Add bread crumbs, stir until golden. Remove from heat and stir in parsley. When fish flakes easily, spread bread crumbs over fish. Return to broiler until crumbs are lightly browned. Serve with juices poured over fish.

**Per serving**
*214 calories*
*18 mg cholesterol*
*339 mg sodium*
*0.5 gm saturated fat*
*3.3 gm fat*

**Exchanges per serving**
*1 fat*
*3 meat*

**On the side** Carrots, steamed just until tender, are a colorful and healthful side dish for this great-tasting fish entree. Add a slice of bread, a glass of milk, and a melange of cantaloupe and honeydew melon balls for dessert and the meal is nutritionally complete.

4 sole fillets

1½ cups herb-seasoned bread crumbs, crushed

3 Tbsp. dry white wine

1 tsp. dried parsley flakes, crushed

4 tsp. margarine

Preheat oven to 350°F. Lay fillets on nonstick baking pan. In bowl, mix bread crumbs, wine, and parsley. Cover fish with crumb mixture. Dot each fillet with 1 tsp. margarine. Bake 15 to 20 minutes.

**Per serving**
*256 calories*
*0 mg cholesterol*
*376 mg sodium*
*1.0 gm saturated fat*
*6.1 gm fat*

**Exchanges per serving**
*½ bread*
*1 fat*
*2 meat*

**On the side** Cook up some new potatoes with rosemary, toss together a salad of your favorite vegetables, pour a cold glass of nonfat milk, and choose your favorite fresh fruit for dessert, and this meal is nutritionally complete.

1 10 oz. pkg frozen spinach, thawed

2 tsp. minced onion

2 Tbsp. chopped green onion

½ tsp. nutmeg

⅛ tsp. salt

4 slices (3 oz. each) fillet of flounder

1 Tbsp. lemon juice

⅛ tsp. paprika

Combine spinach, onion, green onions, nutmeg, and salt. Lay fillets flat on a work surface. Spread a thin layer of spinach mixture over the top surface of fillets. Roll up and fasten with toothpick, if necessary. Place in a nonstick baking pan. Sprinkle with lemon juice and paprika. Bake at 350°F for 20 to 25 minutes.

**Per serving**
*135 calories*
*57 mg cholesterol*
*162 mg sodium*
*0.3 gm saturated fat*
*1.29 gm fat*

**Exchanges per serving**
*2 meat*
*1 vegetable*

**On the side** A side order of rice, and a dessert of mixed berries with nonfat vanilla yogurt make this meal complete nutritionally, appetizing to the eye, and delicious.

# Flounder with Mushroom-Garlic Sauce

*Serves 4*

1 cup water

1½ cups chopped carrots

¼ tsp. salt

1 lb. fresh flounder fillets

Sauce:

½ cup margarine

1½ Tbsp. minced garlic

1½ Tbsp. lemon juice

1 cup sliced fresh mushrooms

In skillet, combine water, carrots, and salt; bring to a boil. Arrange fish over vegetable. Cover and simmer 8 to 10 minutes or until fish flakes easily. Lift fish and carrots out of water; keep warm. In saucepan, melt margarine. Sauté garlic. Stir in lemon juice and mushrooms; heat thoroughly. Serve over fish and carrots.

**Per serving**
*180 calories*
*40 mg cholesterol*
*268 mg sodium*
*0 gm saturated fat*
*0.66 gm fat*

**Exchanges per serving**
*1 fat*
*3 meat*
*1 vegetable*

**On the side** White rice is lovely with this tasty seafood main course. A dessert of baked apples with a glass of milk or some nonfat yogurt make the meal balanced nutritionally.

12 oz. sole or flounder fillets

2 tsp. ground ginger

2 Tbsp. oyster sauce

2 Tbsp. dry vermouth

1 tsp. sugar

1 tsp. soy sauce

Wash fish and cut each piece in half; place in shallow baking dish. Combine ginger, oyster sauce, vermouth, sugar and soy sauce. Pour over fish and bake. Bake at 375°F for 20 to 25 minutes or until fish is flaky.

**Per serving**
*183 calories*
*35 mg cholesterol*
*560 mg sodium*
*0.1 gm saturated fat*
*1.0 gm fat*

**Exchanges per serving**
*3½ meat*

**On the side** Steamed carrots, ½ cup of white rice with saffron, and peaches with cream (nonfat yogurt cleverly disguised, of course), and this meal is nutritionally complete.

2 Tbsp. margarine, melted

1 Tbsp. lemon juice

⅛ tsp. pepper

⅛ tsp. paprika

¼ tsp. basil

⅛ tsp. garlic powder

1 lb. fillet of flounder

¼ cup dry whole-wheat bread crumbs

Combine margarine, lemon juice, pepper, paprika, basil, and garlic. Dredge fish in margarine-herb mixture and roll in bread crumbs. In a shallow baking dish, arrange fish. Spoon remaining margarine mixture over fish. Bake at 475°F for 15 minutes or until fish flakes.

**Per serving**
*208 calories*
*131 mg cholesterol*
*211 mg sodium*
*1.3 gm saturated fat*
*7.3 gm fat*

**Exchanges per serving**
*1 fat*
*3 meat*

**On the side** Julienned zucchini strips mixed with carrots and stir-fried with a little margarine provide a colorful addition to this main fish dish. A serving of white rice, or a slice of bread, some fruit and a glass of milk round out the meal nutritionally.

6 small flounder fillets (2 to 3 oz. each)

⅓ cup minced onion

¼ cup light mayonnaise

¼ tsp. paprika

2 Tbsp. lime juice

⅛ tsp. pepper

⅛ tsp. salt

⅔ cup Parmesan cheese, grated

In a bowl, mix onion, mayonnaise, paprika, lime juice, salt, pepper, and Parmesan cheese. Spread mixture on fillets. Bake at 375°F for 15 to 20 minutes or until brown.

**Per serving**
*135 calories*
*14.5 mg cholesterol*
*198 mg sodium*
*2.4 gm saturated fat*
*5.1 gm fat*

**Exchanges per serving**
*1 fat*
*2 meat*

**On the side** New potatoes with basil, a tossed salad, and a fruity milk shake make this meal nutritionally complete.

⅔ cup low-fat ricotta cheese

1 Tbsp. Romano cheese

⅛ cup green onions, sliced

¼ tsp. dried basil

⅛ tsp. oregano

4 skinless sole fillets (3 oz. each)

⅔ cup spaghetti sauce

½ cup sliced mushrooms

⅓ cup part-skim shredded mozzarella

Preheat oven to 375°F. In bowl, combine ricotta cheese, romano cheese, green onion, basil, and oregano. Place about 2 tablespoons of cheese mixture on one end of each fillet. Roll fillets around cheese mixture; secure with wooden toothpicks. Place in a baking dish and bake for 20 to 25 minutes. Drain liquid off and spoon spaghetti sauce and mushrooms over fish rolls. Sprinkle with mozzarella cheese. Bake for 5 to 10 minutes more. Discard toothpicks before serving.

**Per serving**
*261 calories*
*43 mg cholesterol*
*446 mg sodium*
*4.5 gm saturated fat*
*9.0 gm fat*

**Exchanges per serving**
*1 fat*
*3 meat*
*1 vegetable*

**On the side** This dish looks and taste great with green noodles. Make a dessert dish of melon balls and strawberries with yogurt, and the meal is nutritionally complete.

3 Tbsp. margarine, melted

4 3 oz. sole fillets

½ cup dry white wine

1 Tbsp. lemon juice

1 tsp. dried parsley flakes

1 tsp. dried dillweed

⅛ tsp. thyme

¼ cup chopped green onion

Rinse fillets and pat dry. With melted margarine, baste fillets. Place fillets in 13 x 9-inch baking dish. Pour remaining margarine over fillets. Pour wine and lemon juice over fish. Sprinkle fish with remaining ingredients. Bake at 350°F for about 10 minutes; check. The fish is done as soon as it is opaque and fairly firm to touch.

**Per serving**
*189 calories*
*27 mg cholesterol*
*106 mg sodium*
*1.75 gm saturated fat*
*9.0 gm fat*

**Exchanges per serving**
*½ bread*
*2 meat*

**On the side** Try brussel sprouts, steamed just until tender. They are always good with fish. Round this meal out nutritionally by adding a glass of milk and your favorite fruit for dessert.

2 Tbsp. margarine

2 Tbsp. flour

1 tsp. salt

¼ tsp. nutmeg

½ tsp. dry mustard

1¼ cup skim milk

1 tsp. lemon juice

½ cup shredded part-skim cheddar cheese

Nonstick cooking spray

2 lbs. perch fillets

In saucepan, melt margarine over low heat. Stir in flour, salt, nutmeg, and mustard until smooth. Gradually stir in milk until thickened. Add lemon juice and cheese; stir until cheese melts.Spray a 13 x 9-inch baking pan with nonstick cooking spray. Place fish in pan and pour sauce over fish. Bake uncovered for 50 minutes at 350°F.

**Per serving**
*262 calories*
*180 mg cholesterol*
*595 mg sodium*
*2.0 gm saturated fat*
*7.2 gm fat*

**Exchanges per serving**
*1 fat*
*4 meat*
*½ skim milk*

**On the side** Long-grain wild rice, a tossed salad, milk and fruit complete this meal nutritionally.

# 175  Baked Sea Perch

1 lb. sea perch

⅓ cup white wine

¼ cup sliced onion

¼ cup sliced green onion

⅛ tsp. lemon pepper

1 tsp. minced garlic

⅛ tsp. dried tarragon

½ tsp. dried thyme

¼ tsp. basil

1 tomato, sliced

Place all ingredients into a bowl and marinate for 1 hour. Place fish and marinade into a baking dish and bake for 25 minutes at 350°F.

### Per serving
*184 calories*
*141 mg cholesterol*
*98 mg sodium*
*0.35 gm saturated fat*
*1.4 gm fat*

### Exchanges per serving
*3 meat*

**On the side** Colorful steamed carrots and a serving of white rice make the plate pleasing to the eye and the palate. Mix up a fruit and yogurt dessert and the meal is complete nutritionally.

1 15½ oz. can salmon in spring water

1½ tsp. margarine

½ cup diced celery

½ cup diced green pepper

1 tsp. minced onion

1¼ cup skim milk

1¼ Tbsp. cornstarch

¾ tsp. dillweed

1 cup frozen peas

3 hard-boiled eggs, sliced

Drain salmon. In a saucepan, melt margarine. Add celery, green pepper, and onion; cook until tender. Stir in milk. When hot, add cornstarch and stir constantly until mixture thickens. Season with dillweed. In a 1½ quart casserole dish, arrange half the peas, half the egg slices, and half the salmon. Repeat. Pour sauce over top. Cover and bake at 375°F for 25 minutes.

**Per serving**
*232 calories*
*128 mg cholesterol*
*143 mg sodium*
*1.25 gm saturated fat*
*4.5 gm fat*

**Exchanges per serving**
*½ bread*
*1 fat*
*2 meat*

**On the side** Toss together a salad of fresh, colorful veggies, and choose your favorite fresh berries with yogurt for dessert and this meal is nutritionally complete.

1 15½ oz. can salmon in spring water, drained

1¼ cups whole-wheat bread crumbs

1¼ cups cooked rice

1 egg, slightly beaten

¾ cup skim milk

½ cup chopped onion

1½ Tbsp. lemon juice

½ tsp. dried dillweed

⅛ tsp. ground pepper

Preheat oven to 375°F. In large bowl, combine all ingredients; mix well. Put in 9 x 15-inch nonstick loaf pan. Press down lightly. Bake 45 to 50 minutes or until knife comes out clean.

**Per serving**
*240 calories*
*63 mg cholesterol*
*230 mg sodium*
*0.93 gm saturated fat*
*5.0 gm fat*

**Exchanges per serving**
*1½ bread*
*1 meat*

**On the side** Asparagus as a side dish to this wholesome salmon loaf provides a nutritious and delicious addition to the meal. Create a dessert of mixed melon slices and serve the meal with a glass of cold nonfat milk for complete nutritional balance.

# 178  Salmon with Fruit

1 Tbsp. margarine

1 apple, cut into thin slices

1 pear, cut into thin slices

¼ cup raisins

2 Tbsp. lime juice

⅛ tsp. black pepper

12 oz. salmon fillets

Heat margarine in skillet and add apples, pears, raisins, and lime juice. Season with pepper. Sauté until fruit begins to soften. Place fish on broiler pan and broil on both sides until browned. Pour fruit mixture over salmon.

**Per serving**
*349 calories*
*30 mg cholesterol*
*1118 mg sodium*
*2.2 gm saturated fat*
*12.0 gm fat*

**Exchanges per serving**
*1 fat*
*2½ fruit*
*3½ meat*

**On the side** A raw cabbage salad and a dessert of white rice with milk and cinnamon make this meal nutritionally complete.

1 cup chopped onion

1 9 oz. package frozen green beans, thawed

¾ cup water

1½ Tbsp. soy sauce

½ Tbsp. Worcestershire sauce

1 Tbsp. cornstarch

¼ tsp. dry mustard

¼ tsp. lemon juice

1 15 oz. can salmon in water

1 8 oz. can bamboo shoots

In skillet, cook onions and green beans in ¼ cup water for about 5 to 10 minutes. In a bowl, combine soy sauce, Worcestershire sauce, cornstarch, mustard, lemon juice, and ¾ cup water; mix and set aside. Drain salmon and bamboo shoots. Stir cornstarch mixture in to vegetable mixture in skillet and cook until thickened. Stir in salmon and bamboo shoots. Cover and simmer for 10 minutes.

**Per serving**
*191 calories*
*37.5 mg cholesterol*
*723 mg sodium*
*1.25 gm saturated fat*
*6.25 gm fat*

**Exchanges per serving**
*3 meat*
*1 vegetable*

**On the side** Brown rice looks and tastes just right with this salmon entree. A fruity yogurt dessert completes the meal nutritionally.

1 lb. salmon fillets

¾ cup soy sauce

⅓ cup sherry

1¼ Tbsp. brown sugar

¼ tsp. ground ginger

1 tsp. minced garlic

1 tsp. Worcestershire sauce

2 Tbsp. lemon juice

Mix together all ingredients, except salmon; blend well. Place fish in a large plastic storage bag and put marinade in bag to cover salmon. Marinate in refrigerator for 2½ hours. Drain and broil on each side until done.

**Per serving**
*150 calories*
*63 mg cholesterol*
*2546 mg sodium*
*1.06 gm saturated fat*
*7.2 gm fat*

**Exchanges per serving**
*3 meat*

**On the side** Broccoli florets, gently steamed, a slice of bread and a glass of milk, and a baked apple dessert make this meal nutritionally complete.

1 lb. salmon fillet, skinned and boned

1 10 oz. package frozen spinach, thawed

1 cup chopped onion

¾ cup low-fat yogurt

2 tsp. Dijon-style mustard

2 tsp. honey

½ tsp. dried dill

2 Tbsp. lime juice

Rinse salmon and pat dry. Put spinach and onion in a baking dish. Place salmon on top of spinach and onion. Blend yogurt, mustard, honey, dill and lime juice; spread over salmon. Bake at 350°F for 25 minutes or until fish is flaky.

**Per serving**
*231 calories*
*65 mg cholesterol*
*92 mg sodium*
*1.5 gm saturated fat*
*8.4 gm fat*

**Exchanges per serving**
*3 meat*
*½ milk*
*1 vegetable*

**On the side** Rice and fresh pears complete this meal nutritionally.

# 182 Scallops

1½ lb. scallops

2 Tbsp. margarine

2 Tbsp. lemon juice

1 Tbsp. soy sauce

⅛ cup cooking sherry

1 tsp. dried dillweed

Rinse scallops and pat dry. In skillet, melt margarine;
add scallops and sauté. Add lemon juice, soy sauce,
sherry and dill. Cover and simmer until scallops
are done.

**Per serving**
*222.5 calories*
*56 mg cholesterol*
*529 mg sodium*
*3.1 gm saturated fat*
*6.7 gm fat*

**Exchanges per serving**
*1 fat*
*4 meat*

**On the side** Fresh sliced tomatoes, white rice with saffron, and
honeydew melon slices add color and nutritionally complete
this meal

2½ lbs. scallops

2 cucumbers, cut into 1-inch pieces

⅓ cup vegetable oil

2 Tbsp. lemon juice

1 bay leaf, crushed

⅛ tsp. garlic powder

Thread scallops and cucumbers alternately on each of 6 skewers. Mix together oil, lemon juice, bay leaf and garlic powder. Brush each serving with the mixture. Broil kabobs for 5 to 10 minutes, turning and basting frequently.

## Per serving

*231 calories*
*56 mg cholesterol*
*274 mg sodium*
*1.1 gm saturated fat*
*10.3 gm fat*

## Exchanges per serving

*1 fat*
*4 meat*
*1 vegetable*

**On the side** Rice looks and tastes great with these Scallop and Cucumber Kabobs. Fruit and yogurt complete the meal nutritionally.

# 184 Scallops in Garlic Sauce

1 lb. scallops
4 Tbsp. margarine
1½ tsp. garlic, minced
⅛ tsp. salt
⅛ tsp. lemon pepper
⅛ tsp. paprika

In saucepan, heat margarine and garlic on low heat. Add scallops and cook 5 to 10 minutes or until done. Season with salt, lemon pepper, and paprika. Serve.

**Per serving**
*199 calories*
*37 mg cholesterol*
*391 mg sodium*
*2.0 gm saturated fat*
*12 gm fat*

**Exchanges per serving**
*1 fat*
*3 meat*

**On the side** Zucchini squash, cut in julienne strips and sautéed in a little margarine, a slice of bread or a serving of white rice, and a fruit compote with yogurt for dessert complete this meal deliciously and nutritiously.

1 Tbsp. vegetable oil
1 cup chopped onion
1 tsp. minced garlic
2 cups sliced mushrooms
4 Tbsp. tomato paste
¼ cup dry white wine
1 tsp. dried parsley flakes
1½ tsp. dried oregano
1 can (28 oz.) plum tomatoes
1 lb. sea scallops

In a saucepan, heat oil. Add onion, garlic and mushrooms; cook until tender. Add remaining ingredients, except scallops. Bring to a boil. Reduce heat and simmer for 30 minutes. Add scallops and cook for 5 to 10 minutes.

**Per serving**
*224 calories*
*37 mg cholesterol*
*469 mg sodium*
*0.55 gm saturated fat*
*4.4 gm fat*

**Exchanges per serving**
*1 fat*
*3 meat*
*1 vegetable*

**On the side** White rice is perfect with this scallop dish and provides the bread exchange for this meal. Add a glass of milk and fruit for dessert and you've got all the makings for a nutritionally complete meal.

1 tsp. vegetable oil

2 tsp. minced garlic

1 lb. scallops, rinsed

1 Tbsp. cornstarch

1 cup sliced mushrooms

1 tomato, chopped

¼ cup green onions

1 tsp. dried parsley flakes, crushed

½ tsp. oregano

¼ cup dry vermouth

1½ Tbsp. lemon juice

In a skillet, add oil and garlic. Sauté for a couple of minutes. Add scallops; cook until opaque. Remove and keep warm. Add cornstarch to juices in pan; mix over medium heat until thickened. Add mushrooms, tomatoes, onions, parsley, and oregano. Cook 3 to 4 minutes. Add vermouth and lemon juice; cook for 2 to 3 minutes. Pour sauce over scallops.

**Per serving**
*180 calories*
*24.5 mg cholesterol*
*186 mg sodium*
*0.38 gm saturated fat*
*2.25 gm fat*

**Exchanges per serving**
*3 meat*
*1 vegetable*

**On the side** Rice is a nice side dish with this tasty fish dish. Create a dessert of berries and fruit with yogurt and the meal is nutritionally balanced and delicious.

12 raw jumbo shrimp, shelled and deveined

½ cup melted margarine

1 cup dry bread crumbs

1 tsp. dried parsley flakes

1 Tbsp. finely chopped fresh dill

¼ cup dry white wine

⅛ tsp. pepper

1 tsp. celery seeds

Preheat oven to 350°F. With a sharp knife, split shrimp in half, being careful not to cut all the way through; set aside. Combine margarine and remaining ingredients; mix well. Stuff each shrimp with about 2 tablespoons of the mixture. Place in baking dish. Bake at 350°F for 20 minutes.

**Per serving**
*235 calories*
*130 mg cholesterol*
*215 mg sodium*
*1.3 gm saturated fat*
*8.8 gm fat*

**Exchanges per serving**
*1 bread*
*1½ fat*
*3 meat*

**On the side** Cherry tomatoes with basil are delicious with this succulent shrimp dish. A dessert of mixed strawberries and bananas with yogurt makes the meal nutritionally complete.

¼ cup vegetable oil

½ cup low-sodium tomato sauce

¼ cup soy sauce

1 Tbsp. lime juice

½ tsp. lemon pepper

1 tsp. minced garlic

1 Tbsp. minced onion

1 lb. large shrimp, peeled and deveined

1 lb. scallops

Combine all ingredients, except shrimp and scallops; mix well. In a shallow pan, place shrimp and scallops and pour marinade over. Marinate for 1 hour. Place seafood on broiler pan and broil; turn and brush with marinade.

**Per serving**
*209 calories*
*145 mg cholesterol*
*550 mg sodium*
*1.4 gm saturated fat*
*10.0 gm fat*

**Exchanges per serving**
*2 fat*
*3 meat*

**On the side** Zucchini, cut julienne and stir-fried, is really tasty with this marinated seafood entree. A side order of rice, a glass of milk, and fruit for dessert make the meal complete nutritionally.

3 Tbsp. margarine

16 uncooked large shrimp, peeled and deveined

2 tsp. coriander seeds, crushed

⅛ tsp. salt

⅛ tsp. pepper

⅛ tsp. paprika

3 Tbsp. white wine

In a skillet, melt margarine, add shrimp, coriander, salt, pepper and paprika; stir until shrimp are opaque. Add wine and bring to a boil. Serve.

**Per serving**
*218 calories*
*130 mg. cholesterol*
*177 mg sodium*
*1.2 gm saturated fat*
*9.0 gm fat*

**Exchanges per serving**
*1 fat*
*3 meat*

**On the side** Snow pea pods, simply sautéed, are a delightful accompaniment to Coriander Shrimp. Rice, in ½ cup per person servings, and mixed fruit salad for dessert complete the meal nutritionally.

# 190 Creole Shrimp

2 Tbsp. margarine

1 cup chopped onions

1 cup chopped green pepper

¾ cup chopped celery

1 tsp. minced garlic

1 tsp. thyme

1 cup low-sodium chicken broth

1 Tbsp. flour

3 cups chopped tomatoes

1 tsp. chili powder

⅛ tsp. Tabasco sauce

2 lbs. raw shrimp, shelled and deveined

In a skillet, melt margarine; add onions, green peppers, celery, garlic and thyme until tender. Add chicken broth and blend in flour, stirring constantly. Add remaining ingredients, except shrimp; simmer 20 minutes. Add shrimp and cook for 10 minutes or until shrimp is done.

## Per serving
*257 calories*
*260 mg cholesterol*
*312 mg sodium*
*1.3 gm saturated fat*
*4.0 gm fat*

## Exchanges per serving
*½ bread*
*1 fat*
*3 meat*

**On the side** New potatoes with skins on, boiled, then sautéed whole in a little margarine, are very nice beside this New Orleans' style main dish. Try a mixed fruit salad of celery, apples, and raisins with yogurt to complete the meal.

# 191  Curried Shrimp

2 Tbsp. margarine

¾ cup diced onions

¾ cup diced green pepper

1 apple, peeled, cored and chopped fine

1 tsp. curry powder

1 16 oz. can low-sodium tomatoes

1 lb. raw shrimp, peeled and deveined

⅛ tsp. lemon pepper

In a skillet, melt margarine. Add onion, green pepper, apple, lemon pepper, and curry powder. Stir and cook until onion is tender. Add tomatoes. Break up tomatoes with fork as they cook. Add shrimp. Cover and simmer for 15 minutes or until shrimp is cooked through. Sprinkle with lemon pepper and serve.

**Per serving**
*241 calories*
*173 mg cholesterol*
*259 mg sodium*
*1.4 gm saturated fat*
*8.5 gm fat*

**Exchanges per serving**
*1 fat*
*3 meat*
*1 vegetable*

**On the side** Zucchini with diced tomatoes provides just the right taste to counterbalance the curry flavor of the shrimp. Serve this with pita slices or rice and a melange of exotic fruits to make the dinner an international experience.

1 Tbsp. margarine
3 Tbsp. lemon juice
¼ tsp. salt
¼ tsp. liquid hot pepper sauce
1 lb. medium raw shrimp, shelled and deveined
¼ tsp. dried parsley flakes

In skillet, melt margarine. Add lemon juice, salt, pepper sauce, and shrimp. Stirring occasionally, cook shrimp until shrimp turns pink. Sprinkle parsley on top of shrimp.

### Per serving
*110 calories*
*111 mg cholesterol*
*274 mg sodium*
*0.339 gm saturated fat*
*1.5 gm fat*

### Exchanges per serving
*2 meat*

**On the side** Cherry tomatoes with basil, a serving of rice, a glass of cold milk, and mixed melon balls for dessert make this meal nutritionally complete.

1 can celery soup

1 cup skim milk

3 tsp. lime juice

⅛ tsp. pepper

⅛ tsp. salt

⅛ tsp. paprika

½ lb. shrimp

2 cups cooked rice

1 cup frozen peas, thawed

¼ cup grated Parmesan cheese

Cook soup, milk, lime juice, and seasoning, stirring until well blended. In a 1½ quart casserole dish, pour half of the soup mixture, then add alternate layers of shrimp, rice, and peas. Add the remaining soup. Sprinkle with cheese. Bake, covered, at 350°F for 20 to 25 minutes.

### Per serving
*331 calories*
*81 mg cholesterol*
*1011 mg sodium*
*4.0 gm saturated fat*
*9.4 gm fat*

### Exchanges per serving
*2 bread*
*2 meat*

**On the side** A tossed salad with your favorite dressing, a glass of nonfat milk, and baked apple dessert make this meal nutritionally balanced.

2 lb. uncooked medium shrimp, peeled and deveined

½ cup soy sauce

½ cup chopped green onions

¼ cup sesame oil

¼ cup water

2 Tbsp. minced garlic

2 tsp. ginger

¾ tsp. nutmeg

¼ tsp. cinnamon

Combine all ingredients in a large bowl. Cover and let marinate for several hours. Drain shrimp, discarding marinade. Thread shrimp on skewers. Broil 1 to 2 minutes on each side.

**Per serving**
*200 calories*
*130 mg cholesterol*
*825 mg sodium*
*2.3 gm saturated fat*
*10.0 gm fat*

**Exchanges per serving**
*1 fat*
*3 meat*

**On the side** New potatoes with rosemary are just right with this entrée. The servings of shrimp are large because nobody can eat just a little of this delicious dish. A mixed fruit salad with yogurt dressing completes the meal nutritionally.

8 oz. raw shrimp, peeled and deveined

2 Tbsp. margarine

2 tsp. sesame seeds

¼ cup chopped green onions

3 Tbsp. soy sauce

1 tsp. Worcestershire sauce

½ tsp. ginger

1 cup cooked rice

Cut shrimp into small pieces. In a skillet, heat margarine and sauté shrimp with sesame seeds until shrimp is done. Stir in onions, soy sauce, Worcestershire sauce, and ginger. Stir often. Serve over hot rice.

**Per serving**
*318 calories*
*173 mg cholesterol*
*533 mg sodium*
*2.4 gm saturated fat*
*7.0 gm fat*

**Exchanges per serving**
*1 bread*
*½ fat*
*4 meat*

**On the side** A serving of stir-fried snow pea pods is perfect beside this oriental-style entree. An orange, simply sectioned, is just right for dessert.

1 cup shrimp, peeled, deveined, and cooked

3 cups cooked rice

1 pint light cream

1 tsp. Worcestershire sauce

⅓ cup ketchup

⅛ tsp. Tabasco sauce

1 tsp. soy sauce

Preheat oven to 350°F. In a bowl, combine all ingredients and place mixture into a casserole dish. Heat 30 to 35 minutes or until bubbly.

**Per serving**
*455 calories*
*166 mg cholesterol*
*798 mg sodium*
*14.6 gm saturated fat*
*24.0 gm fat*

**Exchanges per serving**
*2 bread*
*2 fat*
*2 meat*

**On the side** This simple one-dish meal needs only a salad on the side and a fruit for dessert. Remember a glass of milk makes the meal nutritionally complete.

2 Tbsp. margarine

¼ cup sliced mushrooms

⅛ cup chopped green onions

¼ cup chopped green pepper

½ tsp. minced garlic

1 8 oz. can low-sodium tomato sauce

1 cup cooked, small shrimp

1 cup cooked rice

In a skillet, heat margarine. Sauté mushrooms, green onions, green pepper, and garlic until crisp-tender. Stir in tomato sauce and shrimp. Simmer for 10 to 15 minutes. Serve over hot rice.

**Per serving**
*349 calories*
*221 mg cholesterol*
*640 mg sodium*
*2.3 gm saturated fat*
*13.3 gm fat*

**Exchanges per serving**
*1 bread*
*1 fat*
*2 meat*
*1 vegetable*

**On the side** This easy main dish meal is complete all by itself. A glass of milk and your choice of fruit make the meal nutritionally balanced.

1½ Tbsp. margarine

12 oz. fresh shrimp, peeled and deveined

2 tsp. minced garlic

2 tsp. sherry

1 tsp. dried parsley flakes, crushed

In a large skillet, heat margarine. Add shrimp and garlic. Cook and stir frequently until shrimp turns pink. Stir in sherry. Sprinkle with parsley flakes.

**Per serving**
*195 calories*
*130 mg cholesterol*
*178 mg sodium*
*1.05 gm saturated fat*
*6.0 gm fat*

**Exchanges per serving**
*1 fat*
*3 meat*

**On the side** Steamed green beans and white rice go well with this variation of the basic shrimp entree. A mixed fruit salad with yogurt make the meal complete nutritionally.

6 Tbsp. lemon juice

4 tsp. soy sauce

20 oz. shrimp, shelled and deveined

2 medium tomatoes, cut into wedges

1 medium green pepper, cut into larger chunks

1 small onion, cut into wedges

In small bowl, combine lemon juice and soy sauce; add shrimp and coat. On a skewer, thread shrimp, tomato wedges, pepper squares and onion wedges. Alternate ingredients. Broil, turning and basting with reserve marinade until shrimp is firm.

**Per serving**
*163 calories*
*130 mg cholesterol*
*825 mg sodium*
*0.23 gm saturated fat*
*1.0 gm fat*

**Exchanges per serving**
*2.5 meat*
*1 vegetable*

**On the side** These colorful kabobs look great over a bed of white rice, and the rice helps to balance the meal. Add a glass of milk and some fresh mixed fruits for dessert for nutritional completeness.

1 Tbsp. vegetable oil

2 lbs. shrimp, peeled and deveined

¼ cup green onions, sliced

⅓ cup chicken broth, low-sodium

1½ cups frozen peas, thawed

3 Tbsp. soy sauce

½ tsp. ground ginger

1 Tbsp. sherry

2 tsp. cornstarch

1 Tbsp. water

In a skillet, heat oil, add shrimp and green onions, and cook until shrimp turns pink. Add chicken broth, peas, and ginger. Cook until peas are tender. Stir in sherry and cornstarch dissolved in water. Cook until thickened.

**Per serving**
*321 calories*
*222 mg cholesterol*
*330 mg sodium*
*0.3 gm saturated fat*
*2.3 gm fat*

**Exchanges per serving**
*1 bread*
*3 meat*

**On the side** White rice is always right with oriental-style cooking. A mixed vegetable, stir-fried, goes well with this dish also. These plus a glass of milk and your favorite fruit for dessert make the meal complete nutritionally.

24 oz. shelled and deveined jumbo shrimp

4 Tbsp. flour

1 Tbsp. minced garlic

2 Tbsp. vegetable oil

¼ cup dry white wine

1 Tbsp. lemon juice

⅛ tsp. pepper

Dip shrimp in flour. In skillet, sauté garlic in vegetable oil until lightly browned. Add shrimp and sauté until shrimp turns pink. Add wine and bring to a boil. Stir in lemon juice and pepper. Serve.

**Per serving**
*185 calories*
*130 mg cholesterol*
*2 mg sodium*
*0.33 gm saturated fat*
*7.0 gm fat*

**Exchanges per serving**
*½ bread*
*2 meat*

**On the side** Green noodles go well with this version of traditional scampi and they offer a nice alternative to rice. A mixed green salad, a glass of milk, and a fruit for dessert make the meal complete nutritionally.

# 202 Poached Red Snapper

*Serves 4*

4 red snapper fillets

½ cup dry white wine

1 cup water

1 cup sliced carrots

1 cup sliced celery

⅓ cup green onions, chopped

½ tsp. dried thyme

1 bay leaf

⅛ tsp. pepper

In skillet, add all ingredients, except fish, and bring to a boil. Reduce heat and simmer for 15 minutes. Place fish on a rack and lower into broth. Bring to a boil, cover, and simmer for 5 minutes. Serve.

**Per serving**
*178 calories*
*31 mg cholesterol*
*96 mg sodium*
*0.2 gm saturated fat*
*1.1 gm fat*

**Exchanges per serving**
*3 meat*

**On the side** Brown rice is perfect with this poached snapper recipe. A salad of cabbage, carrots, and lettuce with your favorite dressing plus a fruit with yogurt dessert make this meal nutritionally complete.

# 203 Spicy Snapper

4 6 oz. red snapper fillets
1 Tbsp. lemon juice
1 Tbsp. vegetable oil
⅔ cup chopped green pepper
⅔ cup chopped onions
2 Tbsp. white wine
1 tsp. dried parsley flakes
½ tsp. cayenne pepper
1 cup chopped tomatoes
2 Tbsp. grated Parmesan cheese
⅛ tsp. Tabasco sauce

Preheat oven to 350°F. Sprinkle fish with lemon juice.
In skillet, heat oil, stir in green pepper and onions,
and cook until tender. Add fish and cook about a
minute on each side. Add wine, parsley, cayenne,
and simmer for 5 minutes. Transfer to baking dish.
Spoon tomatoes over fish. Sprinkle with cheese and
Tabasco sauce. Bake about 8 to 10 minutes.

### Per serving
*340 calories*
*43 mg cholesterol*
*115 mg sodium*
*3.25 gm saturated fat*
*8.0 gm fat*

### Exchanges per serving
*6 meat*

**On the side** Asparagus, steamed just until tender, a small
baked potato, a glass of milk and your favorite fresh fruit
for dessert make this meal nutritionally complete.

¼ cup sliced green onions

¼ cup sliced green pepper

¼ cup sliced red pepper

1 cup sliced fresh mushrooms

⅛ tsp. lemon pepper

1 lb. snapper

1 dozen green beans, washed and cut in half

½ tsp. lemon juice

¼ tsp. dried tarragon

Preheat oven to 350°F. In bottom of a baking dish, place onions, green peppers, red peppers, and mushrooms. Sprinkle with lemon pepper. Lay fish on top of vegetables. Place green beans on top of fish. Sprinkle with lemon juice and tarragon. Cover and bake for 25 minutes.

**Per serving**
*178 calories*
*55 mg cholesterol*
*105 mg sodium*
*0.35 gm saturated fat*
*1.9 gm fat*

**Exchanges per serving**
*3 meat*
*1 vegetable*

**On the side** White rice or a small baked potato add the starch course, and a glass of milk and a fresh fruit for dessert make the meal complete nutritionally.

4 lemons, cut in ¼ -inch slices

6 3 oz. portions of swordfish

⅛ tsp. salt

⅛ tsp. lemon pepper

1 Tbsp. lemon juice

Preheat oven to 350°F. Take a large piece of aluminum foil and place a layer of lemon slices on half of it. Sprinkle fish with salt and lemon pepper. Lay the fish on top of the lemon slices and then put more slices on top. Sprinkle with lemon juice. Fold the foil over the fish carefully and seal the edges completely. Bake for 20 minutes.

**Per serving**
*164 calories*
*23 mg cholesterol*
*43 mg sodium*
*0.2 gm saturated fat*
*1.3 gm fat*

**Exchanges per serving**
*3 meat*

**On the side** White rice or a baked potato and green beans, cooked to a crispy tenderness, are perfect accompaniments to this lemony-fish dish. A mixed fruit salad with yogurt for dessert makes the meal complete nutritionally.

1 small onion, sliced thin

⅔ cup dry white wine

2 Tbsp. lemon juice

6 swordfish fillets (approx. 3 oz. ea.)

⅛ tsp. salt

½ tsp. lemon pepper

1 cup light sour cream

Cover the bottom of a baking dish with onions. Add wine and lemon juice; stir. Put into 400°F oven and cook for 10 minutes. Arrange fish fillets over onions. Sprinkle with salt and lemon pepper. Bake for 15 minutes covered. Uncover and spread sour cream over fish and broil until cream is lightly brown. Serve.

**Per serving**
*240 calories*
*66 mg cholesterol*
*383 mg sodium*
*2.3 gm saturated fat*
*8.3 gm fat*

**Exchanges per serving**
*1 fat*
*3 meat*

**On the side** Long-grain wild rice is just right with this robust fish dish. A side salad of mixed greens and a fresh pear, sliced and placed attractively on a glass plate with a slight sprinkle of nutmeg, for dessert complete the meal. Remember adding a glass of milk makes this meal complete.

1 lb. swordfish

¼ cup vegetable oil

2 Tbsp. red wine vinegar

1 tsp. garlic powder

2 tsp. Dijon-style mustard

½ tsp. dried basil

⅓ cup chopped onions

1 bay leaf

Combine all ingredients in a shallow dish. Coat swordfish with marinade and let stand at least 1 hour, turning occasionally. Place swordfish on broiling pan and broil on each side, basting occasionally.

**Per serving**
*255 calories*
*43 mg cholesterol*
*65 mg sodium*
*3.5 gm saturated fat*
*10.0 gm fat*

**Exchanges per serving**
*1 fat*
*4 meat*

**On the side** White rice and brussel sprouts go very well with this marinated fish dish. Top off with a melange of fruits and berries with yogurt dressing and the meal is nutritionally complete.

1½ lb. swordfish

1½ Tbsp. lemon juice

2½ Tbsp. light mayonnaise

5 Tbsp. low-fat yogurt

1½ Tbsp. Dijon-style mustard

1½ tsp. dried tarragon

Heat broiler. Cook fish on one side. Pour 1 tablespoon lemon juice over fish. While fish is cooking, combine remaining ingredients; mix well. Cook fish for 1 to 2 minutes on other side, then pour sauce over fish. Continue to cook fish until done.

**Per serving**
*193 calories*
*56 mg cholesterol*
*144 mg sodium*
*2.0 gm saturated fat*
*7.1 gm fat*

**Exchanges per serving**
*1 fat*
*3 meat*

**On the side** A simple baked potato is always good with swordfish. Asparagus spears, steamed just until tender, a glass of milk and your choice of fruit for dessert and the meal is nutritionally complete.

4 swordfish steaks

2 Tbsp. soy sauce

1 tsp. Worcestershire sauce

3 Tbsp. dry white wine

3 Tbsp. lemon juice

1 tsp. minced garlic

½ tsp. lemon pepper

Place swordfish on broiling pan. Combine remaining ingredients. Baste swordfish with marinade and broil until fish is done; baste several times while broiling.

**Per serving**
*160 calories*
*33 mg cholesterol*
*549 mg sodium*
*0.9 gm saturated fat*
*3.4 gm fat*

**Exchanges per serving**
*3 meat*

**On the side** Fresh cooked corn on the cob tastes great with this broiled fish. A tossed salad of mixed greens with your favorite dressing, a glass of nonfat milk, and melon slices for dessert make the meal complete nutritionally.

2 Tbsp. margarine, melted

¼ cup minced onion

1 Tbsp. lemon juice

1 Tbsp. minced garlic

1 tsp. oregano

⅛ tsp. ground pepper

⅛ tsp. lemon pepper

4 trout fillets

½ tsp. paprika

¼ cup whole-wheat bread crumbs

Combine margarine, onion, lemon juice, garlic, oregano, ground pepper, lemon pepper, and mix well. Spoon an equal amount of mixture over each fillet. Sprinkle with paprika; top with bread crumbs. Spray broiler rack with nonstick cooking spray. Place fish on rack. Broil 3 to 4 inches away from heat. Broil until topping is lightly browned and fish flakes easily.

**Per serving**
*254 calories*
*48 mg cholesterol*
*139 mg sodium*
*1.2 gm saturated fat*
*8.9 gm fat*

**Exchanges per serving**
*½ bread*
*1 fat*
*3 meat*

**On the side** Steamed spinach looks and tastes great with this trout dish. Combine strawberries and nonfat milk in the blender and freeze the result for a refreshing mousse for dessert. This simple meal is nutritionally balanced.

# 211 Broiled Fish on Cold Tomatoes Vinaigrette

*Serves 4*

2 Tbsp. vegetable oil

1 Tbsp. vinegar

1½ tsp. ground coriander

¾ tsp. minced garlic

½ tsp. dried parsley flakes

½ tsp. tarragon

1 tsp. oregano

4 trout fillets

2 cups coarsely chopped tomatoes

Beat together oil, vinegar, coriander, and garlic. Add parsley, tarragon and oregano, and mix. Stir in tomatoes. Place fish on broiler pan and brush lightly with oil. Broil fish until done. Pour dressing over fish and serve.

**Per serving**
*178 calories*
*48 mg cholesterol*
*8.7 mg sodium*
*0.9 gm saturated fat*
*7.0 gm fat*

**Exchanges per serving**
*1 fat*
*2 meat*

**On the side** A serving of green noodles, a tossed salad, a glass of milk, and a dessert of mixed melon balls make this meal nutritionally complete.

4 trout fillets

¾ cup soy sauce

¼ cup cooking sherry

1½ Tbsp. lime juice

1 tsp. ground cloves

½ cup vegetable oil

Rinse and pat fillets. In a bowl, mix all ingredients. Place fillets in shallow baking dish. Pour marinade over fish. Let stand for 1½ hours. Spray broiler pan with nonstick spray. Broil fish. Baste occasionally with marinade until fish is flaky.

**Per serving**
*123 calories*
*27 mg cholesterol*
*1125 mg sodium*
*0.3 gm saturated fat*
*1.3 gm fat*

**Exchanges per serving**
*2 meat*

**On the side** Green noodles, a slaw-style salad of cabbage and carrots, a glass of milk, and a baked apple make this meal nutritionally complete.

# 213 Sweet and Sour Fillets

*Serves 4*

2 tsp. vegetable oil

2 Tbsp. minced onion

¼ cup chopped red pepper

1 tsp. minced garlic

¼ cup water

1 tsp. soy sauce

½ tsp. lemon juice

1 Tbsp. sugar

1 Tbsp. vinegar

⅛ tsp. ground pepper

1 tsp. flour, dissolved in 2 Tbsp. water

4 trout fillets

In skillet, heat oil. Add onions, red pepper, and garlic; cook until soft. Add water, soy sauce, lemon juice, sugar, vinegar, and ground pepper. Bring to a boil. Add fillets; cover and simmer until fish flakes easily. Transfer fillets to serving platter; keep warm. Add flour mixture to skillet. Cook, stirring constantly until thickened. Pour over fillets.

**Per serving**
*172 calories*
*48 mg cholesterol*
*92.7 mg sodium*
*0.88 gm saturated fat*
*9.4 gm fat*

**Exchanges per serving**
*1 fat*
*3 meat*

**On the side** A serving of white rice, a side dish of steamed cauliflower, and a dessert of fruity frozen pops complete this meal. Add a glass of milk for total nutritional balance.

2 trout fillets

⅛ tsp. salt

⅛ tsp. lemon pepper

¼ cup fine oatmeal

2 Tbsp. margarine

Season fish with salt and lemon pepper. Coat both sides with oatmeal. Heat margarine in a skillet and sauté trout until cooked through and browned.

**Per serving**
*250 calories*
*48 mg cholesterol*
*370 mg sodium*
*2.6 gm saturated fat*
*10.3 gm fat*

**Exchanges per serving**
*½ bread*
*1 fat*
*3 meat*

**On the side** Freshly sliced cucumbers interspersed with tomato slices look attractive on the plate, taste delicious with this healthy trout dish, and provide the vegetable component needed to balance the meal. Make a drink of 1 cup of skim milk plus a cup of frozen peaches, mixed in the blender until thick and frothy, and this meal is nutritionally complete.

# 215 Creamed Tuna

¼ cup light mayonnaise

2 Tbsp. flour

1 cup skim milk

½ tsp. minced onion

¼ tsp. minced garlic

⅛ tsp. pepper

1 6⅛ oz. can tuna in spring water

1 cup frozen corn, thawed

¼ cup shredded part-skim cheddar cheese

2 whole-wheat English muffins

In saucepan, combine mayonnaise and flour. Gradually stir in milk, onion, garlic, and pepper. Cook over low heat until mixture boils, stirring constantly. Add tuna, corn and cheese. Heat until cheese melts. Serve open faced over whole-wheat English muffins.

## Per serving
264 calories
28.9 mg cholesterol
521 mg sodium
1.1 gm saturated fat
7.0 gm fat

## Exchanges per serving
1 bread
1 fat
2 meat

**On the side** Crunchy carrot and celery sticks and a strawberry freezer drink complete this meal nutritionally.

1 6⅛ oz. can tuna in spring water

1 cup sliced mushrooms

1 can cream of cheddar soup

¼ cup grated Parmesan cheese

¼ cup mozzarella cheese, part-skim, shredded

¾ cup skim milk

2 cups small macaroni

Preheat oven to 350°F. In saucepan, combine tuna, mushrooms, cheddar soup, half of both cheeses, and milk. Stir until heated and combined. Cook macaroni according to package directions; drain. Place macaroni in a casserole dish and pour tuna mixture over macaroni. Sprinkle with remaining cheeses. Bake for 15 minutes or until well heated.

**Per serving**
*240 calories*
*18 mg cholesterol*
*578 mg sodium*
*2.8 gm saturated fat*
*8.8 gm fat*

**Exchanges per serving**
*1 bread*
*1 fat*
*2½ meat*

**On the side** A tossed salad, a glass of milk, and a baked apple dessert complete this meal nutritionally.

8 oz. macaroni

1¾ cup skim milk

3½ Tbsp. cornstarch

¼ cup water

¾ cup sliced fresh mushrooms

¾ tsp. thyme

½ tsp. pepper

1 cup chopped zucchini

1 6⅛ oz. can tuna in spring water

½ cup sliced radishes

Cook macaroni according to package directions; drain and set aside. In saucepan, heat milk. Add cornstarch and water to milk, stirring constantly until it thickens. Add mushrooms, thyme, and pepper. In a 2½ quart casserole dish, arrange macaroni in the bottom, top with zucchini, then place tuna with radishes on top. Pour sauce over the top layer. Cover and bake at 375°F for 40 to 45 minutes or until zucchini is tender.

**Per serving**
*157 calories*
*2.5 mg cholesterol*
*73 mg sodium*
*0 gm saturated fat*
*0.37 gm fat*

**Exchanges per serving**
*1 bread*
*1 meat*
*1 vegetable*

**On the side** Make a drink of 1 cup of skim milk with 1 cup of frozen peaches and this meal is complete nutritionally.

1 7 oz. pkg. elbow macaroni

1 6⅛ oz. can tuna in spring water

1 Tbsp. margarine

¼ cup chopped onion

1 can cream of mushroom soup

¾ cup water

¼ cup shredded part-skim American cheese

1 tsp. dried parsley flakes

Cook macaroni according to package directions. Drain and flake tuna. In a large skillet, melt margarine. Sauté onions. Add soup, water, cheese, tuna, and parsley. Stir until cheese melts. Add macaroni and heat on low for about 10 minutes.

**Per serving**
*190 calories*
*16 mg cholesterol*
*340 mg sodium*
*1.5 gm saturated fat*
*5.2 gm fat*

**Exchanges per serving**
*1 bread*
*1 fat*
*1 meat*

**On the side** A tossed salad of mixed greens, a glass of milk, and an apple, baked with a little cinnamon on top, make this meal delicious and nutritionally complete.

1 6⅛ oz. tuna in spring water, drained

½ cup crushed saltines

1 egg, beaten

⅓ cup skim milk

2 Tbsp. finely chopped onions

¼ tsp. Worcestershire sauce

⅛ tsp. pepper

¼ tsp. prepared mustard

1 Tbsp. margarine

In a bowl, combine all ingredients, except margarine. Shape into 6 patties. In a skillet, heat margarine; add patties and cook over medium heat. Cook and brown on both sides.

### Per serving
*284 calories*
*127 mg cholesterol*
*582 mg sodium*
*2.9 gm saturated fat*
*10.8 gm fat*

### Exchanges per serving
*1 bread*
*3½ meat*

**On the side** Steamed carrots are just right with these tasty tuna patties. They provide the vegetable component for this meal and they look smashing on the plate. A glass of milk and a dessert of mixed berries and melon balls provide the other components that complete the meal nutritionally.

1 cup noodles

1 cup skim milk

1 Tbsp. flour

1 6⅛ oz. can tuna in spring water, drained

¾ cup fresh mushrooms, sliced

1 Tbsp. minced onion

¼ cup finely chopped red pepper

1 tsp. dried parsley flakes

1 tsp. basil

1 tsp. celery seed

⅛ tsp. black pepper

Cook noodles in water until done; drain. In saucepan, add milk and flour; cook until thickened. In bowl, combine tuna, mushrooms, onions, red pepper, and seasonings; mix well. Add milk mixture; mix again. Stir in noodles. Fill baking dish with tuna mixture. Bake at 325° for 40 minutes.

**Per serving**
*289 calories*
*83 mg cholesterol*
*114 mg sodium*
*0.05 gm saturated fat*
*3.7 gm fat*

**Exchanges per serving**
*1½ bread*
*1½ meat*
*1 vegetable*

**On the side** A glass of milk and a fresh fruit for dessert are all you need to make this meal nutritionally complete.

# 221 Tuna Soufflé

*Serves 6*

2 6⅛ oz. cans tuna in spring water
½ cup bran cereal, uncooked
½ cup skim milk
2 Tbsp. minced onion
1 Tbsp. lime juice
1 Tbsp. dried parsley flakes
⅛ tsp. black pepper
1 tsp. celery seed
⅛ tsp. paprika
1 egg white

Heat oven to 325°F. Drain tuna and flake. In a large bowl, mix tuna, bran, milk, onion, lime juice, parsley, pepper, celery seed, and paprika. Beat egg white until stiff peak forms; fold into tuna mixture. Put into 1 quart baking dish. Bake for 40 minutes or until brown.

**Per serving**
*139 calories*
*426 mg cholesterol*
*40 mg sodium*
*0.31 gm saturated fat*
*1.3 gm fat*

**Exchanges per serving**
*1 bread*
*1 meat*

**On the side** Asparagus, gently steamed, is great with this soufflé. A frothy dessert of yogurt blended with pears and topped with cinnamon finishes the meal, refreshes the palate, and nutritionally balances this dinner.

4 tsp. vegetable oil

¾ cup sliced onions

¾ cup chopped tomatoes

¾ cup low-sodium tomato sauce

⅛ tsp. pepper

1 8 oz. can tuna in spring water, drained, flaked

⅛ tsp. hot sauce

4 corn tortillas

⅔ cup skim cheddar cheese, shredded

1 cup shredded lettuce

In skillet, heat oil; add onions and sauté for 5 minutes. Add tomatoes, tomato sauce, pepper, and hot sauce; cook for 5 minutes more. Stir in tuna and cook through. Fill each tortilla with ¼ each of tuna mixture, cheese, and lettuce.

**Per serving**
*252 calories*
*18 mg cholesterol*
*136 mg sodium*
*4.5 gm saturated fat*
*10.8 gm fat*

**Exchanges per servings**
*1 bread*
*1 fat*
*2 meat*

**On the side** A small dollop of cottage cheese with thin slices of avocado and a Mexican-style salad of cucumbers, tomatoes, celery, onions, and green and red peppers with oil-free dressing make this meal an international delight.

1 lb. walleye fillets

1½ Tbsp. margarine

2 cups fresh sliced mushrooms

⅔ cup sliced green onion

⅛ tsp. thyme

¼ tsp. dried crushed tarragon

⅛ tsp. paprika

1½ Tbsp. margarine

Arrange fish on a baking dish. In a skillet, heat margarine and cook mushrooms, onion, thyme and tarragon until tender. Spoon over fish. Sprinkle with paprika. Bake at 450°F for 10 minutes or until fish flakes easily.

**Per serving**
*164 calories*
*97 mg cholesterol*
*117 mg sodium*
*1.0 gm saturated fat*
*15.8 gm fat*

**Exchanges per serving**
*1 fat*
*3 meat*
*½ vegetable*

**On the side** A serving of brown rice, a tossed salad, and a broiled grapefruit with cinnamon for dessert complete the meal. Add a glass of milk and the meal is nutritionally balanced.

1 lb. walleye fillets

¾ cup skim milk

⅔ cup herb-seasoned bread crumbs

¼ tsp. salt

⅛ tsp. pepper

Preheat oven to 500°F. Dip fillets in skim milk and coat with bread crumbs. Season with salt and pepper. Arrange fillets in baking dish. Bake 10 to 15 minutes.

**Per serving**
*149 calories*
*73.75 mg cholesterol*
*333 mg sodium*
*0.4 gm saturated fat*
*1.0 gm fat*

**Exchanges per serving**
*½ bread*
*3 meat*

**On the side** New potatoes in rosemary, steamed broccoli spears, and mixed melon balls with a garnish of fresh mint complete the meal. Add a glass of milk for complete nutritional balance.

1 lb. walleye

1 tsp. dried parsley flakes

½ tsp. salt

⅛ tsp. pepper

½ cup thinly sliced onions

1 small tomato, cut into thin slices

1 Tbsp. lemon juice

1 Tbsp. vegetable oil

Cut fillets into six servings. Arrange fish in baking dish into which the vegetable oil has been poured. Sprinkle with salt and pepper. Top with onion and tomato slices. Sprinkle with lemon juice and parsley. Cover and bake at 375°F for 25 minutes or until fish flakes easily.

**Per serving**
*124 calories*
*73 mg cholesterol*
*52 mg sodium*
*0.28 gm saturated fat*
*2.3 gm fat*

**Exchanges per serving**
*2 meat*

**On the side** Brown rice works well with this festive-looking main dish. A salad of mixed greens and quick-to-fix applesauce from the blender complete the meal. Add a glass of milk and you have it all nutritionally.

2 tsp. margarine

¼ cup minced onion

1¾ cup skim milk

2 tsp. chicken bouillon powder

½ tsp. paprika

2 Tbsp. cornstarch

1 lb. walleye fillets

3 cups sliced potatoes

1 10 oz. package frozen spinach, thawed

In skillet, melt margarine. Add onions and cook until tender. Stir in the milk, bouillon, and paprika. Mix in cornstarch; stir constantly over medium heat until mixture thickens. Cut fillets into ½ inch slices. Arrange potatoes in 2½ quart casserole dish, top with spinach, then fish, then sauce. Cover and bake for 1½ hours or until potatoes are tender. Bake at 375°F.

**Per serving**
*335 calories*
*31 mg cholesterol*
*430 mg sodium*
*0.4 gm saturated fat*
*2.5 gm fat*

**Exchanges per serving**
*1½ bread*
*2 meat*
*½ skim milk*
*1 vegetable*

**On the side** This hearty dish has it all: starch, protein, vegetable, milk. Add a dessert of mixed fruits and the meal is nutritionally complete.

2 tsp. oil

⅔ cup onions, chopped

1 tsp. minced garlic

1 cup chopped tomatoes

¾ tsp. dried basil

¼ tsp. oregano

1 tsp. dried parsley flakes

1½ Tbsp. lemon juice

8 oz. walleye fillet

⅛ tsp. pepper

⅛ tsp. salt

¼ cup water

In skillet, heat oil; add onion and garlic; sauté until golden. Stir in tomatoes, basil, oregano, parsley, and lemon juice. Sprinkle fish with salt and pepper. Lay fish on top of sauce in skillet. Add water; cover and steam fish for 10 minutes or until fish flakes easily.

**Per serving**
*191 calories*
*97 mg cholesterol*
*210 mg sodium*
*0.8 gm saturated fat*
*5.8 gm fat*

**Exchanges per serving**
*1 fat*
*3 meat*
*1 vegetable*

**On the side** Cook up a batch of fresh beets to accompany this updated version of a traditional French recipe. Mix mandarin orange slices, sliced strawberries, and seedless grapes and top with yogurt dressing for a healthy dessert that makes this meal nutritionally complete.

12 oz. walleye fillets

½ cup frozen orange concentrate

⅛ tsp. lemon pepper

⅛ tsp. salt

½ tsp. dried parsley flakes, crushed

⅓ cup dry bread crumbs

1 Tbsp. margarine, melted

Cut fillets into small portions. Combine orange juice concentrate with lemon pepper, salt, and parsley. Dip fish into orange juice mixture, then roll into bread crumbs. Drizzle margarine over fillets. Bake at 500°F for 10 to 15 minutes or until fish flakes easily.

**Per serving**
*381 calories*
*146 mg cholesterol*
*421 mg sodium*
*1.5 gm saturated fat*
*9.1 gm fat*

**Exchanges per serving**
*½ bread*
*1½ fat*
*1 fruit*
*4 meat*

**On the side** Mix steamed broccoli and carrots for a colorful side dish to this healthy dish. Serve the meal with a glass of non-fat milk and this dinner is nutritionally complete.

Nonstick cooking spray

4 walleye fillets

2 Tbsp. sugar

2 Tbsp. lemon juice

1 tsp. Worcestershire sauce

½ tsp. paprika

½ tsp. lemon pepper

Spray pan with nonstick spray. Mix sugar, lemon juice, Worcestershire sauce, paprika, and lemon pepper; set aside. Rinse fillets and pat dry. Place fillets on pan. Brush fillets with sauce. Broil, turning and basting, until fillets are flakey.

**Per serving**
*103 calories*
*73 mg. cholesterol*
*43 mg sodium*
*0.2 gm saturated fat*
*1.0 gm fat*

**Exchanges per serving**
*2 meat*

**On the side** Serve this fish dish with a side of white rice, some steamed carrots, a glass of milk, and fresh pears for dessert and you have a nutritionally complete meal.

# Lamb

2 hard-boiled eggs, chopped
⅔ cup bread crumbs
2 Tbsp. margarine, melted
1 tsp. basil
1 tsp. minced garlic
4 lamb chops
⅛ tsp. paprika

Preheat oven to 400°F. Combine eggs, bread crumbs, margarine, basil, and garlic. Press mixture on top and bottom of each chop. Wrap each chop in foil. Bake for 25 minutes. Sprinkle chops with paprika and broil until browned.

**Per serving**
*424 calories*
*181 mg cholesterol*
*510 mg sodium*
*9.0 gm saturated fat*
*14.0 gm fat*

**Exchanges per serving**
*1 bread*
*1 fat*
*4 meat*

**On the side** Broccoli with garlic, 8 oz. nonfat milk, and a cup of mixed melon balls garnished with fresh mint complete this meal nutritionally.

2 Tbsp. vegetable oil

6 lamp chops

2 cups tomatoes, chopped

1 Tbsp. red wine vinegar

1 tsp. dried basil

1 tsp. ginger

⅛ cup dry vermouth

⅛ tsp. pepper

In a large skillet, heat oil; brown chops on both sides. Remove and place in 9 x 13-inch baking pan. Combine remaining ingredients in the same skillet. Stir and cook for 3 minutes. Pour over chops and bake at 375°F for 35 minutes. Baste meat with sauce occasionally.

**Per serving**
*200 calories*
*51 mg cholesterol*
*179 mg sodium*
*3.3 gm saturated fat*
*12.1 gm fat*

**Exchanges per serving**
*1 fat*
*2 meat*
*1 vegetable*

**On the side** Fresh cooked beets work well with this version of baked lamb chops. A dessert of apples and raisins in yogurt completes the meal.

2 Tbsp. margarine
¼ cup chopped onions
2½ tsp. curry powder
2 lb. lamb, cubed
1½ Tbsp. cornstarch
¾ cup raisins
1¾ cup low-fat yogurt
2 cups cooked rice

In skillet, melt margarine. Add onions and curry powder; sauté. Combine all ingredients except yogurt and rice; simmer until thick and smooth. Remove from heat and stir in yogurt. Serve over rice.

**Per serving**
*375 calories*
*110 mg cholesterol*
*514 mg sodium*
*5.7 gm saturated fat*
*12.3 gm fat*

**Exchanges per serving**
*1 bread*
*1½ fat*
*2 meat*
*½ milk*

**On the side** Minted carrots look great on the plate and add just the right flavor to enhance this spicy dish. Fresh pear slices for dessert and you've got a meal that's delicious and nutritious.

# 233  Dijon-Honeyed Lamb Steaks

2 lbs. lamb steaks
3 tsp. Dijon-style mustard
3 tsp. honey
3 tsp. teriyaki sauce
1 Tbsp. minced garlic
2 Tbsp. low-calorie apricot spread

In bowl, combine all ingredients except lamb; mix well. On broiler pan, place lamb steaks and brush with mustard mixture. Broil 5 to 7 minutes; turn steaks over and baste. Broil until done to taste.

**Per serving**
*197 calories*
*86 mg cholesterol*
*220 mg sodium*
*8.3 gm saturated fat*
*11.1 gm fat*

**Exchanges per serving**
*3 meat*

**On the side** New potatoes with rosemary, green beans and garlic, and apple chunks and raisins with yogurt, topped with cinnamon, make this meal complete nutritionally.

6 large lamp chops
¾ cup canned unsweetened apricot nectar
1 tsp. rosemary, crushed
½ tsp. ginger

Arrange chops on a broiling rack. Combine apricot nectar with rosemary and ginger. Spoon half the mixture over chops. Broil for 4 to 5 minutes. Turn chops and spoon remaining mixture over them. Broil until desired doneness.

**Per serving**
*378 calories*
*86 mg cholesterol*
*62 mg sodium*
*14.8 gm saturated fat*
*32.0 gm fat*

**Exchanges per serving**
*1 fruit*
*3 meat*

**On the side** White rice with saffron, green beans and garlic, and yogurt for dessert make this meal nutritionally complete.

6 loin lamb chops, 1-inch thick
2 Tbsp. margarine
2 tsp. garlic
1 tsp. dried parsley flakes
1 Tbsp. lemon juice

Place lamb chops on broiling pan; broil until desired taste. While chops are broiling, mix margarine, garlic, parsley, and lemon juice over heat. Stir until margarine is melted and thoroughly blended. Pour over chops.

**Per serving**
*394 calories*
*86 mg cholesterol*
*108 mg sodium*
*14.0 gm saturated fat*
*23.0 gm fat*

**Exchanges per serving**
*2 fat*
*3 meat*

**On the side** White rice, asparagus, steamed just until tender, and a mixed fruit salad with 1 Tbsp. white Creme de Menthe (per serving) over the top combine to make this nearly a gourmet meal. Add a glass of milk and the meal is complete nutritionally.

1 lb. ground lamb
⅔ cup grated carrots
1 egg
1 cup finely chopped onions
⅓ cup Parmesan cheese
⅛ tsp. salt
⅛ tsp. pepper
1½ tsp. garlic
½ cup vegetable oil
2 Tbsp. lemon juice

In bowl, combine lamb, carrots, egg, onions, cheese, salt, pepper, and ½ tsp. garlic; blend well. Scoop out rounded tablespoons of the meat mixture and make balls. Spear lamb balls in the center with wooden kabob sticks—3 on a stick. Place in a shallow dish. Combine 1 tsp. garlic, oil, and lemon juice; mix. Pour over kabobs. Broil, turning kabobs and brushing with marinade. Broil to your desired taste.

**Per serving**
*370 calories*
*132 mg cholesterol*
*174 mg sodium*
*9.58 gm saturated fat*
*20.0 gm fat*

**Exchanges per serving**
*1 fat*
*3 meat*
*1 vegetable*

**On the side** Saffron rice, broccoli with garlic, and a dessert mousse of yogurt with pears and honeydew melon, whipped in the blender with ½ tsp. vanilla and fresh mint leaves make this meal complete nutritionally.

# 237  Lamb with Eggplant

1½ lb. ground lamb
1 cup chopped onions
1 small eggplant, sliced
1 cup tomatoes, chopped
1 tsp. garlic
1 8 oz. can low-sodium tomato sauce
⅛ tsp. pepper

In skillet, heat margarine and add lamb; cook until pink color disappears. Add remaining ingredients. Cover and cook over medium heat, stirring occasionally, for 20 minutes or until eggplant is done.

**Per serving**
*319 calories*
*83 mg cholesterol*
*67 mg sodium*
*11.5 gm saturated fat*
*26.5 gm fat*

**Exchanges per serving**
*3 meat*
*1 vegetable*

**On the side** Parsley new potatoes go well with this hearty lamb dish. For dessert make a plate of fresh fruits, sliced, and sprinkle them with poppy seeds. Offer a yogurt dip, and the meal is complete nutritionally.

4 lamb chops, cut 1-inch thick
4 Tbsp. light mayonnaise
3 Tbsp. Dijon-style mustard
3 tsp. lemon juice
⅛ tsp. dried dillweed
⅛ tsp. dried tarragon

Preheat broiler. Place chops on broiling pan and broil for 6 to 10 minutes. In mixing bowl, combine remaining ingredients. Brush chops with sauce while chops are broiling. Pass any remaining sauce or pour over chops.

**Per serving**
*282 calories*
*88 mg cholesterol*
*80 mg sodium*
*15.25 gm saturated fat*
*20.0 gm fat*

**Exchanges per serving**
*1 fat*
*3 meat*

**On the side** New potatoes with rosemary, a side salad of cucumbers, onions, and tomatoes with yogurt dressing, and apples, poached in honey for dessert make this meal nutritionally complete.

4 lamb chops, 1-inch thick
1 Tbsp. sugar
1 tsp. cornstarch
⅔ cup unsweetened pineapple juice
¼ cup chopped red pepper
2 tsp. soy sauce
½ tsp. ground ginger
⅛ tsp. ground cloves

Preheat broiler. Trim fat from lamb chops. Place chops on broiling pan and broil until desired doneness. While chops are broiling, stir together sugar and cornstarch in a saucepan. Stir in pineapple juice, red pepper, soy sauce, ginger, and cloves. Cook and stir until thickened and bubbly. Serve sauce over chops.

**Per serving**
*267 calories*
*75 mg cholesterol*
*468 mg sodium*
*4.75 gm saturated fat*
*13.5 gm fat*

**Exchanges per serving**
*½ fruit*
*3 meat*

**On the side** A serving of white rice, snow pea pods, lightly sautéed so they are still crunchy, and a strawberry milk shake (made with a cup of skim milk and ½ cup frozen strawberries blended until frothy) complete this meal nutritionally.

¼ cup low-sodium tomato paste
3 cups water
1 cup uncooked rice
1 tsp. cinnamon
6 small zucchinis, cut into slices
1 lb. ground lamb
⅛ tsp. pepper
1 tsp. dried parsley flakes

In skillet, brown lamb; drain. Lay zucchini on the bottom of a casserole dish and put lamb on top of zucchini. Mix together tomato paste, water, rice, cinnamon, parsley, and pepper. Pour over lamb and zucchini. Bake at 350°F for 30 minutes.

**Per serving**
*160 calories*
*41.9 mg cholesterol*
*33.9 mg sodium*
*5.8 gm saturated fat*
*13.3 gm fat*

**Exchanges per serving**
*½ bread*
*2 meat*
*1 vegetable*

**On the side** Serve this casserole with ½ slices of a hearty whole-grain bread, a glass of milk, and an apple poached in honey for a nutritionally complete meal.

# Pork and Ham

1 egg white
⅓ cup quick cooking oats
¼ cup raisins
3 tsp. minced onion
2 tsp. prepared mustard
⅛ tsp. pepper
⅛ tsp. salt
1 cup applesauce
¼ tsp. cinnamon
1 lb. lean ground pork

Preheat oven to 350°F. In mixing bowl, beat egg white. Stir in oats, raisins, onion, mustard, pepper, salt, and ¼ cup applesauce. Add the pork and mix well. Shape into a loaf, then place in a baking pan. Bake for 55 to 60 minutes. In a saucepan, combine remaining applesauce and cinnamon. Cook until heated. To serve, slice loaf and serve with heated applesauce.

**Per serving**
*323 calories*
*149 mg cholesterol*
*173 mg sodium*
*3.5 gm saturated fat*
*10.0 gm fat*

**Exchanges per serving**
*½ bread*
*½ fruit*
*3 meat*

**On the side** Baby carrots, sautéed with margarine and ginger-root, go well with this novel variety of meat loaf. Add a glass of milk and this meal is nutritionally balanced.

2 3 oz. pork chops
1 garlic clove
dash salt
dash pepper

Preheat oven to 350°F. Rub chops with garlic.
Sprinkle chops with salt and pepper. Place chops
in baking dish and bake for 40 to 45 minutes or
until chops are done.

**Per serving**
*225 calories*
*70 mg cholesterol*
*50 mg sodium*
*8.9 gm saturated fat*
*15 gm fat*

**Exchanges per serving**
*3 meat*

**On the side** Twice baked potato shells, cooked cabbage, and
apples, honey-poached really set this traditional meal apart
from the average. Add a glass of milk and the meal is nutritionally complete.

# 243 Creole Pork Chops

2 lean pork chops, 1-inch thick
1 Tbsp. vegetable oil
⅔ cup chopped onions
⅔ cup chopped green pepper
¼ tsp. minced garlic
1 Tbsp. margarine
¾ cup chopped tomatoes
2 Tbsp. sweet vermouth
¾ tsp. oregano
⅛ tsp. basil

In a skillet, heat oil and brown pork chops; remove chops from pan. In same skillet, melt margarine; add onions, green peppers, and garlic; sauté until tender. Add remaining ingredients to skillet; simmer for 15 minutes, stirring frequently. Add pork chops and simmer for 25 minutes.

**Per serving**
*300 calories*
*50 mg cholesterol*
*120 mg sodium*
*5.0 gm saturated fat*
*20.0 gm fat*

**Echanges per serving**
*1½ fat*
*3 meat*
*1 vegetable*

**On the side** Serve this colorful dish with white rice, green beans, steamed just until tender, and a side of fresh apple sauce just whipped up in the blender. Add a glass of milk and the meal is nutritionally complete.

6 pork chops, 1-inch thick
3 Tbsp. Dijon-style mustard
¾ cup plain bread crumbs
1½ tsp. curry powder
2 Tbsp. margarine, melted
1 Tbsp. dried, minced onion

Brush chops with mustard. In a dish, combine bread crumbs, curry powder, margarine and onions. Coat pork chops with crumb mixture. Put chops in a baking pan. Bake at 400°F for 35 minutes.

**Per serving**
*315 calories*
*70 mg cholesterol*
*177 mg sodium*
*9.6 gm saturated fat*
*23.5 gm fat*

**Exchanges per serving**
*½ bread*
*1 fat*
*3 meat*

**On the side** Saffron rice, stir-fried cabbage bites, a dessert of baked apples with cinnamon, and a glass of milk make this meal nutritionally complete.

# 245 Fruited Pork Chops

8 lean pork chops
½ cup unsweetened apple juice
1 cup raisins
8 drops Tabasco sauce
¼ cup brown sugar
½ tsp. cinnamon
⅛ tsp. clove
⅛ tsp. nutmeg
⅔ cup water
4 large apples, each cut into 8 wedges

Brown pork chops in skillet on both sides. Arrange chops in shallow baking dish and pour in apple juice, Tabasco sauce, and raisins. Bake for 45 minutes at 350°F. In a bowl, mix brown sugar, cinnamon, clove, and nutmeg. Add apples and coat apples with mixture. Turn chops in baking dish, arrange apples around the chops and sprinkle sugar mixture over apples and chops. Pour water over entire contents. Bake for 15 minutes.

**Per serving**
*360 calories*
*63 mg cholesterol*
*228 mg sodium*
*3.48 gm saturated fat*
*10.1 gm fat*

**Exchanges per serving**
*2 fruit*
*2 meat*

**On the side** A serving of brown rice or a slice of your favorite dark bread goes well with this spicy-fruity dish. Add a cabbage salad or a serving of green beans and a glass of milk and the meal is complete nutritionally.

2 pork loin chops

½ cup sliced carrots

½ cup unsweetened apple cider

¼ cup celery, chopped

⅓ cup chopped onion

¾ cup diced mango

¾ cup diced apple

¼ cup raisins

½ tsp. cinnamon

Place pork chops on broiling pan and broil just until pork chops are lightly browned and set aside. In an 8 x 8-inch baking dish, combine all remaining ingredients; top with pork chops. Cover and bake at 350°F for 35 minutes.

**Per serving**
*370 calories*
*70 mg cholesterol*
*250 mg sodium*
*6.0 gm saturated fat*
*15.0 gm fat*

**Exchanges per serving**
*2 fruit*
*3 meat*
*1 vegetable*

**On the side** Serve this with white rice and a glass of milk and the meal is complete nutritionally.

6 pork steaks
¼ cup flour
2 Tbsp. margarine
¼ cup water
4 Tbsp. brown sugar
¼ tsp. cinnamon
⅛ tsp. ground cloves
1 Tbsp. cider vinegar
dash salt
dash pepper
1 apple, diced

Coat pork with flour. In a skillet, heat margarine and brown steaks. Add water and cook for 15 minutes over medium heat. In a bowl, combine brown sugar, spices, and vinegar. Pour over meat. Salt and pepper. Top with apples. Cover and simmer 15 minutes.

**Per serving**
*345 calories*
*82 mg cholesterol*
*99 mg sodium*
*11.3 gm saturated fat*
*15.0 gm fat*

**Exchanges per serving**
*1 fat*
*4 meat*

**On the side** Serve these tasty pork steaks with green noodles, cooked baby carrots, and a peachy milk shake for a meal that is nutritionally complete as well as palate-pleasing.

2 1-lb. cans black-eyed peas, rinsed and drained
1½ tsp. dried sage
1 8 oz. can low-sodium tomato sauce
1 tsp. garlic powder
1 cup carrots, grated
1 cup lean ham, diced
1½ Tbsp. vegetable oil
⅛ tsp. pepper

Mix all ingredients together in a mixing bowl. Put in a 9 x 13-inch pan. Cover and bake at 350°F for 30 minutes.

### Per serving
*338 calories*
*55 mg cholesterol*
*681 mg sodium*
*6.0 gm saturated fat*
*20.2 gm fat*

### Exchanges per serving
*2 bread*
*1 fat*
*1 meat*
*1 vegetable*

**On the side** Here's a nutritious one-dish meal that needs only an apple-raisin salad and a glass of milk to be complete.

2 3 oz. slices boned, cooked ham
1 cup chunk pineapple in unsweetened juice
4 oz. peeled, cooked sweet potatoes, mashed
1 Tbsp. brown sugar
¼ tsp. ground cinnamon
1 Tbsp. margarine

Preheat oven to 350°F. In a baking dish, place ham and top with pineapple. Spread mashed sweet potatoes over pineapple, sprinkle with brown sugar and cinnamon and dot each with ½ tablespoon margarine. Bake for 20 minutes.

**Per serving**
*177 calories*
*16 mg cholesterol*
*612 mg sodium*
*1.6 gm saturated fat*
*8.1 gm fat*

**Exchanges per serving**
*½ fruit*
*3 meat*
*1 fat*

**On the side** Serve this with a slice of brown bread, a serving of green beans, lightly steamed, and a glass of milk for a nutritionally complete meal.

4 pork loin chops, ¾-inch thick
¾ tsp. orange peel
⅓ cup orange juice
⅓ cup pineapple juice
3 Tbsp. soy sauce
1 Tbsp. honey
⅛ tsp. pepper
½ tsp. minced garlic
1 Tbsp. cornstarch

Trim fat from chops. In shallow baking dish, combine orange peel, orange juice, pineapple juice, soy sauce, honey, pepper, and garlic. Add meat and turn to coat. Marinate for 2 to 3 hours. Place chops on broiler pan. Broil chops until desired doneness. Transfer marinade to a sauce pan. Stir in cornstarch and cook until thickened and bubbly; pass with chops.

**Per serving**
*285 calories*
*70 mg cholesterol*
*669 mg sodium*
*8.9 gm saturated fat*
*12.0 gm fat*

**Exchanges per serving**
*1 fruit*
*3 meat*

**On the side** White rice, zucchini squash, julienned and stir-fried, and a strawberry yogurt dessert makes this meal nutritionally complete.

# 251 Mushroom Pork Chops

4 pork tenderloin chops, ½-inch thick
1 8 oz. can cream of mushroom soup
¼ cup skim milk

In skillet, brown chops on both sides. Combine soup and milk. Pour over chops. Cover, cook for 20 to 25 minutes or until chops are tender.

**Per serving**
*315 calories*
*79 mg cholesterol*
*323 mg sodium*
*2.0 gm saturated fat*
*6.3 gm fat*

**Exchanges per serving**
*1 fat*
*3 meat*

**On the side** Boiled potatoes, cooked baby carrots, a glass of milk, and apples poached in honey for dessert make this meal nutritionally complete.

2 Tbsp. Dijon-style mustard
3 tsp. lime juice
1 tsp. cumin
⅛ tsp. black pepper
1 lb. thin pork chops

Whisk mustard, lime juice, cumin, and pepper. Arrange chops on broiling pan; broil on one side for 5 to 6 minutes with half mustard mixture spread on chops. Turn and spread remaining mixture and broil for 5 to 6 minutes more.

**Per serving**
*301 calories*
*100 mg cholesterol*
*72 mg sodium*
*6.25 gm saturated fat*
*18.0 gm fat*

**Exchanges per serving**
*4 meat*

**On the side** Green noodles, baby carrots, apple sauce from the blender, and a glass of milk complete this meal nutritionally.

1 egg white
⅓ cup chopped onions
¾ tsp. ground oregano
⅛ tsp. salt
⅛ tsp. pepper
1 lb. lean ground pork
½ cup pizza sauce
½ cup part-skim shredded mozzarella cheese
2 cups shredded lettuce

Preheat broiler. In medium-sized mixing bowl, beat egg white. Stir in onion, oregano, salt, and pepper. Add pork and mix well. Shape meat mixture into four patties. Place patties on broiling pan and broil for about 12 to 15 minutes, turning once. Pour pizza sauce over patties and broil for a few minutes more. Sprinkle with cheese and broil until cheese melts. Divide lettuce among four serving plates. To serve, place meat patties on top of lettuce.

**Per serving**
*320 calories*
*94 mg cholesterol*
*399 mg sodium*
*7.87 gm saturated fat*
*20.5 gm fat*

**Exchanges per serving**
*3 meat*

**On the side** Serve these tasty patties on a plate or on a whole-wheat bun, add a tossed salad, and whip up a peachy milk shake in the blender. You've got a meal that's delicious and nutritionally complete.

8 loin pork chops, ⅝-inch thick
½ tsp. ground pepper
2 tsp. crushed dill seed
2 Tbsp. olive oil
1 tsp. minced onion

Rub pork chops well with pepper, dill seed, olive oil, and onions. Broil for 10 minutes or until cooked through.

### Per serving
*315 calories*
*105 mg cholesterol*
*183 mg sodium*
*3.5 gm saturated fat*
*12.0 gm fat*

### Exchanges per serving
*3 meat*

**On the side** White rice, a salad of fresh cucumbers and onions, and a pear, poached in almond extract complete this meal nutritionally.

¾ lb. lean boneless pork, 1-inch thick
½ cup orange juice
1 tsp. finely grated orange peel
¼ cup soy sauce
1 Tbsp. brown sugar
⅛ tsp. ground ginger
1 10 oz. package frozen asparagus
2 carrots, cut into sticks

Cut pork on the bias into 3-inch strips. Combine orange juice, orange peel, soy sauce, brown sugar, and ginger. Place meat in a bowl and pour marinade over meat and marinate for several hours. Drain meat and reserve marinade. Cook vegetables in a small amount of water until crisp-tender. For each kabob, wrap meat strips around 1 or 2 asparagus spears and 1 carrot. Repeat with remaining meat and vegetables. Thread kabobs on skewers. Brush with reserve marinade. Broil until pork is done.

**Per serving**
*294 calories*
*75 mg cholesterol*
*898 mg sodium*
*4.75 gm saturated fat*
*12.1 gm fat*

**Exchanges per serving**
*½ fruit*
*3 meat*
*1 vegetable*

**On the side** Try our yams as a delightful accompaniment to this meal. A serving of cabbage, apple, raisin salad with yogurt dressing makes the meal complete nutritionally.

8 oz. pork cubed steak

1½ cups sliced zucchini

⅔ cup chopped onions

½ cup tomato sauce

¼ cup chopped tomato

¼ tsp. thyme

⅛ tsp. salt

⅛ tsp. pepper

⅔ cup shredded mozzarella cheese, part-skim

2 pita bread rounds, halved

Cut pork into bite-size pieces. In a nonstick skillet, cook meat until no pink remains. Drain off fat. Add zucchini, onion, tomato sauce, tomatoes, thyme, salt, and pepper. Cook over medium heat until vegetables are crisp-tender, stirring occasionally. Divide meat-vegetable mixture among pita halves. Top each pita half with cheese.

**Per serving**

*292 calories*

*68 mg cholesterol*

*342 mg sodium*

*6.25 gm saturated fat*

*14.5 gm fat*

**Exchanges per serving**

*1 bread*

*2 meat*

*1 vegetable*

**On the side** Serve some fresh pineapple slices for dessert and add a glass of milk and the meal conforms to today's standard for total nutritional balance.

3 lbs. meaty pork spareribs
¾ cup apple butter
½ Tbsp. vinegar
¾ tsp. minced onion
½ tsp. garlic powder
1 Tbsp. water

Place ribs, meaty side down, in a shallow roasting pan. Roast at 450°F for 30 minutes. Remove meat from oven; drain. Turn ribs and reduce oven to 350°F. Roast for another 30 minutes. Mix apple butter, vinegar, onion, garlic, and water. Pour mixture over ribs and roast for 30 minutes more.

**Per serving**
*405 calories*
*143 mg cholesterol*
*201 mg sodium*
*9.6 gm saturated fat*
*20.5 gm fat*

**Exchanges per serving**
*2 fat*
*4 meat*

**On the side** Twice-baked yams, cabbage salad, and dessert of baked apple slices with cinnamon round out this meal. Add a glass of milk for total nutritional balance.

POULTRY

1 large chicken breast, skinned, halved
4 tsp. margarine
½ cup low-calorie apricot preserves
2 Tbsp. lemon juice
½ tsp. lemon rind
½ tsp. lemon pepper

Preheat oven to 350°F. Arrange chicken in baking pan and dot with margarine. In a saucepan, combine apricot preserves, lemon juice, lemon rind and lemon pepper; cook over low heat until preserves melt and mixture is blended. Pour over chicken and bake, uncovered, for 35 to 40 minutes. Baste occasionally.

**Per serving**
*371 calories*
*43 mg cholesterol*
*133 mg sodium*
*1.9 mg sodium*
*1.9 gm saturated fat*
*9.8 gm fat*

**Exchanges per serving**
*1 fat*
*1 fruit*
*3 meat*

**On the side** White rice, steamed green beans, and a glass of milk make this meal nutritionally complete and delicious.

2 boneless, skinless chicken breasts, halved
½ cup skim milk
⅓ cup herb-seasoned bread crumbs
⅛ tsp. paprika

Preheat oven to 400°F. Dip chicken in skim milk and roll in bread crumbs. Place chicken in baking pan. Sprinkle chicken with paprika. Bake for 30 to 35 minutes.

**Per serving**
*162 calories*
*70 mg cholesterol*
*138 mg sodium*
*0.5 gm saturated fat*
*3.0 gm fat*

**Exchanges per serving**
*2 meat*

**On the side** New potatoes rosemary, a tossed salad, and a peachy milk shake make this meal nutritionally complete.

3 lb. fryer chicken, cut into pieces
⅛ tsp. garlic powder
1 cup low-calorie apricot preserves
½ cup chopped onions
3 Tbsp. soy sauce
½ cup bottled barbecue sauce

Arrange chicken in a baking dish. Sprinkle with garlic powder. Bake at 370°F for 20 minutes. In a bowl, combine remaining ingredients. Spoon over chicken and bake for 20 minutes more or until chicken is done.

**Per serving**
*305 calories*
*153 mg cholesterol*
*590 mg sodium*
*3.55 gm saturated fat*
*10 gm fat*

**Exchanges per serving**
*1 fruit*
*3 meat*

**On the side** White rice, sautéed vegetables, and a glass of milk complete this meal nutritionally.

2 boneless, skinned chicken breasts, halved
¼ cup low-sodium soy sauce
½ tsp. garlic powder
1 tsp. dried basil

Baste chicken with soy sauce. Sprinkle chicken with garlic powder and basil. Broil chicken. Baste with soy sauce as chicken broils.

**Per serving**
*173 calories*
*73 mg cholesterol*
*825 mg sodium*
*1.7 gm saturated fat*
*5.3 gm fat*

**Exchanges per serving**
*1½ meat*
*1 bread*

**On the side** Fresh corn on the cob, a plate of crisp vegetables with dilled yogurt dip, and watermelon slices (a 4-inch x 8-inch wedge equals one fruit and 110 calories) make this meal balanced nutritionally.

Nonstick cooking spray
2 whole chicken breasts, boneless, skinned, halved
½ cup margarine, melted
¼ cup lemon juice
1 Tbsp. dried parsley flakes
¼ tsp. salt
⅛ tsp. black pepper

Spray broiler pan with nonstick spray. Place chicken on broiler pan. Mix all ingredients together. Baste chicken with sauce. Broil, turning and basting until chicken is done.

**Per serving**
*268 calories*
*74 mg cholesterol*
*209 mg sodium*
*2.3 gm saturated fat*
*12 gm fat*

**Exchanges per serving**
*½ bread*
*3 meat*

**On the side** A serving of white rice, broccoli, steamed just until tender and seasoned with a little lemon juice, a glass of milk and fresh pineapple slices for dessert give this meal nutritional balance.

# 263 Broiled Tarragon Chicken

*Serves 6*

Two 2½ lb chickens, cut into parts and skinned
1 cup chopped onions
¾ cup peanut oil
2 Tbsp. dried tarragon
½ tsp. hot pepper sauce

Combine all ingredients in large bowl. Put chicken in and marinate chicken in refrigerator for about 1 hour, turning the chicken from time to time. Place chicken on broiler pan. Broil; turn and baste with marinade. Broil until chicken is tender.

**Per serving**
*250 calories*
*89 mg cholesterol*
*86 mg sodium*
*1 gm saturated fat*
*9 gm fat*

**Exchanges per serving**
*1 fat*
*3 meat*

**On the side** A serving of white rice, baby carrots simmered with gingerroot, and a strawberry milk shake complete this meal nutritionally.

288

4 oz. curly noodles
1 10 oz. can cream of chicken soup
¾ cup milk
⅔ cup cream-style light cottage cheese
1 cup chopped, cooked chicken
⅔ cup part-skim shredded American cheese
½ tsp. crushed tarragon

Cook noodles according to package directions; drain.
In a bowl, combine cream of chicken soup and milk.
Stir in cottage cheese, chicken, half of the cheese,
and tarragon. Mix in the noodles. Pour mixture into
a casserole dish. Cover and bake at 350°F for 3
minutes. Sprinkle remaining cheese on top. Bake
for 5 minutes more.

**Per serving**
*417 calories*
*108 mg cholesterol*
*1234 mg sodium*
*12 gm saturated fat*
*24 gm fat*

**Exchanges per serving**
*1 bread*
*1 fat*
*4 meat*

**On the side** A mixed vegetable, like green beans and carrots, or
broccoli and cauliflower goes well with this casserole. Add a
glass of milk and some fresh fruit for dessert and the meal is
complete nutritionally.

2 Tbsp. margarine
1½ cups sliced mushrooms
⅓ cup flour
⅛ tsp. salt
⅛ tsp. pepper
2 cups skim milk
¾ cup low-sodium chicken broth
2 cups cubed, cooked chicken
½ cup frozen peas, thawed
2 tsp. sherry
4 slices whole wheat bread, toasted

In a saucepan, melt margarine. Add mushrooms and cook until tender. Stir in flour, salt and pepper. Add milk and chicken broth. Cook and stir until thickened and bubbly. Stir in chicken, peas, and sherry. Heat through. Serve over toasted bread.

**Per serving**
*375 calories*
*107 mg cholesterol*
*473 mg sodium*
*3.6 gm saturated fat*
*16 gm fat*

**Exchanges per serving**
*1½ bread*
*1 fat*
*2 meat*
*½ skim milk*
*½ vegetable*

**On the side** This one-dish meal needs only a plate of fresh mixed fruits and a yogurt dip for dessert and it is nutritionally complete.

2 chicken breasts, skinless, boneless
1½ cups low-sodium chicken broth
1½ Tbsp. lime juice
½ tsp. crushed basil
½ tsp. crushed oregano
⅛ tsp. celery seed
½ tsp. lime rind, grated

Preheat oven to 325°F. Place chicken in shallow baking dish. Combine broth, lime juice, basil, oregano, celery seed and lime rind; pour over the chicken. Cover and bake for 45 to 50 minutes.

**Per serving**
*230 calories*
*61 mg cholesterol*
*78 mg sodium*
*1.4 gm saturated fat*
*5.3 gm fat*

**Exchanges per serving**
*3 meat*

**On the side** Baked potato sticks, fresh cooked spinach, and a peachy milk shake make this meal nutritionally complete.

1 5 lb. roasting chicken

⅛ tsp. salt

⅛ tsp. pepper

½ tsp. dried rosemary

¾ tsp. ground cumin

1 tsp. paprika

1 tsp. minced garlic

4 Tbsp. vegetable oil

Preheat oven to 325°F. Combine in a bowl, all ingredients, except chicken. Rub entire surface of the chicken with seasoned oil mixture. Put chicken in a cooking bag and place bag in roasting pan. Bake for 2½ to 3 hours.

**Per serving**
*322 calories*
*66 mg cholesterol*
*153 mg sodium*
*5.6 gm saturated fat*
*23.5 gm fat*

**Exchanges per serving**
*1 fat*
*3½ meat*

**On the side** A serving of new potatoes with parsley, broccoli with garlic, a glass of milk, and a poached pear give this meal complete nutritional balance.

2 whole chicken breasts, boneless, skinless

3 Tbsp. soy sauce

1 Tbsp. vegetable oil

1 20 oz. package frozen broccoli, thawed

¾ cup low sodium chicken broth

½ cup sliced, fresh mushrooms

½ cup sliced bamboo shoots

2 tsp. lemon juice

¾ Tbsp. cornstarch

Cut chicken into slices. In bowl, combine chicken, soy sauce, and oil; set aside. In skillet, place broccoli and ½ cup broth and stir-fry on medium heat until broccoli is crisp-tender. Increase heat to high; add chicken mixture. Stir-fry for 3 minutes. Add mushrooms and bamboo shoots; stir-fry for 1 minute. Decrease heat. Combine lemon juice, cornstarch, and remaining ½ cup broth. Stir into chicken mixture; heat until thickened.

**Per serving**
*220 calories*
*22.9 mg cholesterol*
*496 mg sodium*
*0.4 gm saturated fat*
*3.4 gm fat*

**Exchanges per serving**
*½ bread*
*2 meat*
*1 vegetable*

**On the side** A serving of white rice, a glass of milk, and a dessert of mixed melon balls and berries balance this meal nutritionally.

1 Tbsp. vegetable oil

1 Tbsp. minced garlic

3 chicken breasts, skinned and cut in halves

¾ cup chopped onion

¾ cup chopped green pepper

1 cup fresh tomatoes, peeled and chopped

¼ tsp. basil

⅛ tsp. pepper

¼ tsp. rosemary

¼ cup dry white wine

Heat oil and garlic in skillet. Add chicken and brown. Remove chicken. Add onions and green pepper; cook until tender. Pour off fat. Return chicken to skillet. Add remaining ingredients. Cover and simmer until chicken is tender.

**Per serving**
*175 calories*
*36 mg cholesterol*
*41.4 mg sodium*
*0.6 gm saturated fat*
*3.9 gm fat*

**Exchanges per serving**
*2 meat*
*1 vegetable*

**On the side** Green noodles go very well with this Italian-style chicken dish. A dessert compote of watermelon and honeydew melon balls and a glass of milk make the meal complete nutritionally.

1 Tbsp. dried dillweed
1 Tbsp. lemon pepper
1 cup Wheaties®, crushed
2 chicken breasts, boneless, skinless, cut in half
1 egg
1½ Tbsp. margarine, melted

Heat oven to 375°F. In shallow dish, combine dill-weed, lemon pepper, and Wheaties. In a bowl, beat egg until mixed. Dip chicken into egg and then into dry ingredients. Place in baking dish. Drizzle margarine over chicken. Bake 35 to 40 minutes.

**Per serving**
*248 calories*
*136 mg cholesterol*
*147 mg sodium*
*6.11 gm saturated fat*
*11.25 gm fat*

**Exchanges per serving**
*½ bread*
*1 fat*
*2½ meat*

**On the side** Add a small dinner roll, cauliflower, steamed just until tender, a glass of milk and a fresh peach for dessert and this meal is complete nutritionally.

1 lb. boneless, skinned chicken breasts
3 cups fresh broccoli spears
3 Tbsp. margarine
½ cup chopped onion
¼ cup flour
1½ cups skim milk
⅛ tsp. black pepper

Preheat oven to 400°F. In nonstick skillet, brown chicken breasts. Steam broccoli spears. In saucepan, melt margarine. Add onions and cook. Stir in flour. Gradually add milk and pepper. Cook until thickened and smooth. In an 8 inch baking dish, place chicken in dish. Sprinkle broccoli over chicken. Pour mixture over chicken and broccoli. Bake 20 minutes until bubbly.

**Per serving**
*335 calories*
*83 mg cholesterol*
*230 mg sodium*
*2.9 gm saturated fat*
*13.2 gm fat*

**Exchanges per serving**
*1 fat*
*3 meat*
*½ skim milk*
*1 vegetable*

**On the side** Roasted potatoes with rosemary add the bread course, and a fruit plate with yogurt dip add a fruit and milk to make this meal nutritionally complete.

2 Tbsp. vegetable oil

1 tsp. minced garlic

1 16 oz. can stewed tomatoes without salt

4 tsp. chili powder

⅛ tsp. ground pepper

2 cups cooked, chopped chicken

½ cup plain low-fat yogurt

2 Tbsp. green chilies

1 Tbsp. chopped green onion

1 Tbsp. minced onion

4 corn tortillas

1 cup part-skim mozzarella cheese

Heat 1 tablespoon oil in saucepan. Add garlic and cook for about 1 minute. Add tomatoes, 3 teaspoons chili powder and pepper. Simmer for about 30 minutes, stirring occasionally. In bowl, combine cooked chicken, yogurt, green chilies, green onions, minced onion, and 1 teaspoon chili powder. Mix well. In skillet, heat remaining oil. Add tortillas and cook each side until soft. Preheat oven to 350°F. Spoon ¼ cup sauce in 8 inch square baking dish. Spread an equal amount of chicken mixture in center of each tortilla. Fold sides over filling. Place tortillas, seam side down in baking dish. Pour remaining sauce over tortillas. Sprinkle with cheese. Bake 30 minutes.

**Per serving**
*326 calories*
*50 mg cholesterol*
*297 mg sodium*
*4.05 gm saturated fat*
*16 gm fat*

**Exchanges per serving**
*1 bread*
*1 fat*
*2 meat*
*1 vegetable*

**On the side** Rice goes well with this meal. Add a glass of milk and a baked apple and the meal is balanced.

¾ cup fresh chopped pineapple
½ cup sliced green onions
⅛ cup chopped celery
1 Tbsp. grated fresh ginger
2 chicken breasts
1 Tbsp. vegetable oil
3 Tbsp. soy sauce

Cover the bottom of a baking dish with pineapple, green onions, celery and ginger. Lay chicken on top. In a small bowl, mix oil and soy sauce. Pour over chicken. Cover and bake for 35 to 40 minutes at 350°F.

**Per serving**
*277 calories*
*85 mg cholesterol*
*85 mg sodium*
*2.1 gm saturated fat*
*11.5 gm fat*

**Exchanges per serving**
*1 fat*
*½ fruit*
*3 meat*

**On the side** White rice, baby carrots, simmered with gingerroot, and a dessert of fresh fruit slices with yogurt dip make this meal nutritionally complete.

1 Tbsp. margarine
⅓ cup honey
1 Tbsp. prepared mustard
⅛ tsp. salt
¼ tsp. curry powder
2 Tbsp. soy sauce
⅛ tsp. pepper
2 large chicken breasts, skinned and cut in half

Preheat oven to 350°F. Melt margarine and mix in remaining ingredients, except chicken. Place chicken in a casserole dish and pour sauce over chicken. Bake 30 to 35 minutes, basting occasionally.

**Per serving**
*211 calories*
*43 mg cholesterol*
*193 gm sodium*
*1.2 gm saturated fat*
*5.3 gm fat*

**Exchanges per serving**
*1 fat*
*2 meat*

**On the side** Saffron rice, snow pea pods, sautéed just until crisp-tender, a glass of milk and a fresh fruit for dessert make this meal complete nutritionally.

2 Tbsp. canola oil

1 lb. boneless, skinless chicken breasts

¼ cup chopped onion

1 tsp. minced garlic

1 cup chopped carrots, zucchini, basil, thyme

1 cup low-sodium chicken broth

⅛ tsp. salt

⅛ tsp. ground pepper

1 tomato, peeled and chopped

⅛ cup low-fat yogurt

⅛ cup skim milk

2 tsp. Dijon-style mustard

2 cups cooked rice

In skillet, heat 1 tablespoon oil. Add chicken and brown on each side; remove to platter. Add remaining oil to skillet and sauté onion and garlic. Add carrots, zucchini, basil and thyme; sauté, stirring frequently. Return chicken to skillet. Add chicken broth, salt and pepper. Simmer for 10 minutes, turning chicken once. Remove chicken and vegetables to platter and keep warm. In skillet, add tomatoes, yogurt, milk and mustard. Increase heat and cook, stirring vegetables until sauce in slightly thickened. Spoon over chicken and vegetables. Serve with rice.

| **Per serving** | **Exchanges per serving** |
|---|---|
| *385 calories* | *1 bread* |
| *98 mg cholesterol* | *1 fat* |
| *472 mg sodium* | *3 meat* |
| *1.9 gm saturated fat* | *1 vegetable* |
| *11 gm fat* | |

**On the side** Add only a glass of milk and a piece of fruit to complete this meal nutritionally.

4 boned, skinned chicken breast halves

⅓ cup low-fat yogurt

4 tsp. flour

⅛ cup water

1 tsp. curry powder

⅛ tsp. garlic powder

⅛ tsp. paprika

⅛ tsp. lemon pepper

2 10 oz. packages frozen broccoli spears

⅛ cup chopped peanuts

Preheat oven to 400°F. Place chicken in shallow baking dish. Cover with foil and bake for 20 to 25 minutes. While chicken is baking, combine yogurt and flour; set aside. In a pan, stir together water, curry powder, garlic powder, paprika and lemon pepper; bring to a boil. Reduce heat and add yogurt mixture. Cook until thickened. Cook broccoli according to package directions; drain. Pour sauce over chicken and top with peanuts; serve with broccoli.

**Per serving**
*229 calories*
*76 mg cholesterol*
*116 mg sodium*
*1.75 gm saturated fat*
*7 gm fat*

**Exchanges per serving**
*1 fat*
*2½ meat*
*1 vegetable*

**On the side** Serve this with brown rice, and offer a plate of fresh fruits with poppy seeds and yogurt dip for dessert and the meal is complete nutritionally.

½ cup skim milk

½ cup cream of celery soup

½ cup cream of mushroom soup

1 cup sliced fresh mushrooms

2 whole chicken breasts, boneless, skinless

Heat oven to 375°F. Mix milk with soups until smooth. Stir in mushrooms. Place chicken in baking dish and pour mushroom mixture over chicken. Bake 35 to 40 minutes.

**Per serving**
*213 calories*
*76 mg cholesterol*
*258 mg sodium*
*2.17 gm saturated fat*
*6.3 gm fat*

**Exchanges per serving**
*½ bread*
*2½ meat*

**On the side** New potatoes, boiled, broccoli, cooked al dente, a glass of milk and a fresh fruit for dessert complete this meal nutritionally.

1 Tbsp. vegetable oil
1½ Tbsp. flour
12 oz. boneless, skinless chicken breasts
½ cup low-sodium chicken broth
¾ tsp. dry mustard
1 tsp. cornstarch
1 tsp. dried parsley flakes
1 Tbsp. sherry
⅓ cup low-fat ricotta cheese
⅓ cup low-fat plain yogurt

In skillet, heat oil. Flour chicken breasts and brown chicken on both sides. Remove and keep warm. Stir in chicken broth, mustard, cornstarch, parsley, and sherry until mixture thickens. Return chicken to pan. Mix ricotta cheese and yogurt until smooth. Stir in ricotta mixture; heat. Serve chicken with sauce.

**Per serving**
*378 calories*
*88 mg cholesterol*
*109 mg sodium*
*5.3 gm saturated fat*
*12 gm fat*

**Exchanges per serving**
*1½ fat*
*4 meat*

**On the side** A serving of white rice, fresh broccoli florets, steamed just until tender, and a peachy milk shake complete this meal nutritionally.

2 cups cubed, cooked chicken

1 15-oz. can garbanzo beans, drained

1 cup part-skim cheddar cheese, cubed

¾ cup sliced celery

¾ cup chopped green pepper

⅛ cup sliced green onions

½ cup light mayonnaise

1½ Tbsp. lime juice

¼ tsp. garlic powder

¼ tsp. chili powder

4 lettuce leaves

In a bowl, combine chicken, garbanzo beans, cheese, celery, green pepper, and green onions. Stir together mayonnaise, lime juice, garlic powder and chili powder. Stir into chicken mixture; toss. Chill. Serve on lettuce leaves.

**Per serving**
*386 calories*
*108 mg cholesterol*
*560 mg sodium*
*10.19 gm saturated fat*
*21.3 gm fat*

**Exchanges per serving**
*1 bread*
*1 fat*
*3 meat*
*1 vegetable*

**On the side** This salad is nearly a nutritionally complete meal all alone. Add a glass of milk and a fruit for dessert and you have it all.

Nonstick cooking spray
8 oz. skinned, boned chicken breasts
⅛ tsp. salt
⅛ tsp. pepper
1 cup drained sauerkraut
⅓ cup shredded, part-skim provolone cheesed
2 Tbsp. low-calorie Russian dressing
¼ cup part-skim Swiss cheese, shredded

Preheat oven to 350°F. Spray baking dish with non-stick spray. Set chicken in bottom of dish and sprinkle with salt and pepper. Spread sauerkraut over chicken and sprinkle with cheeses. Drizzle dressing over cheese. Cover and bake for 20 minutes.

**Per serving**
*515 calories*
*200 mg cholesterol*
*2040 mg sodium*
*3 gm saturated fat*
*15 gm fat*

**Exchanges per serving**
*2 fat*
*4 meat*
*1 vegetable*

**On the side** Serve this with a slice of your favorite brown bread, some beets, a glass of milk, and a baked apple for dessert to complete this meal nutritionally.

# 281 Chicken 'n' Vegetable Skillet

1 10 oz. package frozen brussel sprouts, thawed
2 whole chicken breasts, cut into strips
dash salt
dash pepper
1 Tbsp. vegetable oil
½ cup chopped onion
1½ tsp. lemon juice
¾ tsp. crushed basil
2 cups tomatoes, coarsely chopped

Put brussel sprouts in a colander and run hot water over them; drain and halve. Set aside. Remove skin from chicken; season with salt and pepper. In a skillet, heat oil and cook chicken strips and onion on medium-high heat until done. Stir in brussel sprouts, lemon juice, and basil. Reduce heat and cook for 10 minutes. Stir in tomatoes. Cook for 2 minutes more.

**Per serving**
*164 calories*
*43 mg cholesterol*
*123 mg sodium*
*1.15 gm saturated fat*
*5.75 gm fat*

**Exchanges per serving**
*2 meat*
*1 vegetable*

**On the side** Baked potato sticks are great with this chicken dish. Make yourself a milkshake using 8 oz. nonfat milk, ¼ cup fresh pineapple, and 6 ripe fresh strawberries. Garnish it with some fresh mint from the garden and your meal is nutritionally complete.

1½ lb. chicken breasts, boneless, skinned
⅔ cup oyster sauce
3 Tbsp. soy sauce
3 Tbsp. hoisin sauce*
¼ cup white wine
¼ cup water
⅛ tsp. pepper
¼ cup sliced green onions
1 Tbsp. vegetable oil

Cut chicken in large chunks. In a bowl, combine all ingredients except oil; mix well. Marinate chicken for 10 to 15 minutes. Remove chicken and place in a skillet with heated oil. Pour sauce over chicken and cook for 25 minutes or until chicken is done.

*\*Available in the Oriental food section of most grocery stores.*

**Per serving**
*365 calories*
*145 mg cholesterol*
*286 mg sodium*
*2.6 gm saturated fat*
*8 gm fat*

**Exchanges per serving**
*1 fat*
*3 meat*

**On the side** White rice, stir-fried snow pea pods, and a frozen, blended dessert of fresh pear slices, 2 tsp. Creme de Menthe, and 8 oz. nonfat milk, served like ice cream, complete this meal deliciously and nutritiously.

1 whole chicken
1 can cream of celery soup
1 cup chicken broth
½ cup frozen peas
½ cup margarine
1 cup skim milk
¾ cup flour

Cook chicken in 2 quarts water. When done, remove chicken. De-bone chicken and put in 13 x 9 inch baking dish. Save 1 cup of broth. Combine cream of celery soup, broth and peas; heat over low until mixed. Pour over chicken. Melt margarine in sauce-pan. Add milk and mix in flour; mix well. Spoon over chicken mixture until well-coated. Bake at 400°F for 40 to 45 minutes until golden brown.

**Per serving**
*364 calories*
*84 mg cholesterol*
*331 mg sodium*
*4.46 gm saturated fat*
*18.75 gm fat*

**Exchanges per serving**
*1 bread*
*1 fat*
*2½ meat*
*½ skim milk*

**On the side** Serve this tasty chicken pie with cooked carrots. Make a pretty fruit plate of mixed fruit slices and yogurt dip for dessert. The meal is complete nutritionally.

Dressing:
½ cup plain, low-fat yogurt
1 tsp. finely chopped parsley
1 tsp. sugar
½ tsp. celery seed
2 Tbsp. skim milk
1 tsp. Dijon-style mustard
1 tsp. lemon juice

2 whole-wheat pocket pita breads
½ lb. cooked chicken, cubed
¾ cup alfalfa sprouts
¾ cup broccoli florets
¼ cup onion

In a bowl, combine dressing ingredients; blend well
and refrigerate one hour. Spoon ⅛ cup yogurt mixture into each pocket bread half. Fill each half with
¼ of the chicken, sprouts, broccoli and onions.

**Per serving**
*195 calories*
*25 mg cholesterol*
*207 mg sodium*
*2 gm saturated fat*
*6.5 gm fat*

**Exchanges per serving**
*½ bread*
*1 meat*
*1 vegetable*
*½ skim milk*

**On the side** A glass of milk and honeydew melon slices for
dessert give this meal nutritional balance.

# 285 Chicken Ratatouille

1 cup low-sodium chicken broth
2 whole chicken breasts, boned, skinned, cubed
2 cups sliced zucchini
1 small eggplant, peeled and cubed
1 cup chopped onions
2 cups sliced mushrooms
2 tomatoes, cut into wedges
2 tsp. minced garlic
1 tsp. basil
1 tsp. oregano
1 Tbsp. soy sauce
¼ tsp. cayenne pepper

In large skillet, heat chicken broth and add the chicken. Sauté chicken on both sides. Add zucchini, eggplant, onions, and mushrooms and cook until tender; stir occasionally. Add tomatoes, garlic, basil, oregano, soy sauce, and cayenne. Simmer for 10 minutes.

**Per serving**
*177 calories*
*48 mg cholesterol*
*146 mg sodium*
*0.6 gm saturated fat*
*2.0 gm fat*

**Exchanges per serving**
*2 meat*
*1 vegetable*

**On the side** A serving of white rice, a glass of milk, and fresh fruit for dessert make this meal complete nutritionally.

1 cup low-sodium chicken broth
1 cup chopped onion
1 can sliced water chestnuts
¼ cup chopped red peppers
¾ tsp. sage
⅛ tsp. rosemary
1 10 oz. package frozen peas, thawed
1 12 oz. can low-sodium tomato puree
1 whole chicken breast, skinned, boned, cubed
4 cups cooked rice
6 egg whites, beaten stiff

In a saucepan, heat chicken broth. Add onion, water chestnuts, and red pepper; sauté until thoroughly cooked. Stir in the sage, rosemary and peas; simmer for 5 minutes. Add tomato puree and chicken. Put the cooked rice in a large bowl and mix in tomato-chicken sauce; fold in egg whites. Place in a baking dish, cover, and bake for 30 to 35 minutes at 350°F.

**Per serving**
*268 calories*
*43 mg cholesterol*
*468 mg sodium*
*0.14 gm saturated fat*
*2.6 gm fat*

**Exchanges per serving**
*1 bread*
*2 meat*
*1 vegetable*

**On the side** You need only a milk and a fruit exchange to complete this meal nutritionally.

4 Tbsp. dry bread crumbs
2 Tbsp. grated Romano cheese
½ tsp. dried parsley flakes
½ tsp. dried basil
½ tsp. minced garlic
¼ cup skim milk
4 boned, skinned, chicken breast halves

Preheat oven to 425°F. In a dish, combine bread crumbs, Romano cheese, parsley, basil and minced garlic. Pour milk into another dish. Dip chicken in milk, then roll in the crumb mixture. Place chicken in a baking pan. Bake for 15 minutes or until chicken is tender.

**Per serving**
*177 calories*
*82 mg cholesterol*
*163 mg sodium*
*1.25 gm saturated fat*
*6 gm fat*

**Exchanges per serving**
*3 meat*

**On the side** This tasty chicken dish goes well with green noodles, cauliflower florets, steamed, and, for the fruit and milk choice, try blending fresh melon pieces into a glass of nonfat milk.

4 tsp. light mayonnaise
4 tsp. lemon juice
⅛ tsp. black pepper
⅛ tsp. thyme
⅛ tsp. sage
1 lb. boneless, skinless, cooked chicken, cubed
1 cup diced cucumber
¼ cup diced celery
¼ cup diced carrots
¼ cup chopped onion
1 tsp. dried parsley leaves

In a bowl, combine mayonnaise, lemon juice, pepper, thyme and sage; blend well. Add remaining ingredients and toss well.

**Per serving**
*191 calories*
*74 mg cholesterol*
*27 mg sodium*
*1.61 gm saturated fat*
*5.85 gm fat*

**Exchanges per serving**
*1 fat*
*2 meat*

**On the side** This salad tastes great with lettuce wedges, a slice of bread, a glass of milk, and a fresh orange for dessert.

½ cup low-sodium chicken broth
¼ cup light soy sauce
1 Tbsp. cornstarch
⅛ tsp. black pepper
1 lb. boneless, skinless chicken breasts
1 Tbsp. vegetable oil
2 cups sliced, fresh mushrooms
¼ cup chopped green onion
1 cup chopped green peppers
1 cup chopped carrots
1 cup chopped zucchini
1 tsp. minced garlic
¼ tsp. ginger

Cut chicken into chunks. In a bowl, combine chicken broth, soy sauce, cornstarch and ground pepper. Add chicken, mix well. Refrigerate for about 1 hour. In a large skillet, heat oil. Add mushrooms, green onion, green pepper, carrot, zucchini, garlic and ginger. Cook until crisp-tender; set aside. Add chicken to skillet with marinade. Cook, stirring occasionally until chicken is tender and sauce is thickened. Return vegetables to skillet. Cook until heated.

**Per serving**
*160 calories*
*21 mg cholesterol*
*867 mg sodium*
*1.4 gm saturated fat*
*9.4 gm fat*

**Exchanges per serving**
*2 meat*
*1 vegetable*

**On the side** White rice, a glass of milk and fresh pears complete this meal.

4 boneless, skinned chicken breasts, halved
1 cup low-fat, plain yogurt
1 tsp. ginger
¼ tsp. garlic powder
¼ tsp. ground cloves
¾ tsp. cinnamon
2 bay leaves
⅛ tsp. salt

Cut chicken into finger length strips. Mix together remaining ingredients and marinate for 3 hours. Bake in a casserole dish for 1 hour at 325°F.

**Per serving**
*189 calories*
*73 mg cholesterol*
*67 mg sodium*
*1.3 gm saturated fat*
*8.1 gm fat*

**Exchanges per serving**
*2 meat*
*½ skim milk*

**On the side** White rice with saffron, baby carrots, simmered with gingerroot, and a dessert of fresh fruits, sprinkled with poppy seeds and served with a yogurt dip, complete this tasty meal nutritionally.

2 2 lb. frying chickens

⅛ tsp. salt

⅛ tsp. pepper

⅔ cup orange juice

⅔ cup seedless raisins

⅛ cup chopped chutney

1 tsp. cinnamon

¼ tsp. curry powder

⅛ tsp. allspice

Preheat oven to 400°F. Place chicken in casserole dish and season with salt and pepper. Bake for 20 to 25 minutes. Mix remaining ingredients. Cover chicken with sauce; reduce heat and bake for 50 minutes at 250°F.

**Per serving**
*360 calories*
*134 mg cholesterol*
*177 mg sodium*
*5.8 gm saturated fat*
*15.2 gm fat*

**Exchanges per serving**
*1 fruit*
*4 meat*

**On the side** A serving of white rice, a side of baby carrots, and a glass of milk complete this meal nutritionally.

4 boned, skinned chicken breasts, halved
2 Tbsp. margarine, melted
½ Tbsp. basil
½ Tbsp. tarragon

Place chicken in a shallow baking pan. Mix margarine and herbs together, pour over chicken and bake at 350°F for 45 minutes.

**Per serving**
*190 calories*
*71 mg cholesterol*
*35 mg sodium*
*1.9 gm saturated fat*
*4.1 gm fat*

**Exchanges per serving**
*1 fat*
*2 meat*

**On the side** We like this dish with green noodles, a melange of mixed peppers as the vegetable, a glass of milk and fresh peaches for dessert.

2 large boneless, skinned chicken breasts
⅛ tsp. salt
⅛ tsp. black pepper
3 Tbsp. margarine
3 cups low-sodium chicken broth
¼ cup flour
½ cup vermouth
⅛ tsp. cayenne pepper
1 cup seedless green grapes, halved

Cut chicken breast in half. Season with salt and pepper. Heat margarine in a skillet; sauté chicken until brown. Add one cup chicken broth and simmer for 20 minutes. Whisk together flour, vermouth, and remaining chicken broth. Add to cooked chicken and whisk until smooth. Sprinkle with cayenne pepper. Add grapes. Serve.

**Per serving**
*276 calories*
*43 mg cholesterol*
*185 mg sodium*
*2.1 gm saturated fat*
*11.8 gm fat*

**Exchanges per serving**
*1 fat*
*½ fruit*
*3 meat*

**On the side** White rice or green noodles go well with this entree. We like to serve baby carrots, simmered just until tender with some gingerroot, and offer a dessert of fruit slices, sprinkled with poppy seeds, with a yogurt dip. This complete the meal nutritionally, adds to eye appeal, and really pleases the palate.

9 oz. package frozen spinach

2 Tbsp. margarine

½ cup whole wheat bread crumbs

½ tsp. basil

⅛ tsp. black pepper

2 boneless, skinless chicken breasts, halved

½ cup part skim mozzarella cheese, shredded

Sauté spinach with 1 Tbsp. margarine. In a small bowl, combine bread crumbs, basil and pepper. Coat chicken with bread crumb mixture, pressing firmly. In skillet, heat remaining margarine. Brown chicken on both sides. Spoon spinach onto chicken and sprinkle cheese on top. Cover and cook until chicken is tender.

**Per serving**
*276 calories*
*65 mg cholesterol*
*335 mg sodium*
*5.4 gm saturated fat*
*12.2 gm fat*

**Exchanges per serving**
*½ bread*
*1 fat*
*2 meat*
*1 vegetable*

**On the side** You can choose to complete the bread exchange at this meal by adding a ½ slice of bread or a small dinner roll. A glass of milk and a fruit compote of melon balls and strawberries, sprinkled with crushed mint leaves, add the milk and fruit exchanges and complete the meal nutritionally.

# 295 Chicken with Yogurt

1 cup low-fat plain yogurt
1 tsp. ground ginger
⅔ cup chopped onion
1 tsp. minced garlic
⅛ tsp. pepper
3 boneless, skinless, whole chicken breasts, split
¾ cup bread crumbs
¼ cup margarine, melted

Preheat oven to 350°F. In a dish, combine yogurt, ginger, onion, garlic and pepper. Add chicken and coat well. Dip chicken in crumbs to coat. Place chicken in baking dish. Drizzle with margarine. Bake for 20 to 25 minutes or until chicken is done.

### Per serving
*311 calories*
*71 mg cholesterol*
*205 mg sodium*
*2.5 gm saturated fat*
*9.3 gm fat*

### Exchanges per serving
*½ bread*
*1 fat*
*3 meat*

**On the side** We like to offer slices of pumpernickel or rye bread with this dish, cauliflower and broccoli florets mixed, and a strawberry milk shake to make the meal complete nutritionally.

1 4 lb. skinned chicken, cut into 8 pieces

½ cup ginger brandy

¼ cup honey

½ cup soy sauce

½ cup low-sodium chicken broth

3 Tbsp. lemon juice

½ tsp. ground ginger

⅛ tsp. pepper

Combine all ingredients in large bowl. Refrigerate for several hours. Preheat oven to 350°F. Arrange chicken in shallow baking dish. Brush with brandy mixture. Bake for 40 minutes.

**Per serving**
*258 calories*
*71 mg cholesterol*
*825 mg sodium*
*4.3 gm saturated fat*
*8.3 gm fat*

**Exchanges per serving**
*3 meat*

**On the side** White rice, stir-fried snow pea pods, and a glass of milk work well with this flavorful oriental-style dish. A dessert of pears poached in almond extract completes the meal nutritionally.

2 Tbsp. margarine

2 Tbsp. flour

1½ cup low-sodium chicken broth

1 lb. skinned, boned, cooked chicken, cubed

2½ tsp. dillweed

⅛ tsp. pepper

⅓ cup plain low-fat yogurt

In saucepan, melt margarine. Add flour and stir constantly for 1 minute. Stir in broth and simmer for 5 minutes, stirring occasionally. Add chicken and dill. Simmer until chicken is hot. Season with pepper. Stir in yogurt and heat.

**Per serving**
*218 calories*
*73 mg cholesterol*
*73 mg sodium*
*1.91 gm saturated fat*
*8.35 gm fat*

**Exchanges per serving**
*2 meat*

**On the side** We like this with green noodles as the bread course. Fresh cucumber slices, a glass of milk, and a baked apple round out the meal nutritionally.

2 4 oz. boneless, skinned chicken breasts
1 Tbsp. vegetable oil
2 Tbsp. skim milk
½ tsp. dried basil
2 Tbsp. plain dried bread crumbs
2 Tbsp. grated Parmesan cheese
⅛ tsp. salt
1 Tbsp. lemon juice

In a bowl, combine bread crumbs, cheese, salt and basil; mix. Dip chicken cutlets into milk, then into crumb mixture; coat evenly. In a skillet, heat oil; add chicken and brown on both sides or until chicken is tender. Pour lemon juice over chicken.

**Per serving:**
*242 calories*
*57.2 mg cholesterol*
*347 mg sodium*
*3.5 gm saturated fat*
*13.8 gm fat*

**Exchanges per serving**
*½ bread*
*2 fat*
*3 meat*

**On the side** A small dinner roll, green beans, steamed just until crisp-tender, a glass of milk, and fresh pineapple slices for dessert balance this meal nutritionally.

2 Tbsp. margarine

1½ lb. chicken thighs, skinned

1½ tsp. flour

2 tsp. Worcestershire sauce

1 tsp. dry mustard

¾ tsp. curry powder

1 tsp. light soy sauce

Preheat oven to 375°F. In a small saucepan, heat margarine; add remaining ingredients, except chicken. Stir constantly until mixture is thick and smooth. In a 9 x 9-inch baking dish, arrange chicken in single layer. Pour curry mixture over chicken. Bake for 35 to 40 minutes. Baste chicken occasionally with pan juices.

**Per serving**
*302 calories*
*221 mg cholesterol*
*280 mg sodium*
*3.9 gm saturated fat*
*17.9 gm fat*

**Exchanges per serving**
*1 fat*
*3 meat*

**On the side** A ½ cup of white rice, seasoned with a little fresh parsley, a vegetable course of cauliflower and broccoli florets, steamed just until tender and seasoned with lemon juice, and a peachy milk shake complete this meal nutritionally.

Nonstick cooking spray
3 lb. fryer chicken, skinned, cut up
½ cup onions, chopped
⅓ cup chopped green pepper
1 tsp. minced garlic
1 16 oz. can low-sodium stewed tomatoes
⅓ cup raisins
2 tsp. curry powder
¼ tsp. nutmeg
2 Tbsp. cold water
1 Tbsp. cornstarch
3 cups cooked rice

Spray a skillet with nonstick cooking spray. Brown chicken in skillet on all sides. Add onion, green pepper, and garlic. Stir in tomatoes, raisins, curry powder and nutmeg, and bring to a boil. Reduce heat and simmer for 30 to 35 minutes. Remove chicken. Skim excess fat from sauce. Combine water and cornstarch; stir into sauce and cook until thickened. Serve chicken and sauce over rice.

**Per serving**
*340 calories*
*12.5 mg cholesterol*
*242 mg sodium*
*0.166 gm saturated fat*
*5.0 gm fat*

**Exchanges per serving**
*1 bread*
*3 meat*
*1 vegetable*

**On the side** A glass of milk and a fresh fruit complete this hearty one-dish meal nutritionally.

1 cup whole wheat bread crumbs
1½ tsp. onion powder
¾ tsp. garlic powder
¾ tsp. paprika
1½ tsp. curry powder
¾ tsp. dry mustard
⅛ tsp. pepper
1 cup skim milk
⅛ tsp. Tabasco sauce
2½ lbs. drumsticks, skinless

Combine bread crumbs, onion powder, garlic powder, paprika, curry powder, mustard, and pepper. Place milk and Tabasco sauce in a shallow dish and soak drumsticks. Roll drumsticks in crumb mixture and place in a nonstick baking dish. Bake 25 to 30 minutes at 375°F.

**Per serving**
*256 calories*
*91 mg cholesterol*
*178 mg sodium*
*2.5 gm saturated fat*
*9.31 gm fat*

**Exchanges per serving**
*1 bread*
*2 meat*

**On the side** Corn on the cob, a tossed salad with your favorite low-calorie dressing, a glass of milk, and a baked apple complete this meal deliciously and nutritionally.

# 302 Dijon Chicken

2 boneless, skinless chicken breasts

¼ tsp. black pepper

1 Tbsp. vegetable oil

1 Tbsp. margarine

¼ cup chopped fresh chives

1 Tbsp. lemon juice

1 tsp. dried parsley flakes

3 tsp. Dijon-style mustard

¼ cup low-sodium chicken broth

Sprinkle chicken with pepper. Heat oil and margarine in skillet. Cook chicken until browned and tender; do not over cook. Transfer to warm serving platter. Add chives, lemon juice, parsley, and mustard to skillet. Cook, stirring constantly for about 30 seconds. Stir in broth, stirring gently until smooth. Pour mixture over chicken and serve.

**Per serving**
*230 calories*
*73 mg cholesterol*
*34 mg sodium*
*2.3 gm saturated fat*
*11.5 gm fat*

**Exchanges per serving**
*2½ meat*

**On the side** We like to serve this with baked potato sticks, cherry tomatoes, quickly sautéed with a little margarine and sprinkled with basil, and a peachy milk shake. This completes the meal nutritionally and deliciously.

10 oz. skinned, boneless chicken breasts

1 tsp. margarine

6 broccoli florets

1 tsp. minced garlic

¾ tsp. ground ginger

⅔ cup low-sodium chicken broth

2½ Tbsp. oyster sauce

2 tsp. cornstarch

Cut chicken into strips. In skillet, heat margarine; add chicken and brown on both sides. Remove from skillet. In same skillet, add broccoli, garlic and ginger; sauté. In a mixing bowl, combine broth, oyster sauce, and cornstarch; add to broccoli and return chicken to skillet. Stir until sauce is thickened, then serve.

**Per serving**
*426 calories*
*128 mg cholesterol*
*214 mg sodium*
*2.25 gm saturated fat*
*6.8 gm fat*

**Exchanges per serving**
*5 meat*
*1 vegetable*

**On the side** A serving of brown rice, and frozen peaches, blended in a glass of nonfat milk, add the bread, fruit, and milk exchanges needed to make this meal nutritionally complete.

2 ½ lb. chicken, cut into parts, skinned
2 Tbsp. olive oil
2 garlic cloves, pressed
2 tsp. paprika
2 tsp. rosemary, crushed
⅛ tsp. pepper
⅛ tsp. salt

Rub each piece of chicken with olive oil and garlic. Mix paprika, rosemary, and pepper and salt together. Sprinkle mixture over each piece of chicken. Place in a baking dish and bake at 350°F. for 40 minutes or until chicken is done.

**Per serving**
*354 calories*
*169 mg cholesterol*
*164 mg sodium*
*4.4 gm saturated fat*
*14 gm fat*

**Exchanges per serving**
*1 fat*
*4 meat*

**On the side** Try this with baked potato slices, green beans and carrots, steamed just until crisp-tender, and a strawberry milk shake. We think you'll enjoy this meal, which is nutritionally complete as well as tasty.

⅓ cup long grain rice

1 cup sliced carrots

½ cup sliced green onions

½ tsp. minced garlic

⅔ cup water

3 Tbsp. soy sauce

¾ tsp. five-spice powder

⅛ tsp. pepper

1 whole chicken breast, skinless, halved

Cover a shallow casserole dish with heavy foil, cupping sides of foil. Place uncooked rice in middle. Add carrots, onions, and garlic. In a mixing bowl, combine water, soy sauce, five-spice powder and pepper. Place chicken breasts in center of foil. Pour soy sauce mixture over chicken. Fold two opposite sides of foil together, then fold up ends to seal. Bake at 375°F for 50 minutes.

**Per serving**
*240 calories*
*43 mg cholesterol*
*183 mg sodium*
*0.65 gm saturated fat*
*2.2 gm fat*

**Exchanges per serving**
*1 bread*
*2 meat*
*½ vegetable*

**On the side** A small serving of green beans, steamed just until crisp-tender, a glass of milk, and a baked apple complete this meal nutritionally.

1 tsp. salt

¼ tsp. pepper

¼ tsp. cinnamon

¼ tsp. ground cloves

1 tsp. minced garlic

2 3 lb. frying chickens, skinned, cut into serving-size pieces

2 Tbsp. vegetable oil

¼ cup chopped celery

¼ cup raisins

2 cups orange juice

¼ cup crushed pineapple, fresh

2 Tbsp. cornstarch

¼ cup water

Combine salt, pepper, cinnamon, cloves, and garlic. Rub into chicken pieces. In skillet, heat oil; brown chicken. Add celery, raisins, orange juice and pineapple. Cover and simmer 45 minutes or until chicken is tender. Stir occasionally. Blend cornstarch and water; stir into sauce. Cook, stirring until thickened.

**Per serving**
*273 calories*
*89 mg cholesterol*
*377 mg sodium*
*2.5 gm saturated fat*
*7.5 gm fat*

**Exchanges per serving**
*1 fruit*
*3 meat*

**On the side** A serving of white rice, a glass of milk, and your choice of vegetable complete this meal nutritionally.

# 307 Fruity Chicken

2 chicken breasts, boneless, skinned
1 can (16 oz.) peach halves
4 Tbsp. Dijon-style mustard
½ cup green onions, sliced
1 tsp. soy sauce
¾ cup dry bread crumbs

Preheat oven to 425°F. Place chicken in baking dish. Cover loosely with foil and bake for 25 minutes. Remove foil and place fruit on chicken. Combine mustard, onion, and soy sauce, and spread over chicken. Sprinkle with bread crumbs. Broil until brown.

### Per serving
*375 calories*
*85 mg cholesterol*
*486 mg sodium*
*1.6 gm saturated fat*
*6.3 gm fat*

### Exchanges per serving
*1 bread*
*1 fruit*
*3 meat*

**On the side** A traditional spinach salad goes well on the side with this tasty main dish. Add only a glass of milk and the meal is complete nutritionally.

2½ lbs. skinned frying chicken
⅔ cup low-cal ginger marmalade
1 Tbsp. ginger flavored brandy
1 Tbsp. oil
4 Tbsp. lime juice

Arrange chicken in a large shallow pan. Combine marmalade, brandy, oil and lime juice. Brush on chicken pieces. Bake at 375°F. for 40 minutes. Baste frequently.

**Per serving**
*280 calories*
*78 mg cholesterol*
*75 mg sodium*
*3.2 gm saturated fat*
*12.8 gm fat*

**Exchanges per serving**
*½ fat*
*4 meat*

**On the side** Brown rice, green beans, steamed just until crisp-tender, a glass of milk, and your favorite fruit for dessert combine to make this meal nutritionally complete.

# 309 Glazed Chicken

2 boned, skinned chicken breasts, halved
¼ cup plain low-fat yogurt
3 tsp. brown sugar
3 tsp. Worcestershire sauce
1 Tbsp. minced garlic
⅛ tsp. black pepper
⅛ tsp. Tabasco sauce

In bowl, combine all ingredients, except chicken. Mix well. In shallow baking dish, arrange chicken. Pour half of yogurt mixture over chicken and bake at 350°F. for about 25 minutes or until chicken is tender. Pour remaining yogurt mixture over chicken and broil until lightly brown.

**Per serving**
*188 calories*
*72 mg cholesterol*
*189 mg sodium*
*1.75 gm saturated fat*
*6.1 gm fat*

**Exchanges per serving**
*2 meat*

**On the side** A serving of white rice, lightly sautéed snow pea pods, a glass of milk, and pears garnished with a little mint combine to make this meal nutritionally balanced.

4 whole chicken breasts, boned, skinned, halved
¼ cup margarine
⅓ cup honey
4 Tbsp. Dijon-style mustard
1 tsp. minced garlic
1 Tbsp. lemon juice
2 tsp. curry powder
⅛ tsp. salt

Preheat oven to 350°F. Arrange chicken in a 13 x 9 inch baking dish. Melt margarine in a saucepan; add remaining ingredients and stir until smooth. Pour over chicken. Cook for 25 to 30 minutes, basting frequently.

**Per serving**
*242 calories*
*73 mg cholesterol*
*136 mg sodium*
*2.6 gm saturated fat*
*6.7 gm fat*

**Exchanges per serving**
*1 fat*
*3 meat*

**On the side** Saffron rice, sautéed onions, mushrooms, and green peppers, a glass of milk, and your favorite fruit for dessert finish off this tasty dish and make the meal complete nutritionally.

2 boneless, skinless chicken breasts, cut into chunks
¾ cup chopped green peppers
1 8 oz. can pineapple chunks in unsweetened juice
1 Tbsp. lemon juice
¼ tsp. paprika
4 cups cooked rice

In saucepan, add chicken, green peppers, and pineapple with its juice. Heat to boil. Simmer and add lemon juice and paprika. Cook until chicken is tender. Serve over rice.

**Per serving**
*271 calories*
*425 mg cholesterol*
*491 mg sodium*
*0.65 gm saturated fat*
*2.25 gm fat*

**Exchanges per serving**
*1 bread*
*½ fruit*
*2 meat*

**On the side** Serve this with a tossed salad and a cherry milk shake and the meal is complete nutritionally.

3½ lb. chicken, cut into pieces, skinned
2 Tbsp. vegetable oil
½ tsp. garlic powder
½ tsp. onion powder or salt
½ tsp. pepper
2 tsp. oregano
2 tsp. basil
2 tsp. lime juice
1½ cups chopped fresh tomato

Preheat oven to 450°F. Rub chicken pieces first with vegetable oil, then with garlic powder, onion powder, pepper, oregano, and basil. Place chicken in oven-proof casserole dish. Sprinkle with lime juice. Bake chicken for 20 to 25 minutes. Reduce heat to 350°F. Add tomatoes to the chicken and bake for an additional 20 to 25 minutes.

**Per serving**
*310 calories*
*178 mg cholesterol*
*174 mg sodium*
*4.4 gm saturated fat*
*15 gm fat*

**Exchanges per serving**
*1 fat*
*3 meat*
*1 vegetable*

**On the side** We like to serve this with a baked potato, a vegetable mix of cauliflower florets and carrots, a glass of milk, and fresh fruit for dessert. The meal is nutritionally complete and completely satisfying.

1 whole chicken, cut up
½ cup honey
½ cup margarine, melted
2 tsp. dry mustard

Rinse chicken and pat dry. Combine honey, margarine and mustard; mix. Put chicken in baking dish. Brush honey mixture on chicken. Bake at 350°F for 1 hour. Baste occasionally with mixture.

**Per serving**
*220 calories*
*73 mg cholesterol*
*138 mg sodium*
*2.6 gm saturated fat*
*7.16 gm fat*

**Exchanges per serving**
*½ fat*
*1½ meat*

**On the side** Parsley potatoes, baby carrots, simmered with gingerroot, a glass of milk, and mixed fruit slices for dessert complete this meal deliciously and nutritiously.

# 314 Honey-Lime Chicken

2 boned, skinned chicken breasts, halved
1 Tbsp. margarine, melted
¼ tsp. garlic powder
¼ cup lime juice
5 tsp. honey
3 tsp. Dijon-style mustard

Heat oven to 350°F. In nonstick baking dish, place chicken. Baste chicken with margarine and sprinkle with garlic powder. Bake for about 25 to 30 minutes. In saucepan, combine lime juice, honey, and mustard; heat. Spread mixture over chicken. Broil chicken until lightly brown.

**Per serving**
*212 calories*
*71 mg cholesterol*
*93 mg sodium*
*2.1 gm saturated fat*
*7.6 gm fat*

**Exchanges per serving**
*2 meat*

**On the side** We like to serve white rice, a mixed vegetable of green beans and carrots, a glass of milk, and a compote of mixed melon balls with this tangy entree. The meal is nutritionally complete and satisfying to the eye and the palate.

½ cup chopped onion
½ tsp. minced garlic
½ cup green pepper
2 cups skinned and cooked chicken, cubed
1 Tbsp. vegetable oil
½ tsp. black pepper
1½ tsp. curry powder
1 28 oz. can stewed tomatoes
1 Tbsp. Worcestershire sauce
¼ cup raisins
2 cups cooked rice

In large skillet, heat oil. Add onions, garlic, and green pepper; sauté until onions are tender. Add the remaining ingredients, except the rice. Simmer for 30 minutes. Serve over the rice.

**Per serving**
*323 calories*
*71 mg cholesterol*
*930 mg sodium*
*1.91 gm saturated fat*
*8.3 gm fat*

**Exchanges**
*1 bread*
*2½ meat*
*1 vegetable*

**On the side** This meal is nearly complete in one dish. Serve with a dessert of fruit and yogurt for nutritional balance.

# 316 Lemon-Barbecued Chicken

2½ lb. frying chicken, quartered and skinned
⅛ tsp. paprika
⅛ tsp. cayenne pepper
¼ cup lemon juice
¼ cup honey

Season chicken with paprika and pepper. Place chicken on broiler rack. Combine lemon juice and honey; mix thoroughly. Baste chicken with lemon-honey mixture. Broil 15 minutes; baste occasionally with lemon-honey mixture. Turn pieces over and baste. Broil until chicken is done.

**Per serving**
*300 calories*
*247.5 mg cholesterol*
*192.5 mg sodium*
*3.24 mg saturated fat*
*11.5 gm fat*

**Exchanges per serving**
*4 meat*

**On the side** Corn on the cob, a tossed salad, a glass of milk, and a slice of watermelon for dessert make this a picnic any time of the year. The meal is nutritionally complete and is sure to please the entire family.

1 Tbsp. vegetable oil

1 Tbsp. margarine

3 lb. frying chicken, cut into serving pieces, skinned

⅛ tsp. salt

⅛ tsp. pepper

½ cup chopped green onions

1 Tbsp. dried parsley flakes, crushed

¾ tsp. marjoram

½ cup lemon juice

In skillet, heat oil and margarine. Sprinkle chicken with salt and pepper, and brown on all sides. Sprinkle chicken with onions, parsley, and marjoram. Pour lemon juice over chicken, cover, and simmer 20 to 25 minutes.

**Per serving**
*285 calories*
*213 mg cholesterol*
*307 mg sodium*
*10.7 gm saturated fat*
*18 gm fat*

**Exchanges per serving**
*1 fat*
*3 meat*

**On the side** We like this entree with brown rice, cooked cabbage, and a cherry milkshake.

1 Tbsp. vegetable oil

4 boneless, skinless chicken breasts, halved

1 Tbsp. margarine

⅔ cup diced onions

¾ cup low-sodium canned tomatoes

¾ tsp. basil

⅛ tsp. garlic powder

¼ tsp. thyme

¼ cup sweet vermouth

In skillet, heat oil and brown chicken on both sides. Transfer chicken to a large saucepan. Melt margarine in same skillet and sauté onions. Add to chicken in saucepan. Add remaining ingredients to saucepan and simmer for 30 minutes.

**Per serving**
*219 calories*
*83 mg cholesterol*
*28 mg sodium*
*1.4 gm saturated fat*
*3.75 gm fat*

**Exchanges per serving**
*3 meat*

**On the side** A serving of white rice; sautéed onions, mushrooms, and green peppers, sautéed, a glass of milk, and a pear poached in almond extract complete this meal nutritionally and make it deliciously appealing, as well.

1 Tbsp. margarine
1 cup sliced mushrooms
1½ Tbsp. light cream cheese
¼ tsp. nutmeg
1 Tbsp. minced green onion
⅛ tsp. ground pepper
1 chicken breast, skinned, boned, halved
¼ cup balsamic vinegar

In skillet, heat margarine. Add mushrooms and sauté until liquid is absorbed. Mash cream cheese with nutmeg, green onion, and pepper. Spoon half of the mushroom mixture on each piece of chicken. Put half the cream cheese on top, then loosely fold chicken sides to middle. Place chicken in a casserole dish, seam side down. Pour vinegar over chicken. Bake uncovered at 350°F for 30 minutes.

**Per serving**
*174 calories*
*51 mg cholesterol*
*173 mg sodium*
*2.7 gm saturated fat*
*9.2 gm fat*

**Exchanges per serving**
*2 meat*
*1 vegetable*

**On the side** Green noodles, baby carrots cooked with a little mint, and a dessert of fruit slices, sprinkled with poppy seeds, and served with a yogurt dip complete this meal nutritionally and give it a little touch of elegance well suited for guests.

# 320 Mustard-Coated Chicken

3 Tbsp. Dijon-style mustard
⅔ cup plain bread crumbs
1½ Tbsp. lime juice
5 Tbsp. water
12 oz. boneless, skinless chicken breasts
1 Tbsp. vegetable oil
2 Tbsp. dry white wine

Mix together mustard, bread crumbs, lime juice and water to make a paste. Put half of the mustard coating on one side of each chicken breast. In a skillet, heat oil. Place coated side of chicken in pan. While breasts are sautéing, spread remaining coating on top; brown both sides. Reduce heat and add wine; cook another 5 minutes.

**Per serving**
*299 calories*
*71 mg cholesterol*
*245 mg sodium*
*3.3 gm saturated fat*
*8 gm fat*

**Exchanges per serving**
*4 meat*

**On the side** Parsley new potatoes, fresh tomato slices, a glass of milk, and your favorite fruit for dessert complete this meal nutritionally.

1 Tbsp. vegetable oil
1 lb. chicken breasts, boneless, skinned
1 cup chopped green pepper
¼ cup chopped green onion
1 tsp. minced garlic
1 cup orange juice
1½ tsp. dry mustard
⅛ tsp. salt
⅛ tsp. pepper
3 tsp. cornstarch, dissolved in 3 Tbsp. water
1 small orange, cut into small pieces
⅛ tsp. ginger

Heat oil in skillet. Add chicken and brown; remove. In same skillet, add green pepper, green onion, and garlic. Cook until tender. Return chicken to skillet. Add orange juice, mustard, salt and pepper, and bring to a boil. Reduce heat and simmer for 15 minutes. Transfer chicken to platter; keep warm. Add cornstarch mixture to skillet. Increase heat. Add orange pieces and cook until thickened. Pour over chicken. Sprinkle lightly with ginger.

**Per serving**
*268 calories*
*97 mg cholesterol*
*164 mg sodium*
*1.9 gm saturated fat*
*8.6 gm fat*

**Exchanges per serving**
*1 fat*
*½ fruit*
*2 meat*
*1 vegetable*

**On the side** We prefer white rice and cooked fresh spinach with this delightful entree. Top off the meal with a cherry milk shake for nutritional balance.

1 lb. skinned, boned chicken breasts
⅓ cup low-calorie orange spread
¼ cup light soy sauce
¾ tsp. ground ginger
¼ tsp. garlic powder

In mixing bowl, combine all ingredients, except chicken; mix well. Cut chicken into large cubes. Put chicken in mixture and toss to coat. Marinate in refrigerator for 30 minutes. Transfer chicken to broiling pan. Broil and baste, turning chicken until done.

**Per serving**
*240 calories*
*85 mg cholesterol*
*906 mg sodium*
*1.3 gm saturated fat*
*4.5 gm fat*

**Exchanges per serving**
*2 meat*

**On the side** Wild rice is really nice with this citrus-glazed chicken dish. Steamed broccoli and a dessert of fruit and yogurt complete the meal nutritionally.

¾ cup orange juice
¼ cup honey
4 Tbsp. soy sauce
½ tsp. minced garlic
⅛ tsp. ginger
3 lb. broiling chicken, quartered, skinned

Combine orange juice, honey, soy sauce, garlic and ginger. Stir until honey is dissolved. Arrange chicken on a broiling pan. Pour half of orange juice mixture over chicken. Broil for 5 minutes. Turn chicken over and pour remaining mixture over chicken. Broil until chicken is tender.

**Per serving**
*300 calories*
*153 mg cholesterol*
*561 mg sodium*
*3.4 gm saturated fat*
*12.6 gm fat*

**Exchanges per serving**
*3 meat*

**On the side** White rice, snow pea pods, a glass of milk, and your favorite fresh fruit for dessert are all you need to complete this meal nutritionally.

3 lbs. chicken, skinned

2 cups tomato juice

¾ cup vinegar

2 Tbsp. Worcestershire sauce

2 Tbsp. brown sugar

⅛ tsp. salt

¼ tsp. dry mustard

½ tsp. ground red pepper

⅛ tsp. pepper

1 Tbsp. minced onion

1 tsp. ketchup

Preheat oven to 350°F. In a saucepan, combine all ingredients except chicken. Cook over medium heat, stirring frequently for about 10 minutes. In a 13 x 9 inch baking dish, arrange chicken in an even layer; top with tomato mixture. Bake, basting chicken frequently for 55 minutes.

**Per serving**
*325 calories*
*212 mg cholesterol*
*323 mg sodium*
*4.57 gm saturated fat*
*12.9 gm fat*

**Exchanges per serving**
*4 meat*
*1 vegetable*

**On the side** New potatoes garnished with rosemary, a glass of milk, and fresh strawberries for dessert complete this meal nutritionally.

1 Tbsp. vegetable oil
1 cup chopped onions
½ tsp. minced garlic
4 tsp. paprika
⅛ tsp. black pepper
1½ cups low-sodium chicken broth
1½ Tbsp. cornstarch
2 cups skinned and cooked chicken, cubed
⅔ cup frozen peas
1 cup plain low-fat yogurt
2½ cups cooked noodles

In a large skillet, heat oil. Sauté onions, garlic, paprika, and pepper. Cook until onions are tender. Add broth and cornstarch; stir until smooth. Bring to a boil and add chicken and peas. Boil for 1 minute. Remove from heat and stir in yogurt until blended. Serve over noodles.

**Per serving**
*345 calories*
*100 mg cholesterol*
*250 mg sodium*
*2.21 gm saturated fat*
*9.6 gm fat*

**Exchanges per serving**
*1 bread*
*1 fat*
*3 meat*

**On the side** This main-dish meal goes well with a mixed vegetable of green beans and carrots, a glass of milk, and your favorite fruit for dessert.

2 lbs. chicken, skinned
6 Tbsp. margarine
1 cup chopped onions
2 cups fresh, sliced mushrooms
1 cup chopped celery
4 Tbsp. flour
1 cup low-sodium chicken broth
1 cup skim milk
1 tsp. celery salt
1 tsp. dried tarragon

Cut chicken into serving pieces. Place in shallow pan and bake at 400°F for 15 minutes. Baste with 3 Tbsp. melted margarine and continue baking for 15 minutes longer. Transfer chicken to a casserole dish and set aside. In skillet, heat remaining 3 table-spoons margarine. Sauté onions, mushrooms and celery until soft. Put over chicken, leaving pan drippings. Add flour, chicken broth, and milk to pan drippings, stirring constantly until sauce thickens. Remove from heat and season with celery salt and tarragon. Pour over chicken and bake at 350°F for 20 minutes.

**Per serving**
*290 calories*
*70 mg cholesterol*
*114 mg sodium*
*2.0 gm saturated fat*
*12.0 gm fat*

**Exchanges per serving**
*1 fat*
*3 meat*
*1 vegetable*

**On the side** We like this tasty casserole with a side of saffron rice, a glass of milk, and, if they are in season, some honey-dew and cantaloupe melon slices for dessert.

2 Tbsp. margarine
2 boneless, skinned chicken breasts
¼ tsp. salt
¼ tsp. black pepper
1 lemon

In skillet, melt margarine. Sprinkle chicken with salt and pepper. Brown chicken on each side. Cook until chicken is done. Squeeze lemon over chicken. Simmer for about 2 minutes. Serve.

**Per serving**
*220 calories*
*73 mg cholesterol*
*133 mg sodium*
*2.41 gm saturated fat*
*11.3 gm fat*

**Exchanges per serving**
*1 fat*
*2½ meat*

**On the side** Our favorite accompaniments are green noodles, cooked carrots, and a strawberry milk shake with this quick and easy recipe. They give the meal an appealing appearance to the eye as well as appealing to the palate.

1 Tbsp. Dijon-style mustard
2 tsp. light mayonnaise
2 tsp. plain low-fat yogurt
2 chicken breasts, skinned
1½ cups fine bread crumbs

Preheat oven to 350°F. Mix mustard, mayonnaise,
and yogurt. Spread mixture over both sides of
chicken breasts; dredge in bread crumbs. Place
in a baking dish and cover. Bake for 35 minutes.

**Per serving**
*364 calories*
*86 mg cholesterol*
*666 mg sodium*
*2.1 gm saturated fat*
*8.8 gm fat*

**Exchanges per serving**
*1 bread*
*1 fat*
*3 meat*

**On the side** Cherry tomatoes, lightly sautéed with a little margarine and basil, are delicious with this Quick Baked Chicken
recipe. Add a glass of milk and your favorite fruit for dessert
and the meal is nutritionally complete.

1½ cups crisp rice cereal, crushed
1 6 oz. envelope Italian salad dressing mix
3 lb. broiler-fryer chicken, skinned, cut up
¼ cup margarine, melted
1 tsp. basil

In mixing bowl, combine rice cereal, salad dressing mix, and basil. Brush chicken with melted margarine, then roll in cereal mixture. Place chicken in shallow baking pan. Sprinkle with any remaining crumbs. Bake at 375°F for 50 minutes.

**Per serving**
*397 calories*
*153 mg cholesterol*
*272 mg sodium*
*4.4 gm saturated fat*
*18.6 gm fat*

**Exchanges per serving**
*1 bread*
*2 fat*
*3 meat*

**On the side** A mix of cauliflower and broccoli florets, steamed just until tender, a glass of milk, and your favorite fruit complete this meal nutritionally.

1 Tbsp. vegetable oil
1 Tbsp. margarine
1 tsp. minced garlic
2 Tbsp. lemon juice
¼ tsp. nutmeg
3 lb. chicken
2 potatoes, quartered

In skillet, heat oil and margarine until foamy. Add garlic, lemon juice, and nutmeg. Add chicken to pan, breast side up. Brush with basting mixture. Place chicken in shallow baking dish. Place potatoes around chicken. Bake at 350°F for 35 to 40 minutes. Baste occasionally.

**Per serving**
*409 calories*
*153 mg cholesterol*
*169 mg sodium*
*3.9 gm saturated fat*
*16.0 gm fat*

**Exchanges per serving**
*½ bread*
*1 fat*
*3 meat*

**On the side** Choose your favorite vegetable to accompany this classic roast chicken dish. A glass of milk and some baked apple slices for dessert complete the meal nutritionally.

# 331  Roasted Chicken

2 lbs. whole chicken, skinned

1 tsp. dried thyme

⅛ tsp. pepper

⅓ cup water

¾ cup sliced onion

2 cups frozen brussel sprouts

2 Tbsp. honey

Preheat oven to 350°F. Sprinkle chicken with thyme and pepper. Place chicken in a baking dish. Add water to baking dish and top chicken with onions. Cover and bake about 20 to 25 minutes. Add brussel sprouts around chicken. Drizzle honey over chicken and continue to bake for 20 to 25 minutes longer.

**Per serving**
*336 calories*
*136 mg cholesterol*
*140 mg sodium*
*3.0 gm saturated fat*
*11.3 gm fat*

**Exchanges per serving**
*4 meat*
*1 vegetable*

**On the side** A baked potato, a side salad, a glass of milk, and fresh fruit for dessert complete this classic meal nutritionally.

2 lbs. chicken breasts, skinned
1 can cream of mushroom soup
¾ cup skim milk
¼ cup sliced onion
1 tsp. dried rosemary, crushed
2 cups fresh mushrooms
½ tsp. dried thyme
⅛ tsp. pepper

Preheat oven to 350°F. Place chicken in baking dish. In saucepan, add remaining ingredients. Mix well and heat for 10 minutes. Pour mixture over chicken. Cover and bake for 40 to 45 minutes.

**Per serving**
*351 calories*
*131 mg cholesterol*
*483 mg sodium*
*3.8 gm saturated fat*
*11.6 gm fat*

**Exchanges per serving**
*1 fat*
*3 meat*

**On the side** New potatoes, boiled, then tossed in a pan with a little margarine and some rosemary, a green vegetable of broccoli or green beans, and a frozen fruit yogurt dessert complete this meal deliciously and nutritionally.

6 oz. jar artichoke hearts, drained
2 tsp. cornstarch
¾ tsp. instant chicken bouillon
⅛ tsp. salt
⅛ tsp. pepper
⅔ cup skim milk
1 cup cubed cooked chicken
3 Tbsp. grated Parmesan cheese
¼ tsp. paprika

Cut artichokes into small pieces; rinse and drain in hot water. In a saucepan, combine cornstarch, chicken bouillon, salt and pepper. Stir in skim milk and cook over medium heat until thickened. Stir in cubed chicken and artichoke hearts. Transfer mixture into a casserole dish. Sprinkle with Parmesan cheese and paprika. Bake, uncovered, for 15 minutes at 350°F.

**Per serving**
*328 calories*
*115 mg cholesterol*
*770 mg sodium*
*3.9 gm saturated fat*
*11.8 gm fat*

**Exchanges per serving**
*2 meat*
*½ skim milk*
*1 vegetable*

**On the side** Wild rice is great with this robust recipe. Prepare a dessert plate of fruit slices, sprinkled with poppy seeds, accompanied by a yogurt dip and the meal is nutritionally complete.

# 334 Scotch Chicken

2 boneless chicken breasts
⅛ tsp. salt
⅛ tsp. ground pepper
1 Tbsp. Scotch whiskey
⅓ cup low-sodium chicken broth
1 cup sliced mushrooms
2 tsp. skim milk
1 Tbsp. low-fat cottage cheese
1 Tbsp. low-fat yogurt
⅛ tsp. nutmeg

Season chicken with salt and pepper and place in a nonstick skillet, skin side down. Sear, covered, over high heat for 3 to 4 minutes. Turn chicken over and reduce heat and cook for another 3 to 4 minutes. Remove chicken. Deglaze skillet with scotch. Reduce liquid until it's just a film; stir constantly. Add broth and mushrooms, cover and boil, stirring occasionally. Remove from heat. Stir in milk, cottage cheese, and yogurt. Season with nutmeg. Pour over chicken.

**Per serving**
*195 calories*
*42.5 mg cholesterol*
*672 mg sodium*
*2.1 gm saturated fat*
*5.4 gm fat*

**Exchanges per serving**
*3 meat*
*½ vegetable*

**On the side** Saffron rice, green beans, seasoned with garlic, a glass of milk and your favorite fruit for dessert combine to complete this meal nutritionally.

1⅓ cups water
4½ oz. package Spanish-style rice mix
¾ cup sliced mushrooms
¼ cup diced green chili peppers
4 boneless, skinless chicken breast halves
½ cup shredded part-skim cheddar cheese

Preheat oven to 350°F. Boil water. In baking dish, combine water and rice mixture. Stir mushrooms and chili peppers into rice mixture. Arrange chicken on top of rice mixture and cover with foil. Bake for 40 minutes. Sprinkle with cheese, then bake uncovered until cheese melts.

**Per serving**
*276 calories*
*86 mg cholesterol*
*197 mg sodium*
*1.5 gm saturated fat*
*6.2 gm fat*

**Exchanges per serving**
*½ bread*
*3 meat*

**On the side** A salad of lettuce and tomatoes, a glass of milk, and a dessert of baked apples complete this meal deliciously and nutritionally.

¾ tsp. oregano
¾ tsp. ginger
⅓ cup cornmeal
¾ tsp. basil
1 tsp. minced garlic
½ tsp. lemon juice
4 chicken cutlets, skinned
1 egg white, beaten lightly
½ tsp. Tabasco sauce
½ cup bran flakes, crushed

Combine oregano, ginger, cornmeal, basil, and garlic. Rub lemon juice on chicken cutlets. Mix egg white and Tabasco. Dip chicken in cornmeal mixture, then in egg white mixture; then roll in bran flakes. Place chicken on nonstick baking sheet. Bake at 350°F for 20 to 25 minutes.

**Per serving**
*200 calories*
*21 mg cholesterol*
*274 mg sodium*
*1.0 gm saturated fat*
*2.8 gm fat*

**Exchanges per serving**
*½ bread*
*2 meat*

**On the side** White rice, steamed broccoli florets, and a strawberry milk shake complete this meal nutritionally.

Nonstick cooking spray
2 boneless, skinless chicken breasts
4 Tbsp. sugar
4 Tbsp. lemon juice
2 tsp. Worcestershire sauce
1 tsp. paprika
½ tsp. black pepper
½ tsp. lemon pepper
½ tsp. salt

Spray broiler pan with nonstick spray. Place chicken on pan. Combine all ingredients and mix well. Brush chicken with sauce. Broil, turning chicken and basting with sauce until chicken is done.

**Per serving**
*213 calories*
*73 mg cholesterol*
*627 mg sodium*
*1.41 gm saturated fat*
*5.3 gm fat*

**Exchanges per serving**
*3 meat*

**On the side** Parsley new potatoes, green beans, a glass of milk, and some fresh pineapple slices for dessert are all you need to complete this meal deliciously and nutritionally.

2 lbs. chicken pieces, skinless
1 cup cornflake crumbs
2 tsp. chili powder
½ tsp. ground cumin
¼ tsp. ground red pepper
⅛ tsp. black pepper
¼ tsp. garlic powder

Preheat oven to 375°F. In shallow dish, combine all
ingredients except chicken. Rinse chicken with water,
then roll pieces in the crumb mixture to coat. Place
chicken in nonstick baking pan. Bake 45 minutes.

**Per serving**
*225 calories*
*100 mg cholesterol*
*200 mg sodium*
*1.6 gm saturated fat*
*5.5 gm fat*

**Exchanges per serving**
*3 meat*

**On the side** Serve this spicy dish with a side of white rice,
a serving of green beans, and a cherry milk shake for nutritional completeness and to get raves from the entire family.

2 boneless, skinned chicken breasts

2 Tbsp. cornstarch

3 Tbsp. soy sauce

¼ cup chopped green onions

½ cup chopped green pepper

½ cup chopped red pepper

1 cup sliced, fresh mushrooms

1 Tbsp. vegetable oil

½ cup low-sodium chicken broth

6 oz. package frozen pea pods, thawed

½ cup chopped tomatoes

4 cups cooked rice

Cut chicken into chunks. In bowl, combine chicken, cornstarch, and soy sauce. Over medium heat, cook onions, green pepper, red pepper, and mushrooms in oil until crisp-tender. Remove to a bowl. In a skillet, cook chicken mixture, stirring frequently. Add broth, pea pods, and vegetables from bowl. Cook until chicken is tender. Stir in tomatoes. Heat through, then serve with rice.

**Per serving**
*287 calories*
*26 mg cholesterol*
*245.7 mg sodium*
*4 gm saturated fat*
*10 gm fat*

**Exchanges per serving**
*1 bread*
*2½ meat*
*1 vegetable*

**On the side** This meal needs only a glass of milk and your favorite fruit as dessert to be complete nutritionally.

# 340  Stuffed Chicken

1 whole chicken breast, skinned, halved
4 Tbsp. soy sauce
2 Tbsp. margarine
2 tsp. lemon juice
½ tsp. thyme
⅛ tsp. pepper
¼ tsp. grated lemon rind
¼ cup grated part-skim Swiss cheese
½ tsp. dried parsley flakes

Preheat oven to 375°F. Cut a 2-inch pocket length-wise on each side of chicken breast. In a saucepan, combine soy sauce, margarine, lemon juice, thyme, pepper, lemon rind; bring to a boil. Place chicken in a baking dish. Pour sauce over chicken and bake for 25 to 30 minutes. Remove from oven. Divide cheese and insert into the pockets in the chicken. Return chicken to oven and bake for 10 minutes more, or until cheese melts. Sprinkle with parsley.

**Per serving**
*285 calories*
*59 mg cholesterol*
*363 mg sodium*
*7.7 gm saturated fat*
*22.5 gm fat*

**Exchanges per serving**
*1 fat*
*3 meat*

**On the side** Our preference is for green noodles as the bread course, a tossed salad as the vegetable, a glass of milk, and a mixed fruit salad of apple, peach, orange, and grapes for dessert. This completes the meal nutritionally.

# 341 Supreme Chicken

1 whole chicken breast, halved, skinned
⅛ tsp. salt
⅛ tsp. pepper
2 Tbsp. margarine
2 cups sliced mushrooms
1¼ cup skim milk
1½ Tbsp. cornstarch
1 Tbsp. sherry

Preheat oven to 350°F. Sprinkle chicken with salt and pepper. Place in a baking dish. Dot each with one tablespoon margarine. Bake for 20 minutes. Add mushrooms and bake for 5 to 10 minutes longer. In a saucepan, blend milk and cornstarch until smooth; bring to a boil. Stir in sherry. Pour over chicken. Bake for 5 to 10 minutes more.

**Per serving**
*293 calories*
*37 mg cholesterol*
*396 mg sodium*
*2.9 gm saturated fat*
*15.1 gm fat*

**Exchanges per serving**
*1 fat*
*2 meat*
*1 vegetable*
*½ skim milk*

**On the side** Try this with parsley new potatoes, stir-fried zucchini with tomatoes and a plate of mixed fruit sticks with yogurt dip for a delicious and nutritionally complete meal.

1 large chicken breast, halved, skinned, and boned

1 egg, slightly beaten

3 Tbsp. flour

2 tsp. sesame seeds

¾ tsp. ground ginger

⅛ tsp. cinnamon

1 peach, sliced

⅛ cup sliced green onions

1 Tbsp. vegetable oil

¼ cup ketchup

3 Tbsp. wine vinegar

2½ tsp. brown sugar

2 tsp. soy sauce

½ tsp. minced garlic

1½ Tbsp. white wine

Cut breast into chunks. Combine egg, flour, sesame seed, ginger and cinnamon. Coat chicken with mixture. Heat oil in a skillet and cook chicken. Combine in a blender: ketchup, vinegar, brown sugar, soy sauce, garlic, and wine; blend. Stir in peach. Add sauce and onions to chicken and cook for 5 to 10 minutes.

**Per serving**
*327 calories*
*168 mg cholesterol*
*704 mg sodium*
*2.4 gm saturated fat*
*12.5 gm fat*

**Exchanges per serving**
*1 fat*
*½ fruit*
*3 meat*

**On the side** A serving of white rice, a side of green beans, steamed just until crisp, a glass of milk, and a pineapple slice on the plate as garnish round out this meal.

1 10 oz. package frozen spinach
4 boned, skinless chicken breast halves
⅔ cup skim milk
1½ tsp. cornstarch
2 tsp. instant chicken bouillon granules
¾ tsp. caraway seed
⅛ tsp. paprika
⅓ cup shredded part-skim Swiss cheese

Cook spinach according to package directions; drain. In a nonstick skillet, cook chicken over medium heat, turning occasionally, until tender. Place spinach in a baking dish and place chicken atop spinach. For sauce, combine milk, cornstarch, bouillon, caraway seed and paprika. Cook and stir until thickened and bubbly. Add cheese and stir until melted. Pour sauce over chicken and bake at 375°F for 10 minutes.

**Per serving**
*254 calories*
*79 mg. cholesterol*
*643 mg sodium*
*1.5 mg saturated fat*
*9 gm fat*

**Exchanges per serving**
*3 meat*
*1 vegetable*

**On the side** New potatoes, boiled, then tossed in a little margarine and parsley, are great beside this tasty chicken and spinach mix. Add a glass of milk and your favorite fresh fruit for dessert and the meal is nutritionally complete.

3 Tbsp. minced onion

2 tsp. minced garlic

½ tsp. ground ginger

2 cups low-fat yogurt

½ tsp. coriander

¼ tsp. cumin

1 Tbsp. Worcestershire sauce

½ Tbsp. soy sauce

¼ cup lime juice

⅓ cup orange juice

¾ tsp. paprika

4 whole skinless, boned chicken breasts, halved

Mix onion, garlic and ginger in a bowl. Add yogurt, coriander, cumin, Worcestershire sauce, soy sauce, lime juice, orange juice, and paprika. Blend. Pour yogurt mixture over chicken and marinate in refrigerator for several hours. Remove chicken from marinade and broil until golden brown on each side.

**Per serving**
*214 calories*
*58 mg cholesterol*
*155 mg sodium*
*1.37 gm saturated fat*
*6.3 gm fat*

**Exchanges per serving**
*½ fruit*
*2 meat*
*½ milk*

**On the side** Saffron rice looks and tastes great with this dish. A mix of onions, mushrooms, and green peppers, sautéed with a little margarine, is our vegetable of choice. A fruit plate with yogurt dressing rounds out the meal nutritionally.

1 Tbsp. peanut oil
1 lb. boneless, skinless chicken breasts
1 cup chopped onions
2 cups fresh chopped tomatoes
1 22 oz. can chili hot beans
⅔ cup oat bran
⅓ cup chopped red peppers
1 tsp. chili powder
1 tsp. minced garlic
1½ cup water
⅔ cup part-skim cheddar cheese, shredded

In skillet, heat oil. Cut chicken into thin slices and sauté. Add remaining ingredients, except cheese, and simmer for 25 to 30 minutes. Top with cheese and cover until cheese melts.

**Per serving**
*315 calories*
*58 mg cholesterol*
*359 mg sodium*
*3 gm saturated fat*
*8.8 gm fat*

**Exchanges per serving**
*1 bread*
*1 fat*
*2 meat*
*1 vegetable*

**On the side** A cabbage salad, a glass of milk, and a fresh fruit for dessert complete this zesty meal nutritionally.

2 Tbsp. vegetable oil

1 cup chopped walnuts

3 whole boned, skinned, chicken breasts, cubed

½ cup low-sodium chicken broth

1 Tbsp. cornstarch

1 Tbsp. water

3 tsp. soy sauce

⅛ tsp. pepper

In skillet, heat 1 tablespoon oil and fry walnuts, but don't brown them. Heat remaining oil and stir-fry chicken until browned. Add broth and cook on high heat for 5 minutes. In a bowl, combine cornstarch, water, soy sauce, and pepper. Stir in cornstarch mixture; stir until thickened. Add walnuts.

**Per serving**
*334 calories*
*71 mg cholesterol*
*558 mg sodium*
*4.3 gm saturated fat*
*14.6 gm fat*

**Exchanges per serving**
*1 fat*
*3 meat*

**On the side** This Walnut Chicken recipe goes well with white or brown rice, according to your preference. We also like to serve sautéed snow pea pods to enhance the oriental style of this dish. Add a glass of milk and a fresh fruit for dessert and the meal is complete nutritionally.

2 (1½ lb) Cornish game hens, halved
2 Tbsp. Worcestershire sauce
1 tsp. soy sauce
1 Tbsp. cornstarch
⅔ cup unsweetened apricot nectar
1½ Tbsp. unsweetened apricot jam
1 orange, peeled and cut into pieces

Brush halved hens with Worcestershire sauce and soy sauce; broil until lightly browned on each side. Combine cornstarch, nectar, and jam in saucepan and bring to a boil. Put hens in a baking dish and pour sauce over them. Bake at 350°F for 30 to 35 minutes. Sprinkle with orange pieces and bake for 2 to 3 minutes more.

**Per serving**
*214 calories*
*63 mg cholesterol*
*348 mg sodium*
*0.5 gm saturated fat*
*7 gm fat*

**Exchanges per serving**
*1 fruit*
*2 meat*

**On the side** Boiled squash adds a gourmet touch to these delicious hens. Broccoli spears, steamed just until tender, and a dessert of mixed fruit and yogurt complete the meal nutritionally.

3 18 oz. Cornish game hens
3 Tbsp. cornstarch
2 tsp. dry mustard
¾ cup water
2 Tbsp. vinegar
¼ cup honey
1 tsp. soy sauce
¼ cup unsweetened pineapple juice

Remove giblets; rinse hens and pat dry. Half each hen. Place skin side up on broiler pan. Broil 8 to 10 minutes or until skin is crisp. Heat oven to 325°F. Place halves in a 13 x 9 inch baking dish. In a bowl, combine ingredients; spoon over hens and bake for 45 to 50 minutes. Baste occasionally.

**Per serving**
*318 calories*
*226 mg cholesterol*
*60 mg sodium*
*9.7 gm saturated fat*
*22.3 gm fat*

**Exchanges per serving**
*½ fruit*
*4 meat*

**On the side** Wild rice, a mixed vegetable of green beans and carrots, and a dessert parfait of yogurt, strawberries, and mint make this a meal that is special enough for the most elegant dinner party.

1 24 oz. Cornish game hen
2 Tbsp. margarine
1 medium onion, sliced
2 Tbsp. margarine
¾ cup low-sodium beef broth
⅓ cup dry red wine
1 Tbsp. Dijon-style mustard
1 large carrot, sliced
½ pound spinach

Cut game hen in half. In skillet, heat margarine; brown game hen and onions for about 15 minutes over medium heat. Remove and set aside. In same skillet, stir in broth and bring to a boil. Reduce heat and add wine and mustard. Return game hen and onions to pan and add carrots. Cover and simmer for 15 minutes. Mound ingredients to one side. Push spinach into broth and stir until wilted. Serve game hen and vegetable with broth.

**Per serving**
*468 calories*
*191 mg cholesterol*
*319 mg sodium*
*10.2 gm saturated fat*
*20.8 gm fat*

**Exchanges per serving**
*1 fat*
*5 meat*
*1 vegetable*

**On the side** The recipe is for those intimate meals just for two. Wild rice is our favorite with Cornish game hens. Create your own dessert of yogurt, pears, and almond extract.

# 350 Cranberry Sauced Turkey Steaks

*Serves 4*

4 turkey breast tenderloins
1½ Tbsp. margarine, melted
1 Tbsp. soy sauce
¼ cup cranberry orange sauce
¼ cup orange juice
1 tsp. cornstarch
⅛ tsp. ground cinnamon
⅛ tsp. ground cloves

In a bowl, stir together margarine and soy sauce.
Place turkey on broiler pan; brush with soy sauce
mixture. Broil on both sides until turkey is tender;
brush with soy sauce mixture occasionally. In a
saucepan, add remaining ingredients. Cook and stir
until thickened and bubbly. Spoon over turkey
steaks.

**Per serving**
*141 calories*
*9 mg cholesterol*
*322 mg sodium*
*0.95 gm saturated fat*
*5.0 gm fat*

**Exchanges per serving**
*½ fruit*
*2 meat*

**On the side** Try twice-baked yams as the bread course, cherry
tomatoes cooked gently in a little margarine and tossed
with rosemary, as the vegetable course, and add a glass
of milk and a fresh fruit for dessert to complete this meal
nutritionally.

⅔ cup part-skim cottage cheese
½ cup skim milk
¼ tsp. lemon juice
1 tsp. curry powder
8 oz. skinned and boned, cooked turkey, sliced
⅛ tsp. pepper

In bowl, combine cottage cheese, milk, lemon juice and curry powder; mix with a mixer until smooth. In saucepan, heat cheese mixture, stirring constantly; bring to a boil. Add turkey until heated through. Sprinkle each serving with pepper.

**Per serving**
*110 calories*
*32 mg cholesterol*
*132 mg sodium*
*1.3 gm saturated fat*
*3.0 gm fat*

**Exchanges per serving**
*2 meat*

**On the side** Eggplant adds variety here for the bread course and works well with this curry-flavored turkey dish. A colorful mixed vegetable, like carrots and green beans, or broccoli and carrots, a glass of milk, and a fresh fruit for dessert round out the meal nutritionally.

½ cup low-fat plain yogurt
¼ cup light mayonnaise
1½ Tbsp. skim milk
1 tsp. curry powder
⅛ tsp. pepper
3 cups chopped cooked turkey
⅔ cup halved seedless grapes
⅓ cup chopped water chestnuts
½ cup chopped red peppers
⅛ tsp. nutmeg
6 lettuce leaves

In a bowl, combine yogurt, mayonnaise, milk, curry powder and pepper. Mix well. Fold in turkey, grapes, water chestnuts, and red peppers. Sprinkle with nutmeg. Serve on lettuce leaves.

### Per serving
*260 calories*
*21 mg cholesterol*
*409 mg sodium*
*4.9 gm saturated fat*
*8.1 gm fat*

### Exchanges per serving
*1 fat*
*2 meat*
*1 vegetable*

**On the side** We like to serve this terrific salad with a hearty rye or pumpernickel bread, a glass of milk, and fresh pear slices for dessert. The meal is delicious and is nutritionally complete.

1 cup diced celery

2 tsp. dried minced onion

1 Tbsp. margarine

2 cups water

½ tsp. salt

½ tsp. basil

¼ tsp. oregano

1 lb. can low-sodium tomatoes, reserve liquid

1 cup raw rice

2 5 oz. cans boned turkey

In skillet, combine celery, onion, margarine, water, salt, basil, oregano and liquid from tomatoes. Bring to a boil; add rice and bring to a second boil. Reduce heat and simmer until rice is done. Add tomatoes and turkey. Heat thoroughly.

**Per serving**
*194 calories*
*22.2 mg cholesterol*
*324 mg sodium*
*0.9 gm saturated fat*
*3.7 gm fat*

**Exchanges per serving**
*½ bread*
*1½ meat*
*1 vegetable*

**On the side** Add only a glass of milk, a ½ slice of bread, and a fruit of your choice for dessert and this meal is nutritionally complete.

1½ cups chopped green pepper
1 cup chopped onions
1 cup chopped carrots
⅓ cup water
2 cups peeled, cooked potatoes, diced
12 oz. pre-cooked smoked turkey sausage, sliced

In skillet, combine green pepper, onion, and carrots with water; cover and cook until vegetables are tender-crisp. Add potatoes and sausage until heated through.

**Per serving**
*283 calories*
*57 mg cholesterol*
*873 mg sodium*
*0.9 gm saturated fat*
*11.4 gm fat*

**Exchanges per serving**
*1 bread*
*3 meat*
*1 vegetable*

**On the side** Serve with a glass of milk and a fresh fruit for dessert and you've got a nutritionally complete meal with this easy single dish.

1 Tbsp. vegetable oil

¾ cup diced celery

½ cup chopped onions

2 cups sliced, fresh mushrooms

1 Tbsp. cornstarch

¼ cup soy sauce

¾ cup cold water

¼ cup sliced water chestnuts

2 cups diced, cooked turkey

6 cups cooked rice

In skillet, heat oil. Add celery, onions, and mushrooms; stir-fry until crisp-tender. In bowl, combine cornstarch, soy sauce, and water; mix. Stir cornstarch mixture into vegetables. Cook and stir constantly until liquid is smooth and thickened. Add water chestnuts and turkey. Cook until hot. Serve over rice.

**Per serving**
*285 calories*
*32.3 mg cholesterol*
*735 mg sodium*
*0.7 gm saturated fat*
*4.1 gm fat*

**Exchanges per serving**
*1 bread*
*2 meat*
*1 vegetable*

**On the side** You need only a glass of milk and a fresh fruit for dessert to make this quick and easy meal wholesome and nutritionally complete.

# 356 Spicy Turkey Chili

7 oz. ground turkey
⅓ cup chopped onions
1 cup tomatoes, chopped
⅔ cup low-sodium tomato sauce
½ cup water
2 tsp. chili powder
2 tsp. Worcestershire sauce
½ tsp. vinegar
½ tsp. garlic powder
⅛ tsp. allspice
1 tsp. crushed red pepper

In 3-quart saucepan, over medium heat, cook turkey and onions until turkey is brown. Add remaining ingredients and stir well to combine. Reduce heat and simmer for 30 minutes.

**Per serving**
*262 calories*
*75 mg cholesterol*
*1408 mg sodium*
*1.05 gm saturated fat*
*13.97 gm fat*

**Exchanges per serving**
*3 meat*
*2 vegetable*

**On the side** We like to serve this spicy chili recipe with elbow macaroni (½ cup servings are equal to 1 bread exchange and are about 150 calories; check the package for exact amounts). A glass of milk and apple-cranberry sauce complete the meal nutritionally.

# 357 Spinach Turkey Roll

1¼ lb. uncooked ground turkey
¼ cup chopped onions
1 cup tomato sauce
1 cup whole-wheat bread crumbs
2 eggs
1 tsp. oregano
1 tsp. basil
1 tsp. dry mustard
1 tsp. minced garlic
1½ cup frozen, chopped spinach, drained
½ cup mozzarella cheese, part-skim

Heat oven to 350°F. Combine turkey, onions, ¼ cup tomato sauce, bread crumbs, eggs, oregano, basil, mustard, and garlic; mix thoroughly. On a sheet of foil, pat mixture into a 12 x 8 inch rectangle. Spread spinach over turkey mixture; sprinkle with cheese. Roll turkey up starting on the 8-inch side. Place seam side down on cookie sheet. Bake 60 minutes. Heat remaining tomato sauce and spread over turkey roll.

**Per serving**
*210 calories*
*104 mg cholesterol*
*308 mg sodium*
*1.75 gm saturated fat*
*4.8 gm fat*

**Exchanges per serving**
*½ bread*
*2 meat*
*1 vegetable*

**On the side** Fresh tomato slices, arranged attractively on the plate with this dish, look and taste great. Add a glass of milk and fresh strawberries to complete your meal.

# 358 Sprouts 'n' Turkey Pockets

*Serves 4*

1½ cups low-fat, plain yogurt
1 tsp. Dijon-style mustard
1 tsp. horseradish
2 whole-wheat pocket breads, halved
½ lb. sliced cooked turkey
¾ cup alfalfa sprouts
¾ cup chopped tomato

In a small bowl, combine 8 tablespoons yogurt, mustard, and horseradish; blend well. Spoon 2 tablespoons yogurt mixture into each pocket half. Fill each with ¼ of the turkey, sprouts and tomato. Serve with remaining yogurt.

**Per serving**
*207 calories*
*47 mg cholesterol*
*227 mg sodium*
*1.5 gm saturated fat*
*4.0 gm fat*

**Exchanges per serving**
*½ bread*
*1 meat*
*½ skim milk*

**On the side** We like to serve this pita-style sandwich with fresh cucumber slices. A glass of milk and fresh pear slices for dessert complete the meal nutritionally.

1½ Tbsp. margarine
10 oz. turkey sausage, cubed
⅓ cup diced onion
⅓ cup chopped green pepper
¾ cup sauerkraut, drained
½ tsp. prepared mustard
½ tsp. prepared horseradish
4 whole-wheat pita pockets

In skillet, heat margarine. Add turkey sausage and sauté. Add onions and green pepper and sauté until tender-crisp. Add sauerkraut, mustard, and horseradish, and cook until heated thoroughly. Fill each pita pocket with ¼ of sausage mixture.

**Per serving**
*299 calories*
*48 mg cholesterol*
*1315 mg sodium*
*2.5 gm saturated fat*
*12.2 gm fat*

**Exchanges**
*1½ bread*
*1 fat*
*1 meat*
*1 vegetable*

**On the side** Serve these hearty pita sandwiches with a dessert of plain nonfat yogurt gently mixed with your favorite fresh fruits or berries.

1 lb. ground turkey
¾ cup water
1 envelope taco seasoning mix
2 cups shredded lettuce
⅔ cup shredded carrots
½ cup diced celery
⅔ cup chopped green pepper
⅓ cup chopped onion
½ cup part-skim cheddar cheese, shredded
½ cup part-skim Monterey Jack cheese, shredded
1 cup diced tomatoes
4 corn tortillas, heated and cut into wedges

In a nonstick skillet, cook turkey, stirring occasionally, until browned. Add water and taco seasoning; stir. Bring to a boil; reduce heat and simmer for 15 minutes. In a medium mixing bowl, combine lettuce, carrots, celery, green pepper and onion. Line serving platter with lettuce mixture; top with turkey mixture and sprinkle with cheeses. Sprinkle with tomatoes and serve with tortilla wedges.

**Per serving**
*280 calories*
*110 mg cholesterol*
*697 mg sodium*
*7.8 gm saturated fat*
*18.4 gm fat*

**Exchanges per serving**
*1 bread*
*3 meat*
*1 vegetable*

**On the side** A glass of milk and a fresh fruit complete this meal nicely.

1 small cucumber
1 small carrot
4 oz. light cream cheese
2 Tbsp. skim milk
¼ cup chopped green onion
⅛ tsp. curry powder
1 Tbsp. chopped pimentos
4 6-inch flour tortillas
4 lettuce leaves
8 oz. thinly sliced smoked turkey

Cut cucumber and carrot into thinly sliced sticks. In a mixing bowl, stir together cream cheese, milk, onions, curry powder, and pimentos. Spread mixture on one side of each tortilla. Top with lettuce leaves, turkey, cucumber and carrots. Fold and secure with toothpicks.

**Per serving**
*273 calories*
*65.5 mg cholesterol*
*459 mg sodium*
*0.5 gm saturated fat*
*13.25 gm fat*

**Exchanges per serving**
*1 bread*
*½ fat*
*2 meat*

**On the side** These tortilla roll-ups look great on a plate next to a salad of mixed greens, red and green peppers, and onion slices. Serve a glass of milk and your choice of fruit (we like cantaloupe melon slices) and the meal is nutritionally complete.

2 potatoes, peeled and cubed

½ cup chopped celery

3¼ cup skim milk

1 17 oz. can cream-style corn

2 4 oz. packages turkey breasts, cut into squares

¼ tsp. salt

⅛ tsp. pepper

¼ tsp. nutmeg

In saucepan, cook potatoes and celery in milk until potatoes are tender; mash slightly. Stir in corn, turkey, salt, pepper, and nutmeg. Simmer for 10 more minutes.

**Per serving**

*449 calories*
*139 mg cholesterol*
*660 mg sodium*
*1.7 gm saturated fat*
*6.3 gm fat*

**Exchanges per serving**

*2 bread*
*1 fat*
*2 meat*
*1 skim milk*

**On the side** This robust, dinner in a dish needs only a vegetable and a fruit to make the meal complete nutritionally. We like to make a Waldorf-style salad of mixed lettuce, cabbage, apples, celery, and raisins with a yogurt dressing, but cooked cabbage goes well with this dish, too.

# 363  Turkey in Creamy Orange Sauce  *Serves 2*

1 Tbsp. vegetable oil
12 oz. boneless, skinless turkey breasts
⅔ cup orange juice
1 tsp. cornstarch
⅔ cup low-fat plain yogurt
⅓ cup low-fat cottage cheese
⅛ tsp. black pepper

Heat oil in skillet and brown turkey on both sides.
Mix orange juice and cornstarch and add to skillet;
simmer to thicken and finish cooking turkey. Blend
yogurt and cottage cheese until smooth. Stir into
turkey mixture. Heat thoroughly, but do not boil.
Season with pepper.

**Per serving**
*340 calories*
*88 mg cholesterol*
*124 mg sodium*
*7.2 gm saturated fat*
*10.3 gm fat*

**Exchanges per serving**
*1 fat*
*4 meat*

**On the side** A serving of white rice, refreshing chilled cucumber
slices, and a dessert of yogurt gently blended with fresh
Bing cherries make this an elegant dinner for two that's
also nutritionally complete.

# 364 Turkey Jambalaya

1 Tbsp. margarine
⅓ cup chopped green pepper
⅓ cup chopped onion
¼ cup chopped celery
1 cup chopped tomato
1 cup low-sodium chicken broth
⅔ cup long grain rice
¾ tsp. basil, crushed
¼ tsp. thyme, crushed
⅛ tsp. garlic powder
⅛ tsp. pepper
¼ tsp. hot pepper sauce
1 bay leaf
2 cups cooked turkey, cubed

In skillet, heat margarine; cook green pepper, onion, and celery until tender. Stir in tomatoes, broth, rice, basil, thyme, garlic powder, pepper, and hot pepper sauce. Add bay leaf. Bring to a boil. Reduce heat and simmer for 20 minutes or until rice is tender. Stir in turkey; cook until heated through. Discard bay leaf.

**Per serving**
*312 calories*
*87 mg cholesterol*
*138 mg sodium*
*2.3 gm saturated fat*
*9 gm fat*

**Exchanges per serving**
*1 bread*
*1 fat*
*2 meat*
*1 vegetable*

**On the side** This hearty meal needs only a glass of milk and a fresh fruit for nutritional balance.

Nonstick cooking spray
1¼ lb. ground turkey
¾ cup whole wheat bread crumbs
½ cup chopped onion
¼ cup diced celery
¼ cup chopped carrots
1 tsp. minced garlic
¼ cup skim milk
1 Tbsp. dried parsley flakes
1 egg
⅛ tsp. black pepper
1 tsp. Worcestershire sauce
1 tsp. dried dillweed
½ tsp. sage

Preheat oven to 350°F. Spray 9 x 15 inch loaf pan with nonstick cooking spray. In a large bowl, mix all ingredients; blend well. Spoon into pan and shape into a loaf. Bake 50 to 60 minutes until loaf pulls away from pan.

**Per serving**
*211 calories*
*103 mg cholesterol*
*196 mg sodium*
*1.6 gm saturated fat*
*6.1 gm fat*

**Exchanges per serving**
*2 meat*
*1 vegetable*

**On the side** For nutritional completeness, serve new potatoes with parsley, cooked carrots, a glass of milk, and we like our cranberry-apple sauce, but you may want a fruit of your choice.

# INDEX

A la King, chicken, 290
Amandine, haddock, 165
American Diabetes
    Association, v
Antipasto Salad, 3
Apple butter, ribs with,
    279
Apple chicken salad, 11
Apple-raisin pork loaf,
    263
Apples, red cabbage
    with, 97
Apricot chicken, 283 *258*
Apricot-Cornish game
    hens, 372
Asparagus spaghetti
    toss, 65
Avocado tuna salad in
    pita bread, 49

Bake, chicken, 291,
    360
Bake, zucchini, 108
Baked chicken, 284
    fast, 329
    five-spice, 330
    quick, 353
    spicy, 361
Baked cod, 156
Baked fish, 179
    fillets, 163
    fillets, wine, 162
    with cheese sauce, 176
    with mushrooms, 240
    with sour cream, 223

Baked flounder, 180
Baked haddock with
    vegetables, 164
Baked halibut with sauce,
    170
Baked in a bag chicken, 292
Baked lamb, 249
    with sauce, 250
Baked pork chops, 264
Baked ratatouille and fish,
    158
Baked sea perch, 192
Baked shrimp, 204
Baked swordfish, 222
Baked whole fish, 181
Barbecue-style fried chicken,
    285
Barbecued chicken, lemon,
    341; oven-baked, 349
Barbecued flank steak, 115
Barley veal stew, 146
Basil chicken, 286
Bass, poached whole, 155
Bean pasta stew, 73
Bean sprout fruit salad, 5
Bean, black, chili, 89
Bean, rice and green pea
    salad, 4
Beef and cabbage casserole,
    116
Beef and veal, see pages
    115-152
Beef Burgundy, 117
Beef casserole, 118
Beef kabobs, 119
Beef rice goulash, 120

Beef soup, hearty, 42
Beef Stroganoff, low-fat, 132
Beef teriyaki, 121; with broccoli, 144
Beef with tabbouleh, 143
Beef, vegetable stir-fry, 151
Beef-tomato dinner, 145
Black bean chili, 89
Black-eyed pea and ham casserole, 270
Bread crumb trout fillets, 227
Broccoli and cauliflower salad, 6
Broccoli and chicken, easy, 328
Broccoli and pasta soup, 37
Broccoli potato salad, 23
Broccoli tuna salad, 7
Broccoli, chicken, 293
Broccoli, teriyaki beef with, 144
Broiled chicken, Oriental, 348
Broiled fish on cold tomatoes vinaigrette, 228
Broiled halibut supreme, 171
Broiled lemon chicken, 287
Broiled shrimp and scallops, 205
Broiled sole fillets, 182
Broiled tarragon chicken, 288
Burgers, garden, 126
Burgerwich, 122
Burgundy, beef, 117
Butter, garlic, shrimp in, 215

Cabbage and beef casserole, 116
Cabbage and carrot salad, 8
Cabbage with noodles, 90
Cabbage, red, with apples, 97
Cacciatore chicken, 294
Cakes, tuna, 236
Carrot and cabbage salad, 8
Carrot and potato soup, hearty, 43
Carrot and raisin salad, 9
Carrot-zucchini meat loaf, 152
Casseroles
    beef, 118
    beef and cabbage, 116
    cheesy chicken, 289
    chicken rice, 311
    easy tuna, 233
    eggplant, 91
    German, 127
    ham and black-eyed pea, 270
    mac-tuna, 70
    poultry, 351
    rice, 76
    seafood, 210
    shrimp, 213
    squash and spinach, 100
    tuna noodle, 81
    vegetable, 104
    zucchini, 110
Cauliflower and broccoli salad, 6
Cavatelli salad, 10
Cheese 'n' tuna filled pitas, 59
Cheese and tomato sandwiches, grilled, 50
Cheese sauce, baked fish with, 176
Cheesy chicken casserole, 28

Chicken
  a la king, 290
  and broccoli, easy, 328
  and garbanzo bean
    salad, 304
  and kraut, 304
  and vegetable skillet,
    306
  apple salad, 11
  bake, 291
  bake, Spanish, 360
  baked in a bag, 292
  bean gumbo, 38
  breasts, mushroom-
    stuffed, 344
  broccoli, 293
  cacciatore, 294
  casserole, cheesy, 289
  curry, 324
  cutlets, 295
  Dijon, 327
  divan, 296
  enchiladas, 297
  for two, 298
  honey, 299
  in cream sauce, 300
  in mushroom sauce,
    302
  in mustard cream
    sauce, 303
  Indian style, 301
  Indian, 40
  Mediterranean, 343
  Oriental, 307
  paprika, 350
  pecan salad, 12
  pie, 308
  pockets, 309
  raspberry salad, 13
  ratatouille, 310 285
  rice casserole, 311 286
  Romano, 312

Chicken salad, 313
  Chinese, 15
  salad, warm, 33
  salad, zesty, 34
  stir-fry, 314
Chicken supreme, 366
Chicken Tandoori, 315
Chicken with chutney, 316
Chicken with fresh herbs,
  317
Chicken with grapes, 318
Chicken with spinach, 319
Chicken with yogurt, 320
Chicken, apricot, 283
Chicken, baked, 284
Chicken, barbecue-style
  fried, 285
Chicken, basil, 286
Chicken, broiled tarragon,
  288
Chicken, Chinese ginger, 321
Chicken, creamed, with dill,
  322
Chicken, crumb, 323
Chicken, curry country, 325
Chicken, fast baked, 329
Chicken, five-spice baked,
  330
Chicken, fruited, 331
Chicken, fruity, 332
Chicken, ginger-glazed, 333
Chicken, glazed, 334
Chicken, golden curried, 335
Chicken, Hawaii, 336
Chicken, herbed, 337
Chicken, honey and mustard,
  338
Chicken, honey-lime, 339
Chicken, lemon saute, 342
Chicken, lemon, broiled, 287
Chicken, lemon-barbecued,
  341

Chicken, mustard-coated, 345

Chicken, orange, 346

Chicken, orange-glazed, 347

Chicken, Oriental broiled, 348

Chicken, oven-baked barbecued, 349

Chicken, quick and easy, 352

Chicken, quick baked, 353

Chicken, riced, 354

Chicken, roasted, 355, 356

Chicken, Rosemary, 357

Chicken, saucy, 358

Chicken, Scotch, 359

Chicken, spicy baked, 361

Chicken, spicy, broiled, 362

Chicken, stir-fry, 364

Chicken, stuffed, 365

Chicken, sweet 'n' sour, 367

Chicken, Swiss, 368

Chicken, tangy, 369

Chicken, Texas-style, 370

Chicken, walnut, 371

Chicken, spicy oven-fried, 363

Chickpea vegetable salad, 14

Chickpeas, lasagna with, 69

Chili, black bean, 89

Chili, vegetarian, 107

Chinese chicken salad, 15

Chinese ginger chicken, 321

Chops, lamb, glazed, 253

Chops, lamb, lemon-dill, 257

Chops, lamb, pineapple-ginger, 258

Chops, lamb, with garlic, 254

Chops, pork, baked, 264

Chops, pork, creole, 265

Chops, pork, curried mustard, 266

Chops, pork, fruited, 267

Chops, pork, fruity, 268

Chops, pork, honey-orange, 272

Chops, pork, mushroom, 273

Chops, pork, with dill, 276

Chops, veal, 147

Chowder, fish and pasta, 40

Chowder, shrimp and rice, 44

Chowder, turkey, 387

Chutney, chicken with, 316

Citrus halibut, 172

Citrus salad, zucchini and, 109

Citrus, halibut steaks, 175

Cod, baked, 156

Cold noodle salad, 16

Cold pasta, oriental, 72

Coriander shrimp, 206

Cornish game hen, for two, 374

Cornish game hens, apricot, 372

Cornish hens with pineapple-honey sauce, 373

Country chicken, curry, 325

Crab quiche, crustless, 157

Cracked wheat-rice pilaf, 66

Cranberry sauced turkey steaks, 375

Cream mustard sauce, chicken in, 303

Cream sauce, chicken in, 300

Cream, sour, mushroom steak, 142
Creamed chicken with dill, 322
Creamed tuna, 232
Creamy orange sauce, turkey in, 388
Creamy salmon dish, 193
Creole pork chops, 265
Creole shrimp, 207, 214
Crispy walleye fillets, 241
Crumb chicken, 323
Crumbs, haddock with, 168
Crunchy fish fillets, 183
Crustless crab quiche, 157
Cubed steaks, saucy, 141
Cucumber kabobs, scallops and, 200
Curried chicken, golden, 335
Curried lamb, 251
Curried mustard pork chops, 266
Curried shrimp, 208
Curried turkey salad, 377
Curried turkey, 376
Curry chicken, 324
Curry country chicken, 325
Cutlets, chicken, 295

Deviled drumsticks, 326
Dijon chicken, 327
Dijon-honeyed lamb steaks, 252
Dill, creamed chicken with, 322
Dill, pork chops with, 276
Dill-lemon, lamb chops, 257
Dilled round steak, 123
Dilly-lemon fish fillet, 159

Divan chicken, 296
Drumsticks, deviled, 326

Easy chicken and broccoli, 328
Easy gumbo soup, 39
Easy skillet dinner, 378
Easy tuna casserole, 233
Eggplant casserole, 91
Eggplant Italiano, 92
Eggplant mozzarella, 93
Eggplant Parmigiana, 94
Eggplant, lamb with, 256
Enchiladas, chicken, 297

Fast baked chicken, 329
Fast Stroganoff, 124
Fettuccine with mushrooms, 67
Fettuccine, herbed spinach, 68
Fiesta fish, 242
Fillet, fish, dilly-lemon, 159
Fish Amandine, 165
Fish and pasta chowder, 40
Fish and seafood, see pages 155-246
Fish and vegetables, 160
Fish fillets in sherry mushroom sauce, 173
Fish fillets, baked, 163
Fish fillets, Parmesan, 161
Fish fillets, wine baked, 162
Fish Florentine, 243
Fish fry, oven, 187
Fish Italiano, 166
Fish Provencal, 227
Fish, kettle of, 167
Five-spice baked chicken, 330
Five-spice fish, 174

Flank steak, barbecued, 115

Flounder,
 baked, 180, 181
 Florentine, 184
 Oriental, 186
 oven fried, 187
 Parmesan, 188
 with mushroom-garlic sauce, 185

Fluffy meat loaf, 125

Fort Snelling fish fillets, 191

Fresh vegetable soup, 41

Fried chicken, barbecue-style, 285

Fried walleye fillets, orange, 245

Fruit and spinach salad, 27

Fruit salad, with bean sprouts, 5

Fruit slaw, 17

Fruit, salmon with, 195

Fruited chicken, 331

Fruited pork chops, 267

Fruity chicken, 332

Fruity pork chops, 268


Game hens, Cornish, apricot, 372

Game hens, Cornish, with pineapple-honey sauce, 373

Garbanzo bean salad, chicken and, 304

Garden burgers, 126

Garlic butter, shrimp in, 215

Garlic sauce, scallops in, 201

Garlic tomato sauce, scallops with, 203

Garlic, lamb chops with, 254

Garlic, mushroom sauce, flounder with, 185

German casserole, 127

German style meat loaf, 128

Ginger chicken, Chinese, 321

Ginger-glazed chicken, 333

Ginger-pineapple lamb chops, 258

Ginger-sesame sauce, noodles with, 71

Glazed chicken, 334

Glazed chicken, finger, 333

Glazed lamb chops, 253

Glazed orange chicken, 347

Glazed pork, 269

Golden curried chicken, 335

Goulash, 129

Goulash, beef rice, 120

Goulash, Italian, 131

Grapes, chicken with, 318

Green bean and ham salad, 18

Green pea, bean, and rice salad, 4

Green pepper steak, 130

Green peppers, stuffed, 101

Grilled tomato and cheese sandwiches, 50

Gumbo, chicken bean, 38

Gumbo, easy, 39


Haddock
 Amandine, 165
 baked fillets, 163
 baked, with vegetables, 164

Italiano, 166
kettle of, 167
with crumbs, 168
with vegetables, 169
Halibut steaks a la citrus,
175
Halibut
baked, with sauce, 170
broiled, supreme, 171
citrus, 172
fillets in sherry mush-
room sauce, 173
with spices, 174
Ham 'n' Yam, 271 *249*
Ham and black-eyed pea
casserole, 270 *248*
Ham and green bean
salad, 18
Hamburger, burgerwich,
122
Hamburgers, garden, 126
Hawaii chicken, 336
Hearty beef soup, 42
Hearty potato and carrot
soup, 43
Herb marinade, swordfish
in, 224
Herbed chicken, 337
Herbed spinach fettuccine,
68
Herbs, fresh, chicken with,
317
Honey and mustard chick-
en, 338
Honey, chicken, 299
Honey-lime chicken, 339

Honey-orange pork chops,
272
Honey-pineapple sauce,
Cornish hens with, 373
Hot dish, tuna, 237

Hot shrimp, 209


Indian chicken, 340
Indian-style chicken, 301
Italian goulash, 131
Italiano fish, 166
Italiano, eggplant, 92


Jambalaya, turkey, 389

Kabobs
beef, 119
lamb, 255
pork, 277
scallops and cucumber,
200
shrimp, 216
Kettle of fish, 167
Kraut, chicken and, 305


Lamb casserole, zucchini
and, 259
Lamb chops with garlic, 254
Lamb chops, glazed, 253
Lamb chops, lemon-dill, 257
Lamb kabobs, 255
Lamb steaks, Dijon-honeyed,
252
Lamb with eggplant, 256
Lamb, baked, 249
Lamb, baked, with sauce,
250
Lamb, curried, 251
Lamb, see pages 249-259
Lasagna with chickpeas,
69
Lasagna, vegetarian, 83
Lasagna, zucchini, 84

Legumes and vegetables,
see pages 89-111
Lemon chicken saute, 342
Lemon chicken, broiled,
287
Lemon orange roughy, 177
Lemon veal with spinach,
133
Lemon, spicy walleye
fillets, 246
Lemon-barbecued chicken,
341
Lemon-dill lamb chops,
257
Lemon-dilly fish fillet, 159
Lentil turkey salad, 19
Lentils, 95
Lime juice, roughy with,
178
Lime-honey chicken, 339
Loaf, fluffy meat, 125
Loaf, pork, apple-raisin,
263
Loaf, turkey, 390
Low-fat beef Stroganoff,
132
Luncheon quickie, 380

Mac-tuna casserole, 79
Macaroni salad, 20
Macaroni salad, main
entree, 21
Main entree macaroni
salad, 21
Marinara, scallops, 202
Marinated trout, 229
Meat loaf, 125, 134
Meat loaf, German style,
128
Meat loaf, moist, 136

Meat loaf, zucchini-carrot,
152
Meat loaves, mini, 135
Mediterranean chicken,
343
Medley, pasta, rice, 77
Medley, vegetable, 105
Mini meat loaves, 135
Moist meat loaf, 136
Mozzarella, eggplant, 93
Mushroom pork chops,
273
Mushroom sauce, chicken
in, 302
Mushroom sauce, sherry,
fish fillets in, 173
Mushroom steak, sour cream,
142
Mushroom stuffed chicken
breasts, 344
Mushroom veal steak, 137
Mushroom, toasted sandwich,
58
Mushroom-garlic sauce,
flounder with, 185
Mushrooms, fettuccine with,
67
Mushrooms, snapper with,
221
Mushrooms, walleye baked
with, 240
Mustard and honey chicken,
338
Mustard cream sauce, chicken
in, 303
Mustard pork chops, 274
Mustard sauce, swordfish
with, 225
Mustard, curried pork
chops, 266
Mustard-coated chicken,
345

Noodle casserole, tuna, 81
Noodle salad, cold, 16
Noodles with ginger-
   sesame sauce, 71
Noodles, cabbage with, 90
Noodles, zippy, 85


Oatmeal, trout in, 231
Orange chicken, 346
Orange fried fish fillets,
   245
Orange roughy,
   baked with cheese
      sauce, 176
   lemon, 177
   lime juice with, 178
Orange sauce, creamy,
   turkey in, 388
Orange-glazed chicken,
   347
Oriental broiled chicken,
   348
Oriental chicken, 307
Oriental cold pasta, 72
Oriental fish, 186
Oriental shrimp, 217
Oven fish fry, 187
Oven porcupines, 138

Oven-baked barbecued
   chicken, 349
Oven-fried chicken, spicy,
   363


Pan vegetable pizza, 96
Paprika chicken, 350
Parmesan fillets, 161, 188
Parmigiana, eggplant, 94
Pasta and broccoli soup,
   37

Pasta and fish chowder,
   40
Pasta and rice, see pages
   65-85
Pasta bean stew, 73
Pasta medley, rice, 77
Pasta Primavera, 74
Pasta salad, 75
Pasta shells, stuffed, 79
Pasta spinach salad, 22
Pasta, cavatelli, salad, 10
Patties, pork, pizza-
   sauced, 275
Pea and shrimp salad, 25
Pea soup, split, 45
Peas and tomato sauce with
   spaghetti, 78
Pecan chicken salad, 12
Pepper steak pita pockets, 51
Pepper steak, green, 130
Peppered tuna dish, 234
Peppers, red, stuffed, 98
Peppers, savory, 99
Peppers, stuffed green, 101
Peppers, veal with, 148
Perch, Fort Snelling fillets,
   191
Pie, chicken, 308
Pilaf, cracked wheat-rice, 66
Pineapple-ginger lamb chops,
   258
Pineapple-honey sauce,
   Cornish hens with, 373
Pita bread, avocado tuna
   salad in, 49
Pita pockets with pepper
   steak, 51
Pita, turkey salad in, 62
Pitas, shrimp stuffed, 55
Pitas, stuffed, 384
Pitas, tuna 'n' cheese
   filled, 59

Pitas, tuna, 60
Pizza, pan vegetable, 96
Pizza-sauced patties, ~~275~~ 253
Poached red snapper, 219
Poached whole fish (bass), 155
Pocket, shrimp salad, 54
Pockets, chicken, 309
Pockets, turkey, and sprouts, 383
Porcupines, oven, 138
Pork and ham, see pages 263-279
Pork chops, baked, ~~264~~ 242
Pork chops, creole, ~~265~~ 243
Pork chops, curried mustard, ~~266~~ 244
Pork chops, fruited, ~~267~~ 245
Pork chops, fruity, ~~268~~ 246
Pork chops, honey-orange, ~~272~~ 250
Pork chops, mushroom, ~~273~~ 251
Pork chops, with dill, ~~276~~ 254
Pork kabobs, ~~277~~ 255
Pork loaf, apple-raisin, ~~263~~ 241
Pork patties, pizza-sauced, 275
Pork zucchini, ~~278~~ 256
Pork, glazed, ~~269~~ 247
Potato and carrot soup, hearty, 43
Potato broccoli salad, 23
Poultry casserole, 351
Poultry, see pages 283-390
Primavera pasta, 74
Provencal, walleye, 244

Quiche, crustless crab, 157
Quick and easy chicken, 352
Quick and easy spicy lemon fillets, 246
Quick baked chicken, 353
Quick steak stew, 139
Quickie, turkey, luncheon, 380

Raisin and carrot salad, 9
Raisin-apple pork loaf, 263
Raspberry chicken salad, 13
Ratatouille, baked, and fish, 158
Ratatouille, chicken, 310
Red cabbage with apples, 97
Red peppers, stuffed, 98
Red snapper, poached, 219
Reuben, turkey, 61
Ribs with apple butter, ~~279~~ 257
Rice and shrimp chowder, 44
Rice casserole, 76
Rice pasta medley, 77
Rice salad, 24
Rice stuffing, veal with, 149
Rice tuna salad, 31
Rice, bean, and green pea salad, 4
Rice, beef goulash, 120
Rice, chicken casserole, 311
Rice, cracked-wheat pilaf, 66

Riced chicken, 354
Ricotta sole, 189
Roast chicken, 355
Roasted chicken, 356
Rolled veal loaf, 140
Romano, chicken, 312
Rosemary chicken, 357
Roughy with lime juice, 178
Round steak, dilled, 123

Salad, chicken and garbanzo bean, 304
Salad, chicken, 313
Salad, curried turkey, 377
Salad, pasta, 75
Salad, taco turkey, 385
Salad, zucchini and citrus, 109
Salads, see also pages 3-32
Salmon loaf, 194
Salmon salad sandwiches, 52
Salmon with fruit, 195
Salmon, creamy, 193
Salmon, simple, 196
Salmon, teriyaki, 197
Salmon, yogurt, 198
Sandwiches, see pages 49-62
Sauced tuna pita, 53
Saucy chicken, 358
Saucy cubed steaks, 141
Sauerkraut, chicken and, 305
Savory peppers, 99
Scallops and cucumber kabobs, 200
Scallops in garlic sauce, 201

Scallops Marinara, 202
Scallops with tomato-garlic sauce, 203
Scallops, 199
Scallops, broiled shrimp, and 205
Scampi, shrimp, 218
Scotch chicken, 359
Sea perch, baked, 192
Seafood and fish, see also pages 155-246
Seafood casserole, 210
Sesame shrimp broil, 211
Sesame shrimp, 212
Shells, stuffed pasta, 79
Sherry mushroom sauce, halibut in, 173
Shrimp and pea salad, 25
Shrimp and rice chowder, 44
Shrimp casserole, 213
Shrimp Creole, 214
Shrimp in garlic butter, 215
Shrimp kabob, 216
Shrimp Oriental, 217
Shrimp salad pocket, 54
Shrimp salad, 26
Shrimp Scampi, 218
Shrimp stuffed pitas, 55
Shrimp tarragon salad, 29
Shrimp, baked, 204
Shrimp, broiled, and scallops, 205
Shrimp, coriander, 206
Shrimp, Creole, 207
Shrimp, curried, 208
Shrimp, hot, 209
Shrimp, sesame, 212
Simple salmon, 196
Skillet dinner, easy, 378

Skillet, chicken and
     vegetable, 306
Slaw, fruit, 17
Smoked turkey with
     vegetables, 379
Snapper with mushrooms,
     221
Snapper, red, poached,
     219
Snapper, spicy, 220
Sole fillets, broiled, 182
Sole with wine, 190
Sole, baked, 179
Sole, crunchy, 183
Sole, ricotta, 189
Souffle, tuna, 238
Souffle, vegetable, 106
Soups, see pages 37-45
Sour cream mushroom
     steak, 143
Sour cream, swordfish
     baked with, 223
Spaghetti asparagus toss,
     65
Spaghetti with peas and
     tomato sauce, 78
Spaghetti, summer, 80
Spaghetti, vegetable, 82
Spanish chicken bake,
     360
Spice, five, fish, 174
Spicy baked chicken, 361
Spicy chicken, 362
Spicy oven-fried chicken,
     363
Spicy snapper, 220
Spicy turkey chili, 381
Spinach and squash
     casserole, 100
Spinach fettuccine,
     herbed, 68

Spinach fruit salad, 27
Spinach salad, pasta, 22
Spinach turkey salad, 28
Spinach turkey roll, 382
Spinach, chicken with,
     319
Spinach, lemon veal with,
     133
Split pea soup, 45
Sprout sandwich, 56
Sprouts 'n' turkey pockets,
     383
Sprouts, bean, fruit salad,
     5
Squash and spinach
     casserole, 100
Steak, barbecued flank,
     115
Steak, dilled round, 123
Steak, green peppers, 130
Steak, halibut, a la citrus,
     175
Steak, pepper, pita
     pockets with, 51
Steak, quick stew, 139
Steak, sour cream
     mushroom, 142
Steak, veal, mushroom,
     137
Steaks, lamb, Dijon-
     honeyed, 252
Steaks, saucy cubed, 141
Steaks, turkey, cranberry
     sauced, 375
Stew, pasta bean, 73
Stew, quick steak, 139
Stew, veal barley, 146
Stir-fry chicken, 314, 364
Stir-fry, vegetable beef,
     151
Stir-fry, zucchini, 111

Stroganoff, fast, 124
Stroganoff, low-fat beef, 132
Stuffed chicken breasts, mushroom, 344
Stuffed chicken, 365
Stuffed green peppers, 101
Stuffed pasta shells, 79
Stuffed pitas, 384
Stuffed red peppers, 98
Stuffed tomato, tuna, 103
Stuffed tomatoes, 102
Stuffing, rice, with veal, 149
Summer spaghetti, 80
Sun sandwiches 57
Supreme chicken, 366
Supreme, halibut, broiled, 171
Sweet 'n' sour chicken, 367
Sweet and sour trout fillets, 230
Swiss chicken, 368
Swordfish in herb marinade, 224
Swordfish steaks, 226
Swordfish with mustard sauce, 225
Swordfish, baked with sour cream, 223
Swordfish, baked, 222
Swordfish, broiled, 226

Tabbouleh with beef, 143
Taco turkey salad, 385
Tacos, tuna, 239
Tandoori chicken, 315
Tangy chicken, 369
Tarragon chicken, broiled, 288

Tarragon shrimp salad, 29
Teriyaki beef with broccoli, 144
Teriyaki beef, 121
Teriyaki salmon, 197
Terrific tuna, 235
Texas-style chicken, 370
Toasted mushroom sandwiches, 58
Tomato and cheese, grilled sandwiches, 50
Tomato sauce and peas with spaghetti, 78
Tomato, tuna-stuffed, 103
Tomato-beef dinner, 145
Tomato-garlic sauce, scallops with, 203
Tomatoes vinaigrette, cold, broiled trout on, 228
Tomatoes, stuffed, 102
Tortilla turkey, 386
Toss, asparagus spaghetti, 65
Trout fillets, bread crumb 227
Trout fillets, sweet and sour, 230
Trout in oatmeal, 231
Trout, broiled, on cold tomatoes vinaigrette, 228
Trout, marinated, 229
Tuna 'n' cheese filled pitas, 59
Tuna avocado salad in pita bread, 49
Tuna cakes, 236
Tuna hot dish, 237
Tuna noodle casserole, 81
Tuna pita, sauced, 53
Tuna pitas, 60
Tuna rice salad, 31

Tuna souffle, 238
Tuna tacos, 239
Tuna, antipasto salad, 3
Tuna, creamed, 232
Tuna, easy casserole, 233
Tuna, macaroni casserole, 70
Tuna, peppered, 234
Tuna, terrific, 235
Tuna-stuffed tomato, 103
Turkey chili, spicy, 381
Turkey chowder, 387
Turkey in creamy orange sauce, 388
Turkey Jambalaya, 389
Turkey loaf, 390
Turkey luncheon quickie, 380
Turkey pockets and sprouts, 383
Turkey Reuben, 61
Turkey roll spinach, 382
Turkey salad for two, 30
Turkey salad in a pita, 62
Turkey salad, curried, 377
Turkey salad, lentil, 19
Turkey salad, taco, 385
Turkey spinach salad, 28
Turkey steaks, cranberry sauced, 375
Turkey, curried, 376
Turkey, easy skillet dinner, 378
Turkey, smoked, with vegetables, 379
Turkey, tortilla, 386
Two, chicken for, 298
Two, game hen for, 374
Two, turkey salad for, 30

Veal barley stew, 146
Veal chops, 147
Veal loaf, rolled, 140
Veal steak, mushroom, 137
Veal with peppers, 148
Veal with rice stuffing, 149
Veal with zucchini, 150
Veal, lemon with spinach, 133
Vegetable beef stir-fry, 151
Vegetable casserole, 104
Vegetable medley, 105
Vegetable pizza, pan, 96
Vegetable salad, chickpea, 14
Vegetable skillet, chicken and, 306
Vegetable souffle, 106
Vegetable soup, fresh, 41
Vegetable spaghetti, 82
Vegetables and fish, 160
Vegetables and legumes, see pages 89-111
Vegetables with smoked turkey, 379
Vegetables, baked haddock with, 164
Vegetables, haddock with, 169
Vegetarian chili, 107
Vegetarian lasagna, 83


Waldorf salad, 32
Walleye fillets, crispy, 241
Walleye fillets, spicy lemon, 246
Walleye, baked with mushrooms, 240
Walleye, fiesta, 242

Walleye, Florentine, 243
Walleye, orange fried, 245
Walnut chicken, 371
Warm chicken salad, 33
Wine baked fillets, 162
Wine, sole with, 190


Yam 'n' ham, 271
Yogurt salmon, 198
Yogurt, chicken with, 32

Zesty chicken salad, 34
Zippy noodles, 85
Zucchini
    and citrus salad, 109
    and lamb casserole, 259
    bake, 108
    carrot meat loaf, 152
    casserole, 110
    lasagna, 84
    pork, 278
    stir-fry, 111
    with veal, 150
    summer spaghetti, 80
    carrot meat loaf, 152